Running Weblogs with Slash

chromatic, Brian Aker, and Dave Krieger

O'REILLY®

Beijing · Cambridge · Farnham · Köln · Paris · Sebastopol · Taipei · Tokyo

Running Weblogs with Slash

by chromatic, Brian Aker, and Dave Krieger

Copyright © 2002 O'Reilly & Associates, Inc. All rights reserved.
Printed in the United States of America.

Published by O'Reilly & Associates, Inc., 1005 Gravenstein Highway North,
Sebastopol, CA 95472.

O'Reilly & Associates books may be purchased for educational, business, or sales promotional
use. Online editions are also available for most titles (*safari.oreilly.com*). For more information
contact our corporate/institutional sales department: 800-998-9938 or *corporate@oreilly.com*.

Editor: Laura Lewin

Production Editor: Matt Hutchinson

Cover Designer: Emma Colby

Printing History:

> January 2002:   First Edition.

ISBN: 0-596-00100-2
[M]

Running Weblogs with Slash

Table of Contents

Foreword

When asked to write this introduction I immediately tried to think of a good way to get out of it. Years of running Slashdot has crippled my brain, rendering it incapable of writing anything longer than a single paragraph. Perhaps a nice 20-pt. font would solve this problem! I also considered just using the same sentence 50 times, but I suspected that someone might bother reading it before it went to press, and then the jig would be up. It's awfully hard to fake writing a couple of pages, and I'm nothing if not lazy. But I hope that my laziness will have a bit of a payoff for you at some point.

More than four years ago I registered a domain name. Being the cocky young lad that I was, I decided that I would register the most unpronounceable name I could think of. I didn't know exactly what I would be putting on my site, but I knew that whatever it was, it was going to be a creation purely for the age of the Internet. And part of that was making the name itself a joke (something unpronounceable). I registered what seemed like an appropriately pompous name and proceeded to phase 2 of my master plan.

Owning a domain name has responsibilities besides remembering to turn relay off on your MX and paying your registration fee every year. But even more important then being the lucky recipient of 50 daily pieces of spam addressed to root@ or webmaster@ is the task of populating your domain name with exciting content. Since I had very little of that, I set about creating a tangled mess to make it easier for me to get content with as little effort from me as possible. Had I only known what I was getting myself into, I probably would have canceled phase 2 of my master plan, or at least dramatically altered it until it amounted to "Eat Sandwich."

Slashdot has continued to evolve and change throughout its entire life. In the early days, we were just a few hundred users, and we didn't even need user accounts because we all knew each other. The code adapted through that and countless other changes as we served our first few million pages.* And it followed us as our readerbase grew and changed until I sat back and was just amazed that the discussions were actually just as important, if not more so, as the words I was writing. Years of tweaks followed, some so tiny that probably nobody ever noticed, along with large changes with all the subtlety of an axe slicing through a watermelon. The evolution of a moderation system designed to fulfill our goal made it possible for a variety of readers to experience Slashdot at the level they wanted. It was a discussion board, a newspaper, and an infinite number of variations in between. And it gave them all a reason to hate me for whatever it is I do wrong today.

Slashdot stumbled through countless celebrations and tragedies, from the announcement that Netscape was going to release Navigator as an open source project to Columbine. And at every step of the way we somehow managed to adapt the code to the new challenges at hand.

At first the code was a tangled wreck. It wasn't designed, but like many open source applications, it was evolved. The system was incapable of scaling beyond 100,000 pages a day, which caused a problem because Slashdot's needs were rapidly going far beyond that. After being rewritten to take advantage of *mod_perl,* we could handle 500,000 pages a day, but even that wasn't enough. Following the Andover acquisition in June 1999, I was finally able to hire programmers to take on the task of making Slash a true open source application. Pat and Pudge and later Krow took the trainwreck of code that was Slash 0.2 and 0.3 and turned it into the current versions, and anyone who glanced over those early versions knows what an undertaking that was.

Today Slash does what no other open source weblog can do. Every day it serves nearly 2 million pages to hundreds of thousands of users. It takes hundreds of submissions and lets a handful of authors choose a dozen stories. It lets thousands discuss News for Nerds. Stuff that Matters. And at the end of the day, it allows even a casual reader to browse through stories and maybe see a little more then what a traditional newspaper would provide. It's distributed journalism. And while we definitely didn't invent it, we definitely took it to the next level. And Slash is what makes it possible.

The Internet is a powerful tool that lets computers talk to each other. The Web takes this to the next level by letting people create their own sites to share their stories. But Slash is one of the first applications to take the Net and the Web and let them collaborate to create something that couldn't be done in any other way. Building on Usenet, IRC, and even MUDs, it creates a reasonable system in which the knowledgable and the foolish can mingle, swap places, and somehow produce

---

* This is a fake footnote. I just wanted to do that thing that they do in every O'Reilly book where they put a joke in a footnote.

something that is worth reading. Frankly, it scares me that it works as well as it does.

I can't take credit for it myself. So many people have contributed code and ideas over the years. From Dave and Nate in the early days to Pat, Brian, Pudge, Cliff, and Jamie later on. Each of them contributed in their own way to what is now known as "Slash," and it couldn't happen without them. But Slashdot is only the beginning.

A quick trip to *http://www.slashcode.com/* provides all the evidence you need to know that Slash has gone far beyond what I had originally dreamt of for it. Sites running our code have subjects akin to the original Slashdot, such as nanotech and Perl, but they go far beyond our little niche of the net. Who knew that Slash would serve as a platform that would make it possible for tree huggers, jazz fans, perverts, druggies, and even Canadians to meet online and share what they have in common? Or don't. The Net isn't just for nerds anymore, and I'm glad this code has had a small hand in making that possible. If you're reading this, it means that you have a story to tell, too, some subject that burns inside your heart that you want to open up to the world.

I won't lie (about this anyway). It's not always easy. I've had to get used to daily flames by people who have never met me over things that they know nothing about. I have learned that I am always wrong. But with any luck, between this book, this code, and a little bit of elbow grease, you should be able to get your own site up and running and start getting used to flames and always being wrong, too.

These days I'm a little older, a little wiser. But I'm still pretty cocky. And that unpronounceable domain that I registered has caused me more torture than anything else. Hopefully, what we've learned over the years will make it easier for you to tell your story. The Web is about letting people share their ideas with the world, and this book should help you figure out one of the best ways to do it. But if you're short on words, try using a 20-pt. font.

—Rob "CmdrTaco" Malda

Preface

This book is the product of three authors. Our individual experiences with web publishing, programming, and specifically Slash have shaped our opinions and our prose. We include these brief biographies to explain our biases and decisions, as well as to provide *something* our mothers will understand.

In 1993 Brian "Krow" Aker sat up late with his friends Yazz and Mike at Antioch College connecting their 386BSD box to the network. First came X and then Mosaic. His life changed that evening. It would change again in a few years, when someone mentioned an oddly named web site for news junkies.

In the spring of 1998, chromatic's brother sent him an email from college. He'd come across a web site devoted to all sorts of interesting things, from Linux to LEGO. Run by a couple of college students out of Michigan, Slashdot had no moderation, no user accounts, and rarely saw dozens of comments on a single Story.

chromatic first signed up for a Slashdot account as the site prepared to welcome its 10,000th registered user. One day, Hemos posted a book review and sent out a call for volunteers. chromatic responded, proposing his first review a few months later. Hemos replied, "I have enjoyed your previous work and would be happy to run another review." That lead to a long and occasionally lucrative career providing content for what would quickly become OSDN and built geek credibility.

In the spring of 2000, Dave Krieger met Jeff Bates at a Foresight Institute (*http://www.foresight.org/*) Senior Associates gathering. Inspired, Dave set up Nanodot (*http://nanodot.org/*). His administrative experiences led him to propose this book to O'Reilly and Associates, hoping to make the ever more feature-rich Slash software useful to mere mortals.

Then there's Slashcode. Andover.net employee Patrick Galbraith became the project manager and started recruiting Brian, promising more fun than any generic dotcom could provide. Chris Nandor answered a Boston.pm email posting about Andover jobs. Cliff "Ask Slashdot" Wood and Jaime McCarthy also joined the team. Brian took on the redesign and SQL optimizations, and Patrick and Chris cleaned up the original codebase for the 1.0 release. chromatic submitted a few early patches, moved to Blockstacker's post-Slashdot Everything project, and returned to Slash during research for another book.

Under the talented guidance of Patrick, Chris, and Brian, Slash has matured into a powerful and easy-to-use web application framework. The architecture, installer, and modularity have drastically improved.

Audience

This book is aimed at anyone interested in setting up and running a weblog with the Slash software. This includes system administrators and programmers, but attempts have been made to keep the discussion readable for people who have no desire to compile their own kernels or to rewrite the moderation system. It concentrates more on how to accomplish things than how things work underneath, though it doesn't shy away from the greasy gears and wheels when appropriate.

Unix and Perl experience will help, though neither are required. Familiarity with an existing Slash site is also useful. For the most part, the text assumes the reader has a particular goal in mind, without knowing exactly where and how to start.

Most of this book was written in the heady days leading up to the release of Slash 2.2. Much of the philosophy and most of the interface is similar to Release 2.0. The authors have tried to describe things that will be consistent through future versions and mark things which will likely change in future versions. Until *PSI::ESP* is written, your best bet is to read Slashcode and the *README* file with the current Slash version to see what is new and improved.

What's Inside

Chapter 1, *Slash: an Overview*, begins with an overview of weblogging and Slash. It describes the history of Slashdot, examines the Slash interface from a user's perspective, and gives a big picture overview of the rest of the book.

Chapter 2, *Installing Slash*, walks through the Slash installation process. This includes information on the software prerequisites (Perl, Apache, MySQL) and discusses common configurations.

Chapter 3, *Basic Administration*, takes a first look at the administrative menus. It begins by helping an administrator delegate power and authority and also demonstrates basic Slash customization.

Chapter 4, *Editing and Updating Stories*, examines the story selection and publishing features. It includes the common convenience functions that have grown up over the years.

Chapter 5, *Reviewing and Approving Submissions*, describes the process of publishing Stories recommended by users. Slash has several little-known features for sorting, winnowing, and queueing Stories, all listed here.

Chapter 6, *Comments, Filters, and Content Moderation*, explores the powerful comment and moderation systems in detail. This includes the underlying formulas and functions of moderation and meta-moderation. Yikes.

Chapter 7, *Managing Topics and Sections*, looks at how Slash groups related Stories. This has implications for site organization and future expandability.

Chapter 8, *Managing a Slash Community*, takes a philosophical approach, listing several important questions to answer before a site grows too large. Any successful site must overcome common traps and troubles. Those that can be predicted are presented here.

Chapter 9, *Basic Site Customization*, continues with a foray into site customization. It discusses blocks (those odd boxes in the right and left margins of a site), automatic content retrieval from other sites, and user polls.

Chapter 10, *Advanced Customization*, continues the configuration track, examining blocks and colors yet again. It then delves into practical territory, modifying templates, installing themes, and even creating and installing an example plugin. The chapter finishes with a brief discussion of the Slash features that make internationalization both possible and tricky.

Chapter 11, *Advanced Administration*, concludes the configuration approach, dissecting Slash conventions and utilities. It includes a bestiary of the common daemons that keep a site running. Finally, it describes the form and function of recurring tasks.

Appendix A, *Slash Architecture*, is a blueprint to Slash's grand Gothic structure.

Appendix B, *Common Slash Database Tables*, outlines the schemas for the most important tables in a Slash system.

Appendix C, *The Slash Template Language*, is a gentle introduction to the template language used in Slash. It describes the powerful Template Toolkit features most commonly found in standard Slash templates.

Appendix D, *The Slash API*, categorizes several common functions and methods available to Slash plugins, tasks, and applets.

Appendix E, *Slash Configuration Variables*, lists and explains the default Slash configuration variables.

Conventions Used in This Book

The following formatting conventions are used in this book:

Italic

> Used for file and directory names, pathnames, names of Slash modules and packages, and for important terms when they are first introduced

`Constant width`

> Used for configuration variable names, literal values, database table names, names of Slash functions, and command lines and options that should be typed verbatim

`Constant width italic`

> Used for replaceable arguments within a variable name or a command line

`Constant width bold`

> Used in text that is typed in code examples by the user

To distinguish between Slash elements and non-Slash elements, certain elements within Slash (such as a Story, Topic, or Section) are uppercased. For example, a book author would be lowercased, but an Author on a Slash system is uppercased.

 The owl icon designates a tip, suggestion, or general note relating to the nearby text.

 The turkey icon designates a warning or caution relating to the nearby text.

How to Contact Us

We have tested and verified the information in this book to the best of our ability, but you may find that features have been changed (or even that we have made

mistakes!). Please let us know about any errors you find, as well as your sugges
tions for future editions, by writing to:

O'Reilly and Associates, Inc.
1005 Gravenstein Highway North
Sebastopol, CA 95472
(800) 998-9938 (in the U.S. or Canada)
(707) 829-0515 (international or local)
(707) 829-1014 (fax)

We have a web page for this book, where we list errata, examples, and any additional information. You can access this page at:

http://www.oreilly.com/catalog/runblogslash/

To ask technical questions or comment on the book, send email to:

bookquestions@oreilly.com

For more information about or books, conferences, software, Resource Centers,
and the O'Reilly Network, see our web site at:

http://www.oreilly.com/

Acknowledgments

The authors would like to thank their editor, Laura Lewin, for her steadfast good
nature and adroit management of the project, as well as the entire O'Reilly staff
who performed further magic on this book, including Lenny and Rob. Great
expectations. We also appreciate the eclectic and effective Slashteam: Chris Nandor, Cliff Woods, Jaime McCarthy, Jonathan Pater, Patrick Galbraith, and even Rob
Malda. We kid because we care. Thank you to all Slashcode.com participants, and
to all of the programmers and bugfixers listed in the Slash *AUTHORS* file. These
people do good work. Our technical reviewers offered corrections, suggestions,
and polish. In no particular order, they are: the Slashteam, Jeff Bates, Alvaro del
Castillo, and Aleatha Parker. Thank you.

chromatic's Acknowledgments

Primary thanks go Jeff "Hemos" Bates and Simone Paddock, who have provided
much encouragement and many opportunities. I am fortunate to work with you
and am blessed to call you friends. Much thanks and love to my family, for their
continued support. Thank you to my co-authors. Great work! I offer my apprecia-
tion to other folks at O'Reilly, namely Derrick and gnat. Thanks also to my

professional friends, including those at Foothills, EDC, and Perlmonks, as well as the Wormies and the Farsider fans. Michelle—let's chase the Furies with abandon. To everyone else, if you don't find yourself within these pages in name or in spirit, look harder.

To everyone who participates in this grand meritocracy where we can write the software we use: take a chance, and show other people how they can contribute. Thanks to jlp and p5p (especially ams, jhi, and Schwern). Expect the best of people, and they will make you proud. Pass it along.

Brian "Krow" Aker's Acknowledgments

The first person to be blamed should be Patrick, who got me into this mess in the first place. My apologies to Yazz, who I drag with me into all jobs great and small. Great respect for and a fond love of my fellow Slashdot programmers, who all easily keep me on my toes. Rob and Jeff deserve kudos for sticking with Slashdot and and not letting the Trolls get to them too much. Thanks should go to OSDN who keeps the bills paid so we get paid. I am also thankful for the constant support and bug fixes from MySQL, especially Monty, Sasha, David, and Heikki, who write a truly enterprise-worthy database and have supplied better support then any commercial vendor I have ever had the misfortune to deal with.

I would like to say that I am sorry to everyone who had to deal with other projects I work on getting shoved to the side. My dog Rosayln should be thanked for keeping my feet warm at night, and Nausicaa and Kiki the cats should be blamed for all typos. And no one should ever overlook Christine; she deals with my late-night typing and last-minute requests to review what I write way past her bedtime. I happen to love her.

Dave Krieger's Acknowledgments

I would first and foremost like to thank Christine Peterson of Foresight Institute for her encouragement and advice in the early genesis of this book. Without her, this book would not have come to be. I'd also like to thank my co-authors for pitching in and bailing when the boat began to leak. For aid and comfort, thanks are due to Troy Hudson, Mikey "Bootkid" Miller, Ken Berry, and last and most to Rob Kinninmont, who's twice as good as I deserve.

1

Slash: An Overview

This chapter is a whirlwind tour of Slash. It begins with a short history of Slash, then explores a typical site through the eyes of an average user. It explains the life cycle of a Slash Story, from user submission to published glory, and ends with a skeletal view of the underlying software. Subsequent chapters put meat on these bones. This chapter draws the broad outlines of the map and the major thoroughfares.

The Slashdot Story

The Slash Story begins with Slashdot, one of the most successful news and technology sites on the web. Slashdot's motto says it all: "News for nerds. Stuff that matters." Back in 1997, Rob "CmdrTaco" Malda started a website known as Chips & Dips, served from his student account at Hope College in Michigan. That summer, Malda spent his time writing and updating static HTML files. Every few days, he'd start a new page. Computer programmers like to talk about scalability, the idea that a resource can keep up with increasing demands. Editing HTML by hand is time-consuming and tedious, and quickly scales beyond the attention span of a typical programmer. Computers are fully capable of handling these mundanities.

The site grew in popularity. Malda and his friend Jeff "Hemos" Bates registered the *slashdot.org* domain and moved to a dedicated machine in October 1997. They took the opportunity to automate parts of the publishing process. Malda started learning Perl and enlisted the help of other friends (Patrick Galbraith, Cliff Wood, Jaime McCarthy, and Jonathan Pater) to add templates and a web interface for editing Stories. Soon, they were adding features like madmen—the distinctive visual look of the site, user polls, remote administration, and user comments.

The site became a place to test new ideas, and the coders had to learn to cope with a perpetually growing userbase. Malda discovered *mod_perl* and MySQL, and by April 1998, had ported the software for extra speed and features. His self-confessed first (significant) Perl program grew into a powerful tool for running Slashdot. Somehow, the site put up with a traffic load that could often choke other servers, occasionally eating the entire bandwidth allotment for the city of Holland, Michigan.

These humble beginnings were nothing new, either on the personal or technological levels. Many Horatio Alger stories have come from the heady Internet days of the late 1990s. Some remain. Many modern websites have gone through a similar evolution, from static pages to templates, flat files to database-driven content management systems. Slashdot was different in two important ways.

The Rise of the Weblog

The Internet was once the domain of technically-savvy researchers and students. Only a privileged few were able to enter this freewheeling meritocracy. As with most communication technology, it would soon enter the hands of the common people. A missionary in Bohol can keep in touch with his family and friends via email, and with his supporters through a web page hosted, for free, by a California company.

He still faces several technical barriers, though. He has to know enough HTML to write his web page. He needs access to the machine hosting his site. He must constantly come up with new things to say, or people will stop reading. Solving these problems means that anyone, anywhere, with Internet access, can find his information at any time, day or night.

While the Slashdot crew coded away, several other programmers had similar ideas. Would it be possible to build a program to manage a web site, where people could organize and create things through a web browser instead of HTML editors and FTP clients? What would the resulting site look like? Where would they find fresh content, and what would keep people coming back for more?

One type of site is called the *weblog.** This can be anything from a journal to a stream of consciousness commentary or even a full-blown news site. The important features are a steady stream of fresh content and a willingness to link to other existing sites as a *raison d'être*. Think of the Captain's log on *Star Trek* and how it usually served to introduce and frame the upcoming story, and add in a very quick feedback loop.

---

* To be fair, this term is almost as broadly defined as "peer2peer" or "copy prevention circumvention device."

Weblogs tend to be simple, personal, and immediate, but this is not required. For the most part, weblogs are simple and straightforward. People can publish their thoughts, even for the first time, with almost no training. Within these constraints, sites such as *http://advogato.org/*, *http://blogger.com/*, *http://www.livejournal.com/*, and the venerable *http://slashdot.org/* each serve a different niche.

The main similarities between Slashdot and other news-type weblogs (for example, at the O'Reilly Network, *http://www.oreillynet.com/weblogs/*) is the concept of a *Story*. A Story is usually a link to another web site with a bit of commentary. Built to support a "news" site, Slash formally defines Stories as simple blocks of HTML containing a headline and introduction, an opinion column, a media review, or anything else. Stories are organized by topic and are placed in logical Sections. Readers can comment on Stories and on the comments of other users. An underlying database tracks and manages all of this data. Slash's job is to present everything in a format that's both easily navigable and searchable. Moving closer to personal weblogs, Slash 2.x added user journals. These allow users to record their own thoughts and allow comments from other users. This feature has already proven quite popular at Use Perl (*http://use.perl.org/*).

Slashdot may not have been the first weblog, and it is admittedly not perfect, but its powerful and flexible user comment system was almost unheard of at the time, and is rarely equaled even now. Imagine a city newspaper with letters to the editor attached to every story, in which newsmakers and reporters alike regularly respond! The freewheeling, corner-pub-for-geeks atmosphere the editors try to cultivate doesn't hurt, either. The comment system comes for free with Slash, but the community takes some work.

The Slash Code

Since the Slashdot crew were fierce Linux and Free Software proponents, it was inevitable that readers would ask for their own copies of the Slashdot code. Malda deferred, for a while. It was ugly. It had been patched and repatched to fit the needs of Slashdot alone. It would be nearly impossible to install elsewhere. Besides, running the site was more important and interesting than cleaning things up for a release. People continued to ask.

As the site's influence increased (an interview in Wired magazine! a giant monitor wall at MIT displaying the page! John Carmack posting comments!), imitators and clones appeared. Several new sites began to imitate Slashdot's rather distinctive look. PHP, Java, and even other Perl hackers wrote their own Slash-like software, clearly inspired by what was possible.

Then came Slash, the Slashdot Like Automated Storytelling Homepage. It was hard to read and even harder to install, but it was—more or less—the same software that actually ran Slashdot. Malda and perpetual poll option Jonathon "Cow-boyNeal" Pater had actually delivered the goods. This original release had a not-entirely undeserved reputation for unreadability. People downloaded it anyway, and a hardy few used it to build their own sites.

Slash Matures

Slashdot has always believed in free speech. Even after user accounts were added in August 1998, users without accounts were still allowed to make stunningly brilliant, if anonymous, comments. Of course, the same mechanism that protects a free-speaking whistleblower gives bored 15, 25, or even 85-year-old readers the chance to spew inanities, vulgarities, and redundancies, even in a Story memorializing a computing pioneer. The Slash developers realized that a little community moderation was in order.

The point of *moderation* is to pick out hidden gems on the sandy beach of comments. A secondary goal is to mark the dross clearly enough, so that only people who want raw, unfiltered opinions can see it. Originally, a hand-picked crew of long-time readers performed this filtering. The ranks swelled as the experiment continued. Finally, Slashdot opened the floodgates to all registered users in good standing. In theory, the community as a whole would develop coherent standards to separate the wheat from the chaff.

In June 1999, Slashdot announced that it had been sold to a technology and online-content company called Andover.Net. Having turned down several other offers, Malda and Bates negotiated a shrewd deal. They would maintain editorial independence, while receiving the financial backing to continue doing what they loved. This brought another round of upgrades and additional authors, and kept the site running.

If Slashdot has proved one thing about Internet communities, it's that there are at least as many opinions as there are participants. While many thousands of people enjoy reading Slashdot without ever posting, thousands do comment. *Meta-moderation* came about to help curb possible abuses of rogue moderators and to test the grand experiment. Again, users in good standing could review existing moderations, judging them as fair or unfair. In theory, the system balances itself. In practice, site administrators can tweak dozens of variables to modify the system.

With these powerful new features, users again clamored for fresh code. Perhaps remembering the pain of the last releases, Malda again deferred. Andover.Net decided to make Slash a business project. They hired two noted and very capable Perl hackers, Chris "Pudge" Nandor and Brian "Krow" Aker, to oversee the project, and launched the Slashcode site (*http://slashcode.com/*) to help the process.

Things were still rough, but they improved quickly after the release of Slash 0.9 in January 2000.

Today, Slash is much more than a weblog. It's a web application platform, to throw around a buzzword or two. It separates presentation from content, has a database abstraction layer, performs powerful caching, hooks directly into the Apache web server, and can be extended to do just about anything a web application could be expected to do. It can serve content in various languages, perform various maintenance tasks automatically, and, if tuned correctly, serve millions of pages per day.

Perhaps best of all, it's free in every sense of the word. You can download it at no charge. You can modify it to your heart's content. You can sell it, if you find buyers, and you can distribute your changes.* This was true of the earliest releases and has not wavered in subsequent releases (Slash 1.0 escaped in March 2000, with Slash 2.0 following in May 2001).

The power of Slash to spread a message, to start discussions, and to build communities around the world is available to anyone willing to learn.

Becoming a Slash Guru: A Roadmap

The ideal place to start is to explore an existing Slash site. It will demonstrate the current possibilities, perhaps inspiring fresh ideas. There's no shame in imitating a successful site, either. Imitation is the sincerest form of flattery, and sincere flattery is usually good currency for the technical crowds.† Being a user on another site gives a unique perspective. How does the site work? Who does it attract? How has its focus changed over time? How does it handle conflict and growth? You will probably also come up with a list of things you'd handle differently. They may be philosophical, or they may be as simple as a different color scheme or as complicated as a new moderation system.

Most users don't get to see the seamy underbelly of Slash. Site administrators spend most of their time working with a special interface. The underlying metaphor of Stories comes into play. The essential mechanisms are exposed as pulleys and trapdoors. Slash has a staggering wealth of editorial tools, but just knowing what's available returns things to manageable levels.

With theories and introductions out of the way, it's time to install the beast. All of this power comes at a price—someone has to understand the underlying

---

* For more information about these rights, see the *COPYING* file in the Slash distribution. The Free Software Foundation (*http://www.fsf.org/*) and Open Source Initiative (*http://www.opensource.org/*) web sites explain the philosophical and pragmatic reasons behind this concept, respectively.

† (Root) Beer and pizza also work.

components well enough to put them together. The Slash team has spent a tremendous amount of time smoothing things out. Gone are the days of reading Malda's mind. With a little Unix experience, a handy installation guide, maybe some junk food to bribe your local teenaged hacker, Slash will be up and running.

Of course, the default installation produces a rather generic site, looking just like unconfigured Slashcode and behaving much like Slashdot does. Site customization will fill the days of the site administrators. The first order of business is to recruit other people to ease the administrative burden. The second is to fill in some of the blanks. Slash has dozens of configuration options, and it's easy to control everything from presentation to algorithmic behavior.

With surprisingly little experience, administrators can quickly begin to post Stories. Slash's most developed and polished feature gives Authors power to schedule, promote, annotate, and weed out everything from user suggestions to original content. A normal, Slashdot-like site will rely heavily on Stories. It's what weblogs do.

Slash's powerful user comment system is arguably its biggest draw. It has a wealth of options for viewing and posting comments. It is easily customized to user preferences. It has powerful features for filtering out unwanted content, and it has a powerful moderation system. Understanding the comment system is essential to developing a good community, and part of being a good host is guiding the conversation. The types of things discussed influence the site audience, which influences the types of things discussed. To help organize things, Slash provides two axes for Story classification. Understanding the feedback loops and exploiting the taxonomy will help you shape your site's evolution.

To avoid devolution into messy anarchy, a site must consider its purpose. Why does it exist? A simple hobbyist site has different goals than a mainstream journalism site, but they both must address similar questions to earn the loyalty of their users. Asking these questions before trouble starts could save a lot of time and grief.

As the site grows, the details will become more important. Publishing information is one thing, doing it with style is another. Without commentary, a weblog is just a bookmark list. Without context and direction, it's just a voice crying in the wilderness. Slash allows users many customization options, but administrators must make the raw materials available. As usual, Slash makes some common tasks easy.

A certain class of people finds the guts of a thing fascinating. Slash obliges them, with miles of dark, squalid entrails to explore. The rest of the world just needs to know how it works. A little preventative maintenance keeps a site running smoothly, and learning the basics of Slash anatomy makes this possible. It also lays the groundwork for advanced surgery, like grafting on an extra arm.

Sites evolve, and many move into new ecological niches. Others run up against artificial boundaries. As free software, Slash can be modified to change with the site. The task may seem imposing, but a moderate Perl programmer armed with a good idea and a map can drastically change the look and feel of the site, add new behavior, or even modify the underlying code directly. It's not only possible, it's recommended and encouraged. If you're not the person to do this, several others are capable and willing to do it for you. The price may even be right.

The Slash User Interface

The original and most popular Slash site is Slashdot, and most users first encounter Slash there. The site's homepage looks something like Figure 1-1. (The default appearance of a newly installed Slash site is slightly different.) The most important page feature is the central column, which lists Stories in reverse chronological order. Each Story is introduced in a separate box. This introduction may, in fact, be the entire Story. The box also provides other information, including the Story's title, date, and time of publication; the number of comments made on the Story so far; and the person responsible for the Story.

Other navigational aids surround the Story column: links to site features, live headlines pulled from other sites; a Search form, a multiple-choice user poll, and a list of older Stories that have been pushed off the homepage by newer ones.

The *Read More . . .* link in any Story box leads to that Story's individual page. This displays the full Story along with user comments. Story content may be limited to the "Intro" text (displayed on the homepage), or it may include "Extended" text (displayed only on the Story page). An HTML form beneath the content allows you to add a comment or to change the presentation of existing comments.

Comments may be viewed in threaded, nested, or flat formats, or may be suppressed entirely. They may also be sorted by the date and time of posting or by their *moderation score* (an aggregate value of other users' opinions of the comment). Users can also suppress the display of comments with scores below a certain threshold value. Chapter 6 describes the comment and moderation system in full detail.

Slash User Preferences

Slash allows users to create their own accounts, which can be used to store site customizations. Each registered user will have a unique *nickname* which will be attached to his comments. Users who do not register share a common generic account called "Anonymous User". (The site administrator may change the label of this account.) Only registered users can participate in comment moderation and

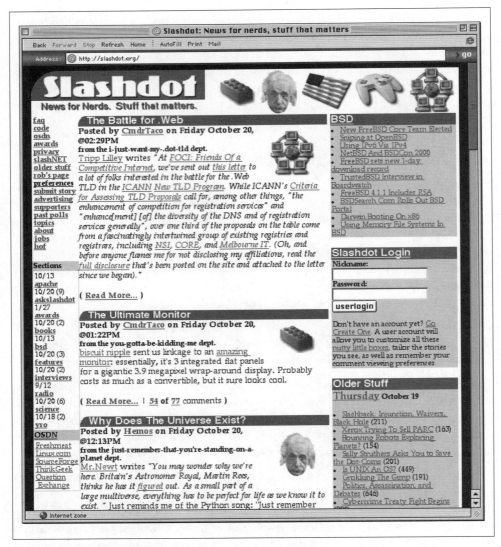

Figure 1-1. The Slashdot homepage

save their viewing preferences. Slash can also be configured to prevent unregistered users from posting comments.

Slash uses browser cookies to identify registered users. These cookies can persist across browser sessions (for home or work machines) or can be discarded when the user closes the browser (in public labs and cafes). In spite of (or because of) this, these cookies should not be considered a high-security access mechanism. Slash trades security for convenience and ease of use. Keep your passwords safe. Users who have not logged in will see the Login Slashbox on most pages (see

Figure 1-2). This allows registered users to enter their name and password. Users without an account can click on *Go Create One* in the Login Slashbox or on the *preferences* link on most pages to reach the Login/Register page shown in Figure 1-3.

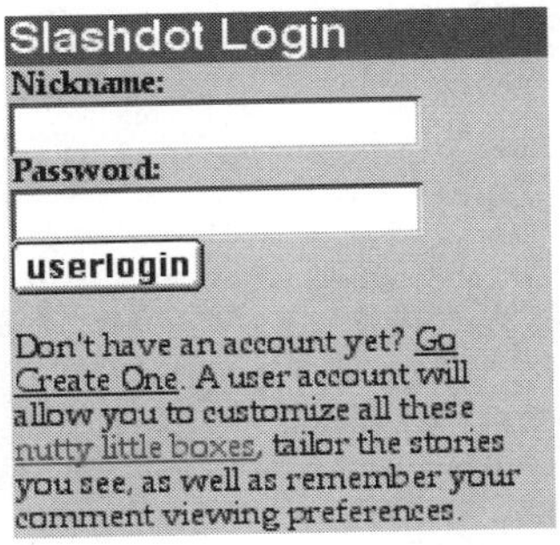

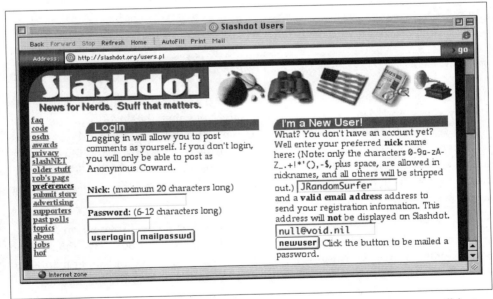

Figure 1-2. The Login box at Slashdot

Figure 1-3. A non–logged-in user who clicks the preferences link on any page will be presented with a login form (left) and a registration form (right)

To register, enter your desired nickname and a valid email address in the I'm a New User! form (on the right in Figure 1-3), and click Newuser. Both values must be unique within the system. If so, Slash will generate an initial password for your account and mail it to the provided email address. Check the address carefully. If it is invalid, you will not receive your password. If either value has been used already, Slash will prompt you to choose something more unique. After receiving the Lovecraftian password, you can log in and change it to something more pronounceable, if you so desire.

Logged-in users can click on *preferences* to customize their user preferences (see Figure 1-4). A series of links across the top of the page divides these options into related categories. The first category is *Homepage*, which controls the appearance of the default page. (In the case of Slashdot, this would be *http://slashdot.org/.*)

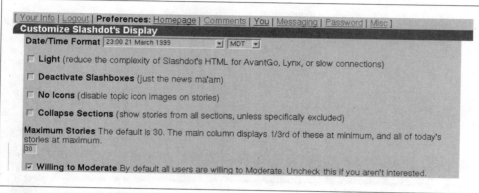

Figure 1-4. The top of the homepage customization form

The Date/Time menus allow users to choose the format and time zone used to display times and dates throughout the site. Note that the given options in the form do not reflect the current date and time. Instead, they're merely examples. The Light checkbox reduces the complexity of the site's pages, using fewer graphics and simpler HTML. This is very handy for users with low-bandwidth connections, or for visually impaired users. No Icons suppresses the display of Topic icons, which can also improve download time.

Maximum Stories limits the number of Stories and headlines displayed on the front page in both the center column and in the Older Stuff Slashbox. One-third of the Stories will be displayed normally, with their title, date, author, department, and blurb. The rest of the Stories will appear as headlines only in the Slashbox. Given the default value of 30, 10 Stories will appear in the center column, with 20 headlines in Older Stuff. A good rule of thumb is that Maximum Stories should be 1.5 times the number of Stories published between visits. (If you visit a site once per day and it publishes 10 Stories per day, set this value to 15 to buy yourself some breathing room. Occasionally, a web publisher will get to work early.)

The Willing to Moderate checkbox allows users to abstain from becoming a content moderator. If this box is unchecked, the user will never be asked to moderate comments, but if it is checked, the user may never become a moderator (the section "Gaining Moderator Access" in Chapter 6 discusses the criteria for selecting moderators).

The Exclude Stories Section (see Figure 1-5) lets users exclude Stories from the homepage. Every Slash Story has an Author, a Topic, and a Section. *Authors* are Slash users credited with posting (or writing) Stories. *Topics* are categories used to classify Stories by content, such as "Space Exploration" or "Aardvark Jokes." *Sections* are logical categories, used to group Stories or Topics according to some additional criteria. Sections have their own home pages, which list the most recent Stories of the Section. Users can exclude Stories associated with a particular Author, Topic, or Section by checking the appropriate checkbox and clicking the Save button.

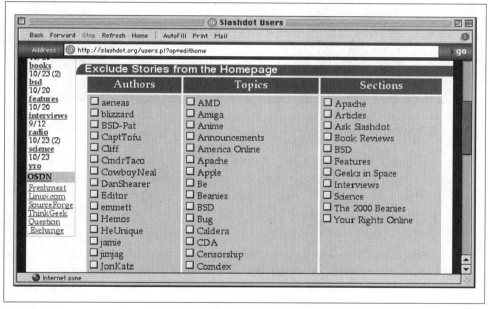

Figure 1-5. Registered users can exclude Stories from display on the homepage by Author, Topic, or Section

Further down the page, Customize Slashboxes (see Figure 1-6) lets users choose which Slashboxes will appear on their homepages. Slashboxes contain either content retrieved from other web sites or static blocks of HTML (the section "Secrets of Headline Swapping: XML, RDF, and RSS" in Chapter 9 describes how live Slashboxes are updated). Static Slashboxes can contain links to popular Stories, links to other sites, site-specific notes, or any other HTML.

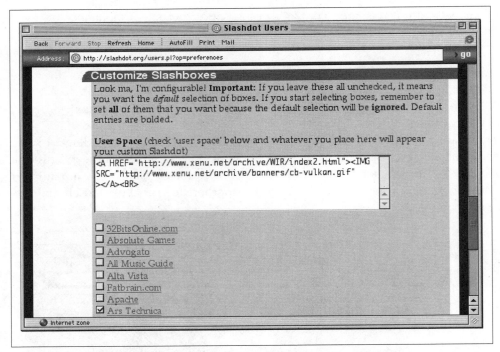

Figure 1-6. The Customize Slashbox checkboxes and the User Space Slashbox text area

A new user will see no Slashboxes checked. In this case, Slash will use a default set of Slashboxes, visible by bold titles in Figure 1-6. Checking any box will override the default selection, and only those Slashboxes explicitly checked will be shown. For example, if a new user checks the Poll Slashbox, it will be the only Slashbox shown on the homepage.

The User Space Slashbox lets users create their own custom static Slashboxes. Any HTML in the text area will be displayed on the homepage if the user checks the User Space checkbox. Figure 1-7 shows the Slashbox generated by the HTML input from Figure 1-6. This figure also highlights the three buttons in each Slashbox's titlebar. These allow users to control the order in which Slashboxes appear on a customized homepage. Clicking the upward-pointing triangle on the left swaps that Slashbox with the one above it, shifting it up one position in the column. The downward-pointing triangle on the right shifts it downward by one. The X in between deletes that Slashbox from the homepage, just as if the user had unchecked it on the Customize Homepage form. The site administrator can customize the appearance of these controls.

Figure 1-7. The custom User Space Slashbox generated by the input shown in Figure 1-6, with the positional widgets circled

The *Edit User Info* link (see Figure 1-8) allows users to modify their public profiles. Users can provide their Real Name if they choose. Their Email Address appears here. Slash can automatically obfuscate this in an attempt to avoid unsolicited commercial email. The Homepage field can contain a link to a personal or favorite web page. The Sig contains a signature which Slash will append to all comments, and the Bio will be displayed on the user page. Users can also provide a Public Key (a PGP or GPG key), allowing other users to contact them in a cryptographically private fashion.

Editing chromatic (9471) chromatic@wgz.org

You can automatically login by clicking This Link and Bookmarking the resulting page. This is totally insecure, but very convenient.

Real Name (optional)

Your Email Address
(required but never displayed publicly, unless you specify so in your comment preferences. This is where your passwd is mailed. If you change this address, a notification will be sent, and you will need follow the enclosed instructions to re-register)

`chromatic@wgz.org`

Homepage (optional:you must enter a fully qualified URL!)

`http://wgz.org/chromatic/`

Sig (appended to the end of comments you post, 120 chars)

```
<BR>-- <BR>
chromatic the <A
HREF="http://wgz.org/chromatic/">revolutionary</A>
```

Bio (this information is publicly displayed on your user page. 255 chars)

```
<B>Karma</B> $1.024 (mostly the sum of moderation done to
users comments)<P>

Slashdot <A
HREF="http://slashdot.org/index.pl?section=books">Book
Reviewer</A>, Perl <A HREF="http://perlmonks.org/">Monk</A>,
```

Public Key

```
-----BEGIN PGP PUBLIC KEY BLOCK-----
Version: GnuPG v1.0.4 (GNU/Linux)
Comment: For info see http://www.gnupg.org
```

Save User

Figure 1-8. The Edit User Info form

Most of the requested user information can be fake, if so desired. However, two fields should be handled with care. On the Password page, both fields must match, or the old password will remain in effect. If you accidentally change this to an unknown or to an unrememberable value, you will be unable to log into the site.

The other important field is the Real Email field. A user can retrieve a lost or forgotten password from the Login form on the Login/Register page (see Figure 1-3). Place the account nickname in the Nick field and click the mailpasswd button. This causes the server to email the current password to the specified email addres. Changing Real Email to an invalid or inaccurate address will cause this and any other site mailings to fail. Handle this field with care.

Besides screening articles by Topic, Section, or Author, users can view lists of Stories in one of these categories. Following the *Topics* link in the left or bottom navigation bar displays a page (*/topics.pl*)* listing the site's defined Topics and their icons (see Figure 1-9). Clicking on the name or icon for any Topic displays a reverse-chronological list of the titles of Stories on that Topic; each title is a link to the individual page for that Story. Similarly, the *Authors* link in either main navigation menu leads to a page that lists the site's Authors (*/authors.pl*), with some biographical information and links to lists of Stories posted by each Author, and a Sections page (*/sections.pl*), which provides links to lists of Stories assigned to each of the site's Sections.

Additionally, those fields of the Edit User Info page that will be displayed on the site (such as the Bio) are filtered to remove Javascript and other potentially page-breaking HTML.

User Polls

One popular feature of Slash (and Slashdot) is the ability to attach a multiple-choice user poll to the homepage or to a specific Story. Polls appear in a Slashbox beside the main content column (see Figure 1-10). Users vote by selecting the

---

* Unless otherwise noted, all URIs of this form are relative to the root of the site. If the site's root is *http://firewheel/*, the Topics page will be at *http://firewheel/topics.pl*. For the Ghostwheel site at *http://firewheel/ghostwheel/*, the Topics URI is *http://firewheel/ghostwheel/topics.pl*.

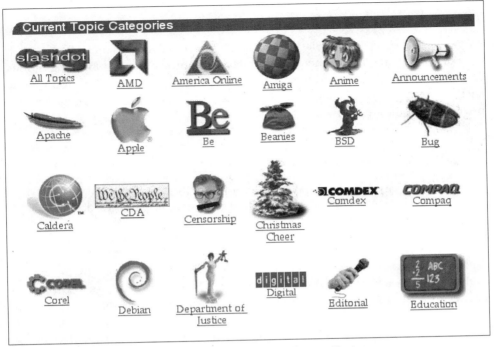

Figure 1-9. A fraction of Slashdot's Topics, as displayed on its Topic page

radio button next to their preferred response, and clicking the Vote button. This leads to a page showing a bar graph tabulating the results of the poll to date. Slash makes few attempts to prevent ballot-stuffing by automated bots or determined humans, so the results should not be used for any serious purpose. The section "Managing User Polls" in Chapter 9 covers everything worth knowing about Slash polls.

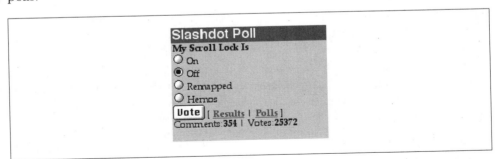

Figure 1-10. A Slash poll

The Slash Author Interface

As mentioned earlier, each Slash site has a set of privileged users, called Authors (or Editors), charged with the responsibility of approving and publishing Stories. Some Authors may have additional privileges such as modifying the site's appearance, deleting user comments, adding or deleting Slashboxes, or regulating the privileges of other Authors.

 The phrase *Slash site administrator* can be a little misleading. There is no special "Administrator" entity in the software, merely Authors of varying levels of privileges. "Slash site administrator" is shorthand for "any of the site's Authors who has sufficient privileges" for the operation under discussion.

Authors are simply regular users with additional access bestowed by an existing Author with the ability to do so. Thereafter, these users have access to the Author interface (at the relative URL *admin.pl*), which provides access to site administration functions. Depending on their access level, Authors have an additional row of links to administrative options at the top of the page. The Author interface uses a simpler layout with a grayed-out color scheme to distinguish it from regular pages (see Figure 4-1). Furthermore, a logged-in Author sees special interface elements on every page of the site that do not appear for run-of-the-mill users, such as the Author menu, a row of HTML links to the various pages of the Author interface. The links available in the Author menu vary depending on the privileges of the Author viewing it. For example, only Authors with the highest possible privilege level will see the *Authors* or *Vars* links.

The homepage of the Author interface is the Stories list, available via *admin.pl* or through the *Stories* link in the Admin menu. The Stories list provides Authors with a quick overview of recent publishing activity on the site. The *New* link allows an Author to create a new Story from scratch. The *n Submissions* link leads to the Story queue, where users have submitted n articles. This is the most important source of new content for many Slash sites. Chapter 4 describes the mechanisms of the Slash publishing cycle in detail. The next section presents a broad overview of the publishing cycle.

Home links to the site's homepage, while *Help* links to a terse help file for Authors, located at the relative URL */slashguide.shtml*. *Topics* links to the Topics page, which displays the names and icons of all Topics defined for the site. Each icon is a link to a reverse-chronological list of Stories published on that Topic; each name is a link to an HTML form for editing or deleting that Topic or changing the icon associated with it. Similarly, the *Sections* link displays a list of the site's Sections and provides the ability to modify and delete them. See Chapter 7 for more details.

The *Templates* link allows Authors to modify the site's templates. This is a very powerful feature. Templates control the appearance, layout, and wording of most of the site's common interface elements: the structure of Story boxes and Slashboxes, general page layouts, and other types of generated pages. Additionally, they control the wording of standard forms and messages such as the Login box and the email accompanying a new user's password. They have more powerful uses, too. *Blocks* lets Authors modify the contents (or, for live Slashboxes, content sources) of Slashboxes and other simple site components. *Site Colors* provides a special interface to modify one of these blocks, which contains the HTML hex triplet values (e.g., #FFFF00 for yellow) for the colors used in rendering the site. The section "Section Blocks: Colors and Boxes" in Chapter 10 describes color blocks, while the section "Blocks and Slashboxes" in Chapter 9 discusses the mechanics of block editing.

The *Vars* link allows site administrators to change the values of important configuration variables. These control, for example, whether Anonymous Users can comment on Stories or if non-Author users can view submissions currently in the queue. Chapter 3 discusses the how and why of basic Slash administration in depth.

Similarly, the *Authors* link is available only to the most privileged Authors. It provides the interface to create and delete Author accounts as well as to manage their privileges. The section "Editing Authors" in Chapter 3 discusses the mechanics of the interface; the section "Managing Authors" in Chapter 8 outlines principles for choosing and managing Authors.

Comment Filters

Depending on the level of maturity of your site's audience (and let's face it, if your site is open to the public Internet, your audience is guaranteed to include a number of folks who haven't progressed much since their toilet training), you may be troubled with various kinds of comment postings that, shall we say, don't add much to the discussion: posts composed solely of non-alphanumeric or whitespace characters; ASCII drawings of Homer Simpson, Mickey Mouse, or more scatological subjects; or posts with an empty subject or empty body. Slash provides a highly configurable mechanism, *comment filters*, to catch these kinds of posts when they're entered and chuck them back at the poster with a helpful explanation. Each comment filter is made up of a Perl regular expression, a field of the comment to apply it to, and numerical parameters governing the sensitivity of the filter ("Do non-alphanumeric characters make up over 30% of this post?"). The *Comment Filters* link provides Authors with access to the interface for establishing and modifying comment filters. The entire comment system, including filtering and moderation, is covered in Chapter 6.

The Slash Publishing Cycle

Like living organisms, political movements, and dot-com startups, Slash Stories have a well-defined life cycle (see Figure 1-11). They are born (usually as user submissions), they mature (when published by an Author), they live productively for a while (as users add comments and moderate those comments), and, after a full life, they go to heaven (are archived, where no more comments can be added).

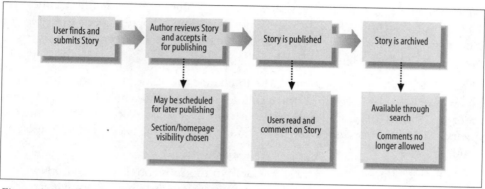

Figure 1-11. The life cycle of a Slash Story and comments

Most Slash sites operate somewhat like community newspapers. The people in a small town have a number of shared concerns that arise from living in the same legal jurisdiction, in the same school district, and so on. A small-town newspaper serves as both a mirror held up to that community and a speakers' platform for the people to conduct public business and make their voices heard. Readers can write letters to the editor or opinion essays for the editorial page, or just call the attention of the newspaper staff to issues they feel deserve coverage. In the case of a Slash site, the common unifying factor of its audience is less likely to be geographic proximity than a social or technical topic of common interest, but Slash sites (and other kinds of public weblogs) provide the same mechanisms of reportage and discussion that a good small-town newspaper provides for its community.

A Story usually starts off as a user submission. Each Slash page has a *Submit Story* link where anyone, even Anonymous Users, can suggest a story to the site Authors. This can be as simple as a URL to something interesting elsewhere on the web or as complex as a 4,000-word essay in plain text or jazzy HTML. Submitted stories live in a database table. Site Authors view this queue of submissions, choosing which stories to publish. Slash can be configured to allow the public to view the submission queue. Normally only the Authors can see it.

Site Authors can select, preview, edit, and publish user submissions when they're satisfied. New Stories appear at the top of the list on the homepage and on the homepage of their respective Sections. A Story ages and moves further down the homepage as newer Stories are posted. Eventually, it slides off the main page, becoming a headline in the Older Stuff Slashbox before leaving the front page entirely. Older articles are still available through the site's Search facility and the *Older Articles* link in Older Stuff.

Slash allows users to comment on Stories. Comments resemble "Letters to the Editor" in a newspaper or magazine. While a traditional editorial staff must evaluate the feedback and choose what to publish, Slash makes this feedback immediately available, if the site administrator allows it. Readers can do their own evaluation through the comment moderation system. A particularly insightful or funny comment will garner moderation points from appreciative readers and move up in the moderation rankings; obtuse, off-topic, or flameworthy posts will lose points and subside into invisibility.

Eventually, the Story is no longer current news. With new Stories published all the time, fewer people read and comment on the older Stories. After living for a certain number of days (set by the site administrator), the *dailyStuff* program, run nightly by the *slashd* daemon process, accompanies the Story to its heavenly rest. The Story becomes a static web page with its comments to date, in flat form. It is still viewable, but no longer alive. No new comments can be added. Think of the Story as having been embalmed and put on display, like V. Lenin or W. Disney— informative, and hence still useful, but no longer dynamic and vital.

The Slash Architecture

In Version 2.0, Slash underwent a complete architectural overhaul. The new Slash provides features such as themes, database abstraction support, an API for the database, use of the Perl Template Toolkit, an improved and streamlined installation process, hooks to support addition of third-party modules, and better support for hosting multiple Slash sites.

Slash has always been Free Software, available under the GNU General Public License. With the open-sourcing of the MySQL database, all of Slash's underlying infrastructure is now open source as well. Slash is built on the Apache web server, the *mod_perl* Apache module, and a relational database that speaks Structured Query Language (SQL). (MySQL is supported out of the box. Some work has been done to port things to the excellent PostgreSQL database, though it lags behind. Oracle has some preliminary support.)

At the bottom of the traditional software architecture "layer-cake" diagram (see Figure 1-12) squats the operating system. Slash was born on Linux and has been run successfully on FreeBSD, OpenBSD, and several commercial flavors of Unix, including Solaris and HP-UX. As of this writing, Mark Breitenbach (*geo@other.org*) has ported Slash 1.x to NT; track the progress of the port at *http://geo.trippy.org/ nt-slashcode/*.

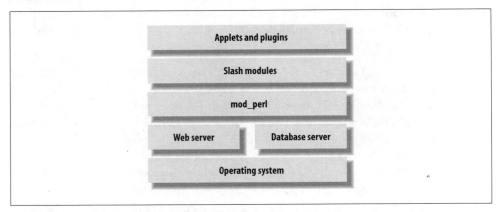

Figure 1-12. Diagram of Slash software infrastructure and architecture

The web server and database server sit on top of the operating system. Slash requires Apache, the world's most widely used web server, compiled with the *mod_perl* module, which adds a Perl virtual machine running inside the Apache process. This enables Perl applications such as Slash to run as persistent "applets" instead of forked-off children using the Common Gateway Interface (CGI). When Apache starts, it compiles and loads these applets, initializing them (including retrieving configuration data). They remain in memory to handle client requests. This spends more memory on Apache child processes but improves performance by avoiding the delays of loading, compiling, and initializing a separate CGI process for each client request.

Any of several SQL-compliant database servers may be used with Slash. Slash initially worked only with MySQL, but the 2.0 redesign added a layer of abstraction to enable easy porting to other SQL databases. The database stores all of the information that makes up the site: Stories and comments, user data and preferences, layout templates, comment filters, and poll results.

Slash itself is made up of four kinds of Perl programs:

Applets

> The Perl programs that run inside the Apache web server process. Like CGI programs, each has a URL and is executed when the web server receives an HTTP GET or POST request for that URL from a web browser. The applet then

generates an HTML page which is sent back to the requesting client. Examples of Slash applets are *index.pl*, which generates each user's custom view of the site homepage, and *article.pl*, which does the same for individual Story pages.

Tasks

Programs that run independently from the web server. The *slashd* daemon schedules and runs them. Tasks are small programs that perform various system tasks, often updating site content or keeping things in order. For example, the *portald* task fetches RDF-format content from elsewhere on the web to update Slashboxes, and generates the site's own RDF file for others to grab. The section "Setting the Tone" in Chapter 8 explains these programs at length.

Utilities

Standalone programs that run on an as-needed basis when invoked by site administrators or daemons. We have already discussed the *dailyStuff* program, which sends out nightly headline mailings. Other utilities are provided for analyzing suspiciously high levels of activity and other common tasks.

Modules

Perl libraries defining objects and functions used by the other programs. The most important of these are, in brief:

Slash.pm

The original workhorse, this is the standard entry point for common, high-level functions called by applets and plugins. These range from operations such as "give me the HTML for pop-up menu of the site's Sections" to "give me an HREF link tag to Story ID *foo*." Most of these functions live in other packages; *Slash.pm* exports them for convenience.

Utility.pm

Defines lower-level functions called by *Slash.pm*, such as "tell me who the current authenticated user is, if any." Functions in *Utility.pm* are used both within Apache (i.e., by applets) and from other processes (such as the daemons and utilities).

DB.pm

Provides high-level database functions such as "fetch block *motd* from the database." *DB.pm* doesn't actually implement any of these functions itself. Instead, there is a separate, specific library for each of the supported databases (*MySQL.pm*, *PostgreSQL.pm*, etc.); when anybody asks *DB.pm* for anything, it delegates the job by cleverly choosing the right database-specific module from which to inherit that subroutine.

Display.pm

This module (and its friends) add support for the Perl Template Toolkit by Andy Wardley (*http://search.cpan.org/search?dist=Template-Toolkit*), "a collection of modules which implement a fast, flexible, powerful and

extensible template processing system." This system defines components of web pages containing embedded variable references which are
replaced with the corresponding values when the page is requested and
viewed. Appendix C discusses working with the Template Toolkit in Slash.

Apache.pm

Apache's module interface lets programmers change just about any
aspect of the web server's behavior. The Slash modules *Slash::Apache*,
Slash::Apache::User, and *Slash::Apache::Log* use this interface to get under
Apache's hood and handle some of Slash's needs earlier in the request-
handling process than could be done otherwise. *User.pm* gets Apache to
handle user authentication against the Slash user database, *Log.pm* handles
any logging that should go to the Slash database instead of the standard
Apache logs, and *Apache.pm* makes it easier to configure Apache to run
multiple Slash sites on the same machine.

Appendix A catalogues the main modules and describes their main functions. Two
other types of components are necessary for site operation: themes and plugins.
Themes are bundles of templates and applets that control the presentation of data.
Plugins are bundles of applets and data that add new behavior to a site. The
default Slash behavior (Slashcode-clone) is itself implemented with the Slashcode
theme and the Admin plugin.

2

Installing Slash

Installing Slash is not difficult, but there are multiple steps and several possible complications. This chapter describes the complete process, from downloading Slash and all of its requirements through compilation and installation. Please note that this chapter does not cover everything there is to know about configuring and using these tools.* It does walk through the basic steps to get a Slash server up and running.

The Slash install process improved greatly for the 2.0 release. The latest distribution includes a GNU makefile, plus a Perl script (*install-slashsite*) for customizing the installed Slash server with site-specific information, such as the machine's *fully qualified domain name* (FQDN) and the name of the local Slash user. These should work on any free Unix system; however, they are guaranteed only on GNU/Linux systems. ("Linux" is used as a convenient shorthand for "an operating system containing tools from the GNU project, built around the kernel named Linux".)

Before You Begin

Because this chapter can't reasonably go all the way back to the Big Bang, it assumes certain things. You should already have a working and compatible Unix-like operating system. As with most Unix software, you will need root access, along with at least some basic system administration experience. If you're new at this, read the instructions completely before beginning an installation, then follow along.

---

* That information resides in the books *Apache: The Definitive Guide* by Ben Laurie and Peter Laurie; *MySQL and mSQL* by Randy Jay Yarger, George Reese, and Tim King; and *Programming Perl* by Larry Wall, Tom Christiansen, and Jon Orwant—all published by O'Reilly & Associates.

In addition, prepare the following information:

- The installed location of the Slash files, also known as the *Slash home direc-tory*. The default, */usr/local/slash/*, is highly recommended. Subsequent exam-ples assume this to be the case. If you use another location, modify them accordingly. Earlier versions of Slash installed into */home/slash/* instead.

- The Slash system account name. By default, this is `slash`. This user will own all files and directories associated with Slash. Machines running multiple Slash sites should have a different system user for each site.

- The fully qualified domain name of the server. This is the machine name that will appear after `http://` in URLs pointing to the site. For example, Slashdot's FQDN is (more or less) *slashdot.org*. It must be a valid DNS name for the net-work on which the site will serve requests.

- The directory containing source code for the installed components. The exam-ples to follow assume that the directory is */usr/local/src/*, with a named subdi-rectory for each different software package. (For example, Slash would be in */usr/local/src/slash-2.2.0/*, Apache in */usr/local/src/apache-1.3.22/*, and so forth.)

Getting Help

Slash is a complex piece of software, depending on several other complicated pieces of software. Most of the questions from new users come during the installa-tion phase. You are expected to read this chapter before installing Slash. You are expected to read the installation instructions that come with Slash before attempt-ing to install it. The same very helpful people who might be willing to help you with a hirsute problem have already provided many answers to common prob-lems. Do yourself a favor and ask good questions (*http://perl.plover.com/Ques-tions.html*).

With all of the ex-help-desk angst out of the way, there are several avenues of assistance available for MySQL, Perl, *mod_perl*, Perl modules, and Slash itself.

Getting help on MySQL

The MySQL programmers maintain a useful website at *http://www.mysql.com/*. This page features prominent links to online documentation as well as to MySQL mail-ing lists. The searchable manual is quite good. The `mysql` and `msql-mysql-modules` are probably the most appropriate mailing lists.

Getting help on Perl

Perl has a wealth of fabulous resources, starting with the standard documentation. The *perldoc* command displays and searches over 1,500 pages of included documentation. Start with *perldoc perldoc* for an overview. The same program handles documentation for all properly installed Perl modules. For example, to read about *DBIx::Password*, type *perldoc DBIx::Password*. There's also a voluminous FAQ, accessible through *perldoc perlfaq*.

There are several other venues for Perl support. Web sites such as Perl Monks (*http://perlmonks.org/*) and Perldoc (*http://www.perldoc.com/*) are good places to ask advice from other programmers or to browse documentation from several different versions of Perl. Mailing lists can be found at *http://lists.perl.org/*. Good places to start, ordered by increasing specialization and complexity, are beginners, dbi-users, msql-mysql-modules, mod_perl, and template-toolkit.

Getting help on Apache and mod_perl

The Apache web server homepage can be found at *http://httpd.apache.org/*. It has links to a FAQ and copious online documentation (*http://httpd.apache.org/docs/*). The Tutorials section is particularly good, especially "The Idiot's Guide to Solving Perl CGI Problems". Don't let the name put you off—at least one author had to read it several times while debugging his first Perl CGI program.

mod_perl has its own web site at *http://perl.apache.org/*. Like the web server site, there are plenty of links to mailing lists, online documentation, and FAQs. This is the first place to look for *mod_perl* answers. Other worthwhile sites are Apache Toolbox (*http://www.apachetoolbox.com/*), which takes all of the pain out of compiling the web server, and Stas Bekman's excellent *mod_perl Guide* (*http://perl.apache.org/guide/index.html*).

Getting help on Slash

Slashcode (*http://slashcode.com/*) is the premier site for all things Slash. Besides listing all sorts of useful developer links, it is a good place to ask questions of the Slash community at large. Of course, the Slash format does not always lend itself to immediate answers. For quicker results, there are several mailing lists available on the SourceForge project page (*http://sourceforge.net/projects/slash/*). The slashcode-general list handles general discussion, including installation questions. slashcode-development is for those hearty souls writing plugins and messing with Slash internals. Scary.

There is also a dedicated Slash IRC channel on the OpenProjects Network. Named #Slash, it often hosts several of the Slashteam members as well as dedicated Slash administrators. The channel inhabitants are happy to answer good questions, but may have low tolerance for questions answered in the documentation. (There is room for grace where the documentation is confusing or out-of-date.)

Finally, Slashcode also links to several other sites willing to provide Slash customization and Slash hosting. If the prospect of running your own site is appealing, but the nuts-and-bolts installation and configuration leave you cold, you can pay a modest fee for someone else to do this for you. As of this writing, at least three companies were capable of doing this.

Getting the Software

The starting place for all things Slash is *http://slashcode.com/*, the Slashcode web site. Slash-based, naturally, it serves as a community newspaper for Slash site administrators and operators, and is the definitive source of the most up-to-date information about installing and maintaining Slash. After your site is up and running, submit a "YASS" (Yet Another Slash Site) announcement for free advertising. For now, simply locate and download the latest stable release.

The current stable release of Slash is always available for download from Source-Forge. This is a free service for open source projects, funded by Slashdot's parent organization. The Slash developers use SourceForge for development mailing lists, bug tracking, and download services. The Slash project page on SourceForge is at *http://sourceforge.net/projects/slashcode/*. (Slashcode's Quick Links Slashbox has a convenient link to this page.) Scroll down to "Latest File Releases" and choose the *Download* link for "slashcode". ("Slashcode-dev" is the latest development version for the next release and may not be stable enough for regular use.) As of this writing, the current stable release is Slash 2.2.3, with a development release of 2.3.0.

The most recent version of Slash will appear at the top, with older versions following in reverse order. The version numbers in the "Release & Notes" column are links to the *README* file for each release. The filenames, of the form *slash-VERSION.tar.gz*, are links to the actual distribution files themselves. Save the appropriate file to the source directory.

Source distribution files with the *.tar.gz* extension are called *tarballs*. They are created by first archiving source directories with the Unix *tar* utility, then compressing them with the GNU *gzip* utility. To unpack a tarball:

```
# cd /usr/local/src  (the source directory)

# gzip -d slash-2.n.n.tar.gz  (this will create the tar file slash-2.n.n.tar)
```

```
# tar xvf slash-2.n.n.tar (this will create the directory slash-2.n.n and its subdirectories)

# cd slash-2.n.n (this moves into the unpacked slash directory)

# ls -F
Bundle/   INSTALL          MANIFEST   Slash/   httpd/         sql/
CHANGES   INSTALL.bender   Makefile   bin/     public_html/   utils/
COPYING   INSTALL.debian   README     docs/    sbin/
```

 The GNU *tar* utility can untar and uncompress a file in one step, with the –z flag: `tar xvfz slash-2.n.n.tar.gz`.

Be sure to read the *README* and *INSTALL* files. They contain the most current installation information relevant to the downloaded version. The *INSTALL* file outlines the steps for building and installing not only Slash, but also Apache, Perl, and the supported database. You may find the HTML version much more readable because it has additional formatting. It is located at *docs/INSTALL.html* in the source distribution or can be read online at *http://slashcode.com/docs/INSTALL.html*.

The *INSTALL* file also lists the most recent versions of the underlying components known to be compatible with Slash. Newer versions of Apache or MySQL will likely work with no problems, but only the listed versions have been tested and proven to be good. Finally, *INSTALL* includes URLs where these programs may be downloaded.

The Short Version

The basic steps for installing Slash and its components are:

1. Prepare the ground. Create system users, make home directories for software, and set file and directory permissions appropriately.

2. Prepare the database. Install the database software, create a database user account for the site, and create and populate the basic Slash tables. The distribution includes canned SQL scripts to make this easy. This chapter assumes you're using a MySQL database. Other software will be similar, but please refer to its documentation and the current version of *INSTALL* for any known caveats.

3. Install Perl, Apache, and *mod_perl*. Although many Unix-like operating systems come with Perl already installed, building Apache with *mod_perl* requires the Perl source.

4. Install the Perl modules that Slash requires. This is also easy, thanks to Andreas König and his marvelous CPAN module, which can find and install Perl modules. (The CPAN, or Comprehensive Perl Archive Network, is a repository of reusable Perl components.) Slash includes a CPAN Bundle file, which lists the modules to be installed.

5. Make and install Slash. Thanks to the makefile provided with recent Slash releases, this part is so easy a typing poodle could do it. (Be sure to get video if this actually happens.)

6. Run *install-slashsite* to configure each individual Slash site on a machine. This Perl script asks for the server name and the name of the virtual database user. It automagically updates the Apache configuration file and Slash configuration variables as needed. The *install-slashsite* script also installs any optional Slash modules.

7. Check the Apache configuration. The previous step should automatically update Apache's configuration file. It needs to know where to find Slash-specific directives for each installed site.

8. Start up the server and play.

Power-users who've already installed Unix software many times will probably find *INSTALL* sufficient. The rest of this chapter provides a bit more hand-holding for less confident or less experienced souls.

The Details

As mentioned previously, most of the installation steps require root access. For users without prior administrative experience, this can be a daunting task. The O'Reilly and Associates guides *UNIX in a Nutshell* and *Running Linux* are both good Unix references.

Preparing the Ground

The first step is to create a unique Unix user account, not associated with a human user. Running server daemons such as Apache or *slashd* as root is a serious security risk. The *system user* will own all files associated with Slash, and the Slash daemons will run as if this user had executed them. Most Unix systems provide a nobody account for this purpose. Another good option is to create a new user named slash. The more services running as nobody, the more damage an attacker can do if he gains access to the account.

The slash user needs to belong to a group as well. This is convenient and practical. Any other user with membership in the slash group can work with Slash files and directories that allow group access. The easiest way to create a new group is with the *groupadd* command, provided by some operating systems (it handles details such as choosing the next available group number automagically):

```
# groupadd slash
```

If this command is not available, manually edit the */etc/group* file. Add a line defining the slash group. On the *nanodot.org* machine, this line is:

```
slash:x:501:dkrieger
```

This means that the user named dkrieger is in the slash group. The group number is 501, the lowest unused number above 500. (On many Linux machines, group and user numbers below 500 are reserved for special system groups and users. This can vary between operating systems.)

Next, create the slash user. Most Linux systems provide the helpful *useradd* command:

```
# useradd -g slash -d /usr/local/slash slash
```

The -g command-line option supplies the default group for the new user. -d specifies the user's home directory. Finally, slash is the username to add.

In the absence of *useradd*, editing the */etc/passwd* file can accomplish the same thing:

```
slash:x:505:501::/usr/local/slash:/bin/bash
```

Here, 505 is the next available user ID number, and 501 is the user's default group ID (the newly created slash group). As discussed previously, */usr/local/slash/* is the Slash home directory. It should be the home directory for the slash virtual user.

For advanced users: with multiple web servers serving the same Slash site, mounting files with NFS, the slash user and group IDs must match on all machines.

Create the empty Slash home directory:

```
# mkdir /usr/local/slash
```
(or the preferred location)

Change the owner and group of the directory as appropriate:

```
# chown slash:slash /usr/local/slash
```

Bestow read and execute rights (on the directory, not from the files):

```
# chmod a+rx /usr/local/slash
```

Create the directory where Apache will be installed:

```
# mkdir /usr/local/apache
```

If you would like to store individual site log files outside of the Apache tree, create a new directory for them:*

```
# mkdir /usr/local/apache_logs  (instead of apache/logs)
```

Installing MySQL

Though MySQL makes binary distributions for most operating systems, building it from source avoids several hassles. For example, the Perl MySQL database modules need MySQL headers to build properly. Be a good citizen and download the source from one of several mirror sites, listed at *http://www.mysql.com/downloads/ mirrors.html.* Choose a nearby mirror, follow the *Downloads* link, and look for the specific release mentioned in the Slash *INSTALL* file (usually the current stable version). Download the tarball to the source directory, then unpack it:

```
# tar xvzf mysql-VERSION.tar
# cd mysql-3.nn.nn
```

The *INSTALL-SOURCE* file will have specific instructions for installing that release of MySQL. The basic steps are:

```
# ./configure
# make
# make install
# scripts/mysql_install_db
# vi /usr/local/mysql/bin/safe_mysqld  (edit safe_mysqld to add time zone control
    required by Slash)
# /usr/local/mysql/bin/safe_mysqld &
```

The first three steps are commonplace when installing Unix software from source code. The *configure* script looks for everything needed to compile and to install MySQL. It generates a *makefile*, complete instructions for the *make* utility to compile, link, and install the software. The *make* command actually compiles the source code, using options determined by *configure*), then links the files to create

---

* This is to accommodate the multiple-web-server configurations described earlier. A running Apache server must be able to write log files. If the web server binaries and configuration files are shared over the network via read-only NFS, each machine must have its own unshared directory to run. Relocating the *logs* directory outside of */usr/local/apache/* makes this possible.

executable binaries. If *make* succeeds, run *make install*, which will install the binaries and libraries and supplementary files into their new home.*

The next two steps are like plugging in MySQL and turning it on: the shell script *mysql_install_db* creates MySQL's internal database (appropriately named mysql). The mysql table within this database keeps track of other databases, users and their rights, and user database tables. *safe_mysqld* starts the MySQL server daemon (*mysqld*). Before running *safe_mysqld*, edit the file and prepend these two lines:

```
TZ=GMT
export TZ
```

These instruct MySQL to use Greenwich Mean Time (Universal Time) and to notify other processes of this setting. Using GMT in MySQL allows Slash users to customize their display according to their own time zones.

After starting the MySQL daemon, the database processes should appear in the Unix process table:

```
# ps -Af | grep mysql
root     7878       1   0 Apr24 ?        00:00:00 sh /usr/local/bin/safe_mysqld --
root     7896    7878   0 Apr24 ?        00:00:00 /usr/local/libexec/mysqld --base
root     7898    7896   0 Apr24 ?        00:00:00 /usr/local/libexec/mysqld --base
root     7899    7898   0 Apr24 ?        00:00:00 /usr/local/libexec/mysqld --base
root     7983    7898   0 Apr24 ?        00:00:04 /usr/local/libexec/mysqld --base
```

Once MySQL is running, add the slash database and user. This is easier than it sounds. First, create a database:

```
# mysql -u root -p
```

This command starts the MySQL client, logging in as the root user. It will prompt for the MySQL root password, which was set during the MySQL installation. Next, create a MySQL user with access to this database:

```
CREATE DATABASE slash;
GRANT ALL ON slash.localhost TO 'slash' IDENTIFIED BY 'newpassword';
FLUSH PRIVILEGES;
```

This creates a new database called slash, and a new MySQL user named slash, with a password of newpassword. This user will only have access to the slash database from the local machine (localhost). Consult the MySQL documentation to enable network access securely and safely. The final command tells MySQL to refresh its internal data structures so that the server will recognize the new user without having to be restarted. Note that the username within MySQL is not tied to

---

* Some makefiles also provide a set of tests to verify proper operation of the software. Run *make test* after *make*, and MySQL should report several successes. If more than a handful of tests fail, refer to the MySQL support pages.

the Unix username that owns the Slash files and directories. To use a different database name, username, or password, simply change the command as appropriate. For example, to create a database named george, with a user named george possessing a password of newpassword, use:

```
CREATE DATABASE george;
GRANT ALL ON george.localhost TO 'george' IDENTIFIED BY 'newpassword';
FLUSH PRIVILEGES;
```

To change a user's password, use the MySQL command shell:

```
# mysql mysql (start the MySQL command shell)
Reading table information for completion of table and column names
You can turn off this feature to get a quicker startup with -A

Welcome to the MySQL monitor.  Commands end with ; or \g.
Your MySQL connection id is 25 to server version: 3.22.32

Type 'help' for help.

mysql> (this is the MySQL command prompt)
```

Replace newpassword with the new password:

```
mysql> UPDATE USER SET Password = password('newpassword') WHERE user = 'slash';
Query OK, 1 row affected (0.00 sec)
mysql> FLUSH PRIVILEGES;
Query OK, 1 row affected (0.03 sec)
```

Don't forget the *flush privileges* command! Keep track of the new password. The *install* script will need it later to populate the Slash database tables.

Building Apache with mod_perl

Apache is the world's most popular web server (running over 60% of all web sites, according to the Netcraft survey, *http://www.netcraft.com/*) as well as one of the most successful open source software projects to date. Apache's modular architecture makes it convenient for programmers to add to or to modify the functioning of the web server. In particular, the mod_perl Apache module executes Perl programs as persistent applets instead of as separate CGI programs. Even better, it allows programmers to create Apache modules in Perl to extend fundamental Apache operations such as user authentication and URL translation. Appendix A describes the Slash Apache modules.

Building the *mod_perl*-enhanced Apache executable requires the source code for both Perl and Apache. For Perl, start with the Perl language web site at *http://www.perl.com/* and follow the *Downloads* link. Locate the tarball for the Perl version mentioned in *INSTALL* (usually the "stable release"). Download this file and unpack it into the source directory.

The Apache web site is *http://www.apache.org/*. Be a good neighbor and download the Apache source from a mirror site near you (listed on the Apache site at *http://www.apache.org/mirrors/*).

Finally, download the *mod_perl* tarball from the *mod_perl* web site, *http://perl.apache.org/*.

Each of these distributions has its own *README* and *INSTALL* files. Read these for the latest news, release notes, and up-to-date installation instructions. The basic steps to install Perl are much like those for installing MySQL:

```
# rm -f config.sh Policy.sh (remove old configuration files)
# sh Configure -de (scout out the system for required libraries and tools)
# make
# make test (the coolest part of the process)
# make install
```

The –de options to *Configure* allow it to rely on its defaults and to proceed without asking several questions. This will work fine for most users and systems. Advanced users can omit these options and supervise *Configure*'s many configuration options. (Most Perl hackers use the defaults.)

When running one site across multiple web servers, installing Perl in the Apache directory tree (i.e., */usr/local/apache/lib*) can simplify matters. This will share Apache and Perl across all servers, ensuring a consistent environment. To control the placement of the Perl libraries, run *Configure* without the –d option. See the Slash *INSTALL* file for details.

Slash installs its core libraries into Perl's *site_perl* directory. If you have multiple versions of Perl installed, be aware that the version you use to install your site will be the version that has access to the libraries.

After installing Perl, build the web server. The *mod_perl* installer also knows how to configure, build, and install Apache. Apache supports several build methods, but this is the recommended procedure for Slash. First, configure any Apache modules not shipped with Apache to be compiled into the server (the section "Customizing Template Behavior" in Chapter 10 discusses a potential supplementary module). When that is complete, enter the *mod_perl* source directory:

```
# cd /usr/local/src/mod_perl-n.n
```

The *mod_perl* installation uses a Perl script called *Makefile.PL* instead of a *Configure* shell script, but the basic procedure is the same:

```
# perl Makefile.PL APACHE_SRC=/usr/local/src/apache-n.n.n DO_HTTPD=1 \
    USE_APACI=1 PERL_MARK_WHERE=1 EVERYTHING=1 \
    APACHE_PREFIX=/usr/local/apache
```

(The backslashes at the end of each line indicate that the entire command is one logical line. They can be omitted in shells that wrap arbitrarily long commands, such as the GNU version of *bash*.)

Makefile.PL accepts many key=value command-line options.* Of the options shown here, DO_HTTPD=1 means "build Apache, too"; USE_APACI=1 means "use the Apache AutoConf-style Interface (APACI)," a highly flexible and convenient configuration method that supplanted an older method involving manual editing of a build configuration file; and EVERYTHING=1 enables all of the Apache handlers used by the *Slash::Apache* modules, plus other features Slash uses such as server-side includes written in Perl. APACHE_SRC tells the installer where to look for the Apache source code, and APACHE_PREFIX tells it where to put the finished Apache installation. Modify these locations as necessary.

Finally, use *make* to build, test, and install Apache with *mod_perl*:

```
# make
# make test
# make install
```

The Slash authors recommend this process even if Apache has already been built with *mod_perl*. Some users have reported that the Apache/*mod_perl* bundle shipped with Debian GNU/Linux 2.2 (Potato) does not need reconfiguration.

Installing Slash's Required Perl Modules

Slash requires the following Perl modules (and all of their prerequisites):

libnet	Digest-MD5	MD5
Compress-Zlib	Archive-Tar	Storable
MIME-Base64	libwww-perl	HTML-Tree
Font-AFM	HTML-FormatText	XML-Parser
XML-RSS	DBI	Data-ShowTable
Msql-Mysql-modules	DBIx-Password	ApacheDBI
libapreq	AppConfig	Template-Toolkit
Mail-Sendmail	MailTools	Email-Valid

---

* The *mod_perl* installation process, including all of its command-line options, is documented in Chapter 2 and Appendix B of *Writing Apache Modules with Perl and C* by Lincoln Stein and Doug MacEachern (O'Reilly).

| Image-Size | Time-HiRes | TimeDate |
| DateManip | Time-modules | Schedule-Cron |

Either download, unpack, configure, make, test, and install each of these separately, or use the *Bundle::Slash* file from the CPAN.

The CPAN is the Comprehensive Perl Archive Network, a system of repositories and mirrors for storing and distributing Perl modules. The *CPAN.pm* module automates the process of locating and installing modules that have been published through the CPAN archive. The following installs the Perl modules Slash needs using CPAN and the Slash bundle:

```
# cd /usr/local/src/slash-2.n.n (or your own Slash home directory, if different)
# perl -MCPAN -e "install 'Bundle::Slash'"
```

The -MCPAN command-line option tells Perl to use the CPAN module, while -e executes the quoted command. CPAN should have been installed with the standard Perl distribution. If it has not run before, it will ask for some configuration information. The defaults usually work just fine.

CPAN will recursively try to fetch any missing modules required by Bundle::Slash. At the conclusion of the bundle installation, it will report whether it successfully installed all of the required modules. If it failed to locate or to install a module, it's possible to install the module manually. See *perldoc perlmodinstall* for the gory details. Some Perl modules have prerequisites and will fail with diagnostic errors. For example, *XML::Parser* requires the *expat* C library (*http://expat.sourceforge.net/*), and the MySQL modules require the MySQL headers.

The *DBIx::Password* module has an interactive installation procedure. This module keeps track of database connection parameters (user and database names, as well as passwords) by associating them with virtual users. It can also hide passwords from prying eyes. It needs several items relating to the MySQL account created earlier. For Virtual User, choose a name to identify the new connection. slash is a good choice. The DBI driver must correspond to the database type (mysql). The database machine name must be valid and resolve to the machine containing the database. If the database and web server exist on the same machine, use localhost. Finally, the database name, username, and password must match those set up in the section "Installing MySQL" later in this chapter.

If you run into trouble installing any or all of these modules, see the *perlmodinstall* file. You can also reinstall *Bundle::Slash* with no ill effect. Installed modules of the latest version will be skipped safely.

Making and Installing Slash

The Slash installation procedure should be familiar by now, since it resembles the standard Unix practices. There is no *configure* file because there are only four common options. These may be changed by editing the makefile manually or by passing them as arguments to *make* and *make install*:

```
# cd /usr/local/src/slash-n.n.n
```

For example, to install Slash to */home/slash* instead of to */usr/local/slash*, edit the makefile and change the PREFIX line accordingly. These options are a couple of lines from the top of the file.

```
PREFIX = /usr/local/slash
```

Next, run *make install*. On Solaris, Debian GNU/Linux, or Red Hat Linux 7.0 or newer, add the extra option INIT=/etc:

```
# make install INIT=/etc
```

The makefile supplied with recent versions of Slash performs a lot of tasks that formerly had to be done manually. It creates and installs the *init* scripts that restart the MySQL, Apache, and Slash daemons when the machine is rebooted. It installs the Slash Perl modules (including plugins) in the *site_perl* directory associated with the current Perl version. It also installs the Slash Perl applets and supporting files in the Slash home directory (*/usr/local/slash* by default).

Installing the Slash Site

The *install-slashsite* script creates a Slash site, populating the directories and database. It requires one command-line argument: the name of the Slash virtual user created with *DBIx::Password*:

```
# cd /usr/local/slash (the Slash home directory)
# ./bin/install-slashsite -u slash (or the virtual user name)
```

The script will ask for the fully qualified domain name that is associated with the site. This must be a valid machine name resolvable by domain servers serving the clients that will be allowed to connect. (If the site will be available to the Internet at large, the root name servers must know about the domain name. If it will be available only to local clients on an intranet, an internal name server must know about the name.) The script will guess an appropriate hostname with the Unix *hostname* command, but it may choose incorrectly. For example, Nanodot runs on a machine known as *kryten.foresight.org* but answers requests as *nanodot.org*.

```
What is hostname of your slash site
        (e.g., www.slashdot.org)? [guess.domain.com] slashsite.domain.com
    (or hit Return to accept the default)
```

Next, the script asks for the name of the Slash user account and group. The default is nobody, but the earlier example (in the section "Preparing the Ground" earlier in this chapter) used slash. Either way, the group and username should have limited privileges and should not be allowed to log into a shell. This makes it less vulnerable to intrusion.

```
What user would you like to run your slash site as? [nobody]
   (hit Return to accept the default)
What group would you like to run your slash site under? [nobody] (hit Return)
```

The script prompts for changes to the site's unique URL. From here, Slash can be configured to listen on a TCP/IP port other than the default of 80. Most users will not change this setting.

```
OK, I am planning on using slashsite.domain.com as the unique name
for the slash site.  If this is not ok, you need to fill in
something else here. [slashsite.domain.com] (hit Return to accept the default)
```

Next, the script displays available site *themes*. Themes were introduced in Slash 2.0 to allow administrators to bundle their own custom look-and-feel settings. Themes can include new data for the database, new static and dynamic web files, and often several new templates. The default theme, slashcode, looks just like *http://slashcode.com/*. Other themes are available for internationalization and localization purposes.

```
Which theme do you want to use?
( )1.    slashcode "The sturdy default
( )2.    pudgeworld "Nicer than The Big Dig"
( )3.    krooooow "Sandals and Cutoffs"
1
```

Also new in Slash 2.0, plugins are optional modules that add functionality to Slash. Several modules ship with Slash. The installer produces a menu from which the administrator can choose any or all available plugins. Enter the number of the plugin you wish to install, either in one comma-separated list or one at a time. Type a to install all of them. Type q and hit Return to end.

```
Please select which plugins you would like ('*' marks default).
( ) 1.   Admin "Admin Interface"
( ) 2.   BunchaBlocks This is a bunch of portald blocks you can add
( ) 3.   CheesyPortal CheesyPortal is a script to get an overall look at portal boxes
( ) 4.   Journal "Journal system for users"
( ) 5.   Ladybug "Ladybug bug tracking"
( ) 6.   Search Slash Search is the default search engine for Slash.
1,2,4,6
q
```

Next, choose whether to copy the plugin files into the site's home directory or create symbolic links to the files. Using links obviously saves disk space, but the real benefit is that a plugin can be updated once, within the Slash home directory, and all installed sites will automatically get the newest version. Disk space is cheap, but administrative time and effort is still a precious commodity.

The final questions set up the administrative account within the new site. This user will have complete, unfettered access to the system. Choose a username, a good account password, and provide a valid administrative email address. Slash will send system reports and other notices to this address.

```
OK, we need to create an admin account;
give us a name (8 characters only please). [nobody] perldiver
What is the password for the account? ('QUIT' exits): ez2guess
What is the email address of the account? [perldiver@slashsite.domain.com]
perldiver@pobox.com
```

install-slashsite will install the templates and plugins, inserting some basic configuration data into the database. Provided everything works correctly, it will also create or edit Apache configuration files for Slash in general as well as the currently configured site. As Slash supports running multiple virtual sites on the same machine, each unique site has its own set of directories under the Slash home directory. The example installation would create */usr/local/slash/slashsite.domain.com/* with subdirectories including *htdocs/* (containing the Perl applets and static HTML and image files for the site) and *logs/* (for task and plugin logs).

Configuring Apache

Apache needs to know where the Slash files live and what to do with them. To accomplish this, simply add the additional Slash directives to *httpd.conf*, the web server configuration file. This file lives in the *conf/* subdirectory of the Apache home directory. (By default, this is */usr/local/apache/conf/httpd.conf*, unless changed during the build process.)

The simplest approach is to append the following line to *httpd.conf*:

```
Include "/usr/local/slash/httpd/slash.conf"
```

Any subsequent changes made with *install-slashsite* will automatically be reflected in the *slash.conf* file. Simply restart Apache to implement them.

Running Apache with the –S option is handy for debugging:

```
# /usr/local/apache/bin/httpd -S
DRIVER mysql:slash
[Thu Dec 21 17:27:54 2000] [alert] httpd: Could not determine the server's
fully qualified domain name, using 127.0.0.1 for ServerName
```

This causes Apache to parse your configuration file (without starting up a server process) and report any errors in it. For further troubleshooting, check the network configuration of the machine, including valid hostnames and IP addresses, and the Apache documentation.

Starting the Server

The installation process should have installed the necessary files to start Apache and the Slash daemons when the server boots. Manually rebooting the server will accomplish this (*shutdown -r now*, on most Unix systems). It's also easy to start the daemons manually:

```
# /etc/rc.d/init.d/httpd start
DRIVER mysql:slash
/etc/rc.d/init.d/httpd start: httpd started
# /etc/rc.d/init.d/slash start
Starting slashd slash: ok PID = 2274
```

(On Solaris, Debian GNU/Linux, or Red Hat 7.0 systems, the scripts are located in */etc/init.d* instead of */etc/rc.d/init.d*.)

If the server starts successfully, the Slash site should be visible at its homepage (*http://slashsite.domain.com/* in the example installation). It will resemble the standard homepage (see Figure 2-1).

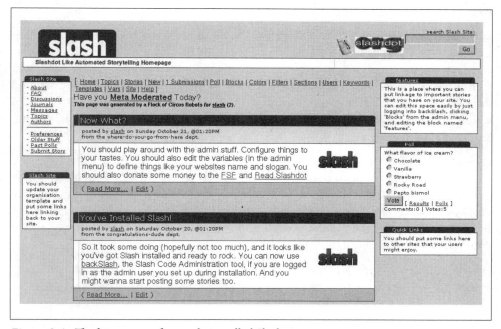

Figure 2-1. The homepage of a newly installed Slash site

If the existing *httpd.conf* file has a global Perl handler declaration, Apache may process each request with both *Apache::Registry* and Slash. If this happens, a second page with HTTP headers will follow the normal page in the browser. To fix this, comment out the first two lines of *slash.conf*:

```
# AddHandler perl-script .pl
# PerlHandler Apache::Registry
```

Advanced Installations

The simplest Slash installation features one site running on one web server. This is not a limitation of the software. Thanks to advanced features of Apache and the Perl DBI modules, as well as clever coding, Slash can be used to run several smaller sites on one machine (in a managed hosting situation, perhaps), as well as one large site served by several machines. It's even possible to mix the two configurations.

Multi-Machine Sites

Because it was designed to run Slashdot, the Slash software is scalable from a single machine to large web site clusters. Based on the level of traffic you expect, you can choose from several possible server configurations. Most new sites start with low requirements and can live comfortably on a single, properly tuned machine.* Figure 2-2 shows other available options. Putting the database on a separate machine, connected via a high-speed network, will alleviate some processing and memory crunch.

Larger sites might run several web servers with a single database. In this case, the individual servers would mount an NFS directory served by one machine (which may or may not itself be a web server), and access a database on another machine. This is the configuration Slashdot itself uses. For extremely high traffic sites, it's possible to use database replication to reduce the backend bottleneck. If your site is this successful, buy several copies of this book.

Heavy-traffic sites can get a speed boost by serving images and static content from a separate web server. This allows a small and fast server to cache and dole out

---

* Chris Nandor points out that the default Apache and MySQL configurations can easily overwhelm a machine with low memory if it experiences a spike in requests. Stas Bekman's excellent *mod_perl* guide (*http://perl.apache.org/guide/*) offers several performance-tuning suggestions.

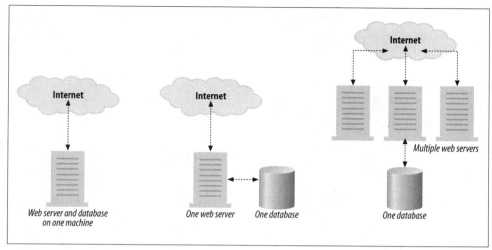

Figure 2-2. Several possible Slash configurations, scaling with the expected web traffic

unchanging information as quickly as possible, reserving the heavy-but-powerful *mod_perl* and Slash processes for dynamic content. Be sure to modify the imagedir Slash configuration variable to point to the root URL for the image server. Most of the other standard performance improvement suggestions also apply.

Running Multiple Virtual Slash Sites

It's possible to run multiple Slash sites on the same machine. Administrators running only one Slash site on a server can skip to the next chapter and start configuring things. The installation process must be repeated, and Apache needs additional configuration. For each additional Slash site:

1. Create a virtual user. Each unique Slash site must access the database as a separate user. To enable a second site catering to otter fanciers, an administrator might create a new virtual user named otter. If both sites are closely related, otter might use the slash group:

   ```
   # useradd -g slash otter
   ```

   Otherwise, it needs a group of its own:

   ```
   # groupadd otter
   # useradd -g otter otter
   ```

2. Create a separate database and database user. Copy the *slashdb_create.sql* script and replace all instances of slash with otter (as in the "george" example in the section "Installing MySQL" earlier in this chapter). This will allow

the database user named otter to access the database server. Don't forget to set otter's password in the database:

```
# mysql mysql (start the MySql command shell)
(...)
mysql> update user set Password = password('sleek&furry')
where User = 'otter';
Query OK, 1 row affected (0.00 sec)
mysql> flush privileges;
Query OK, 1 row affected (0.03 sec)
```

3. Run *install-slashsite* to set the values for the new site:

```
# cd /usr/local/slash
# ./bin/install-slashsite otter
What is hostname of your slash site
        (e.g., www.slashdot.org)? [guess.domain.com] otter.domain.com
(etc.)
```

4. As with the first site, the domain names of all subsequent sites must be valid and should resolve to an IP address on which the server listens.

5. Check the virtual host configuration. *install-slashsite* will create a new site directory and create an Apache-style configuration file there. It will even include the file within the *slash.conf* file included in *httpd.conf*. Look over the new site file to verify the settings. Rerun */usr/local/apache/bin/httpd -S* as necessary. The *slash.conf* file preloads several important Perl modules and also tells Apache to include the specific configuration file for each individual site. The example *otter.conf* files might contain the following:

```
# Any Other Options
LimitRequestBody 75000
# PerlFreshRestart On


<VirtualHost 192.168.0.77>


    # edit all of these values
    ServerAdmin otter@domain.com
    DocumentRoot /usr/local/slash/otter.domain.com/htdocs
    ServerName otter.domain.com
    ErrorLog /usr/local/apache/logs/otter-error_log
    CustomLog /usr/local/apache/logs/otter-access_log common


    SlashVirtualUser otter


    PerlSetupEnv      On
    PerlSetEnv              TZ GMT
    SlashCompileTemplates   Off


    PerlAccessHandlerSlash::Apache::User
    PerlCleanupHandler      Slash::Apache::Log
    PerlCleanupHandler      Slash::Apache::Log::UserLog
```

```
AddType  text/xml .rdf
AddType  text/xml .rss
AddType  text/xml .xml
AddType  text/xml .mml

AddType  text/html        .shtml
AddHandler       server-parsed       .shtml

AddType  text/html        .inc
AddHandler       server-parsed       .inc
```

`</VirtualHost>`

6. This example assumes that this server has only one IP address. If the server has multiple network interfaces, Slash can listen on any of them. For each network address, add a `NameVirtualHost` directive in *httpd.conf* and a `Listen` directive in */etc/apache.listen*. Also, each `ServerName` needs to resolve to the IP address given in the enclosing `<VirtualHost>` directive.

   Test the configuration with:

   # **/usr/local/apache/bin/httpd -S**

7. Restart the Slash and Apache servers. The safest way to do this is to run the *init* scripts for these daemons with the *stop* and then *start* parameters. (The scripts also take a *restart* paramater. When using Apache with *mod_perl*, this often has undesired effects on memory usage and module compilation.)

   # **/etc/rc.d/init.d/httpd stop**
   (will be /etc/init.d/httpd on Solaris, Debian, Red Hat 7.0)
   /etc/rc.d/init.d/httpd stop: httpd stopped

   # **/etc/rc.d/init.d/httpd start**

   /etc/rc.d/init.d/httpd start: httpd started
   # **/etc/rc.d/init.d/slash restart**
   Stopping slashd slash: ok.
   Starting slashd slash: ok PID = 32694
   DRIVER mysql:slash

3

In this chapter:
- *The Admin Menu*
- *Editing Authors*
- *Modifying Configuration Variables*

Basic Administration

While site users only see the front end of Slash, administrators and Authors have a special interface called *backSlash*, which controls everything from posting Stories to managing Authors. The first order of business on any new site is to create new Author accounts and modify the default configuration to fit the site's true goals. This chapter describes the web interface for managing Authors and variables. Subsequent chapters describe the rest of the Slash administrative interface, but the following functions provide the most basic level of control over the operation of the server.

The Admin Menu

Any logged-in Author will see a special row of links below the main title banner on any page. This is the *Admin menu*. If the heart of Slash administration is the backSlash interface, its nerve center is the Admin menu. It holds the keys to unlock the remote administration features provided by the *admin.pl* applet.

Editing Authors

A Slash Author account is simply a user account that has been granted additional privileges. Versions of Slash before Release 2.0 had separate accounts, in which an Author had to log on first as a user and then as an Author. Current versions of the software removed this distinction, turning Authorship into a user attribute. This is much more convenient.

Each user account within Slash has an assigned security level or *seclev*. This is an integer between 0 and 10,000. Regular users start with a seclev of 1, and the Anonymous User has a seclev of 0. Authors must have a seclev of at least 100. In addition, a special Author flag is set on their accounts. In a fresh Slash installation, there is only one Author. The administrative account created during the site installation stage will have a user ID of 2 and a seclev of 10,000.

Think of a 10,000-point seclev as the root account on a Unix machine. Its wielder is allowed to do powerful things because he is not prevented from doing stupid things. Consequently, the initial administrative account has full access to every function of the web interface, including promoting and demoting other Authors and modifying site configuration variables. A seclev can exceed 10,000, but this bestows no additional privileges. You're either omnipotent or you're not.

Only the most trusted Authors should be allotted this power. In particular, Authors at seclev 10,000 can change their security levels—and those of other Authors. Be very cautious. Any Author with this power can easily and quickly seize the reins of power (such as they are), demoting all other Authors. It is advisable to restrict this power to those who will use it wisely and benevolently, like famous Slash gurus. The section "Managing Authors" in Chapter 8 has other advice on selecting and cultivating Authors.

Also, if you accidentally reduce the initial account's seclev before creating any other Authors with this power, you will have to modify the users table in the database to recover from your mistake.*

Authors with seclev 10,000 will see the User Admin menu (Figure 3-1) on most pages belonging to the *users.pl* applet. This is the most convenient way to upgrade and edit any user on the system. The single textbox is a multipurpose widget, allowing a user to be selected by UID, nickname, or network ID. Slash does its best to guess the contents, but prefers UIDs. Click the Edit User button to edit the user's public information (nickname, email address, homepage). Administrators have the power to modify the profile of any other user, including other Authors but excluding the Anonymous User. This can be handy to reset invalid email addresses or edit a Bio or Sig that violates site rules. The site's owner gets to make the rules.

The User Info button brings up a page used to modify the user's system information, as shown in Figure 3-2. The Seclev field controls the user's security level. Only specific values have meaning; seclevs between 1 and 99 confer no special powers. The Author flag bestows the ability to post and edit Stories. The Save Admin button updates the database with the new user information. Again, raising the seclev of a user too high affords the opportunity for mischief. Lowering the seclev of a user too low can render portions of the site unreachable.

---

* This is where the root user metaphor breaks down. The server administrator wields ultimate power. It should never be necessary to use this, but it's there.

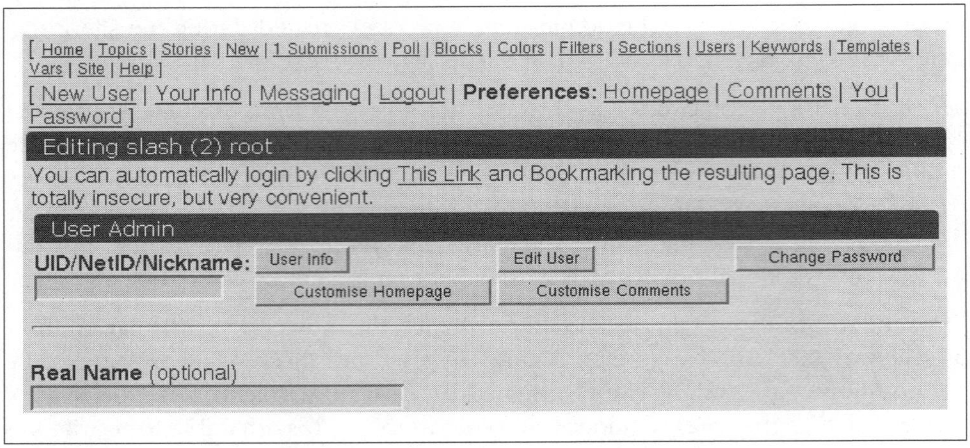

[Home | Topics | Stories | New | 1 Submissions | Poll | Blocks | Colors | Filters | Sections | Users | Keywords | Templates | Vars | Site | Help]
[New User | Your Info | Messaging | Logout | **Preferences:** Homepage | Comments | You | Password]

Editing slash (2) root

You can automatically login by clicking This Link and Bookmarking the resulting page. This is totally insecure, but very convenient.

User Admin

UID/NetID/Nickname: User Info   Edit User   Change Password

                          Customise Homepage   Customise Comments

Real Name (optional)

Figure 3-1. The User admin menu

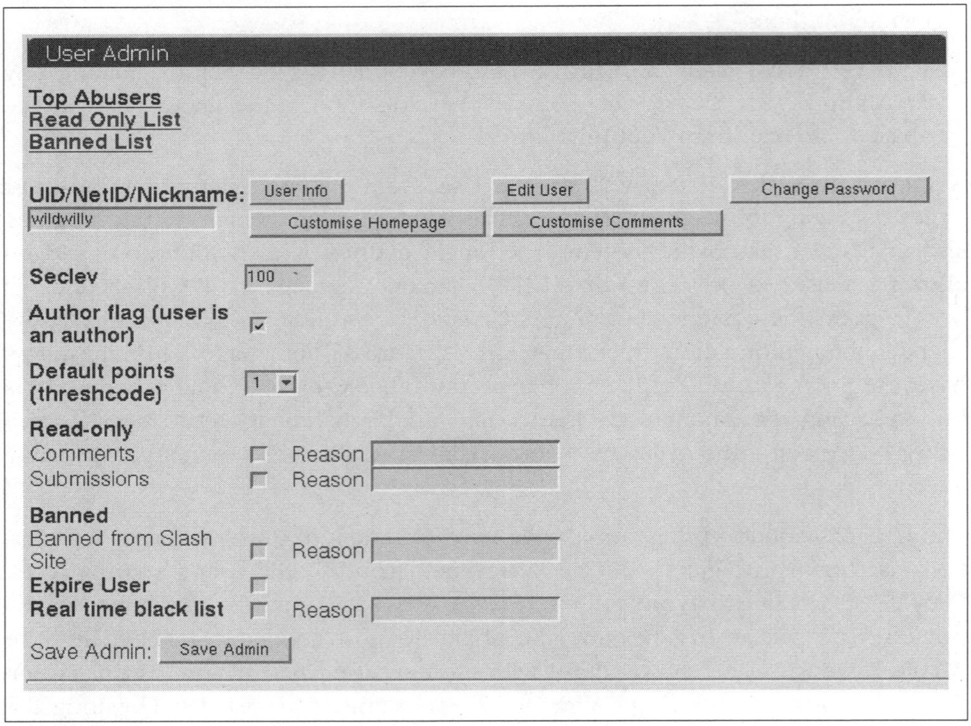

User Admin

Top Abusers
Read Only List
Banned List

UID/NetID/Nickname: User Info   Edit User   Change Password
wildwilly   Customise Homepage   Customise Comments

Seclev   100

Author flag (user is ☑
an author)

Default points   1 ▾
(threshcode)

Read-only
Comments   ☐   Reason
Submissions   ☐   Reason

Banned
Banned from Slash   ☐   Reason
Site
Expire User   ☐
Real time black list ☐   Reason

Save Admin: Save Admin

Figure 3-2. The User management interface

The other widgets of this page exist to curb abusive users. For example, the Default points value determines the initial score of the user's comments. The Read-only checkboxes can be used to bar a user from posting comments or submitting stories. Banned will cut off all access to the site. Setting Real time black list prevents the user from being selected as a moderator or from meta-moderating. Each of these settings has an optional Reason field. If a user has broken the rules, it is wise to specify exactly which rule has been broken. The final option is Expire User. If checked, this will require the user to validate his account before she is allowed back on the site. Use this if you suspect someone has cracked a user's password and is committing mischief as the user. The section "IPIDs, NetIDs, and blacklists" in Chapter 8 discusses anti-abuse features in more detail.

Specific Author abilities kick in at the following seclevs:

seclev	Ability
100	View Admin menu
100	View Stories list
	Edit Stories
	Use block editor
	Post new Stories (if user has `Author` flag set)
	Create and edit polls
	Unlimited moderation (if `authors_unlimited` variable is true)
	Delete posted comments
500	View and approve submissions
	Edit templates
	Edit site colors
1,000	Manage Sections
	Manage comment filters
10,000	Manage Authors
	Edit variables
	Edit Topics
	Ban user
	Edit IP block list
	Expire user Session
	Set default user comment score
	Set user read-only flags

Blocks and templates also have seclevs. Only Authors with a seclev above 100 and the seclev of the block or template may edit the component. That is, an Author at level 150 cannot edit a block at level 200.

Modifying Configuration Variables

Configuration variables control important aspects of the site's behavior. For example, the `allow_anonymous` variable controls whether anonymous users can post comments. Earlier versions of Slash stored these variables in a special file. They moved into the database with Version 2.0, and the Slashteam added a browser-based interface. The *Vars* link in the Admin menu leads to the Variables interface (see Figure 3-3).

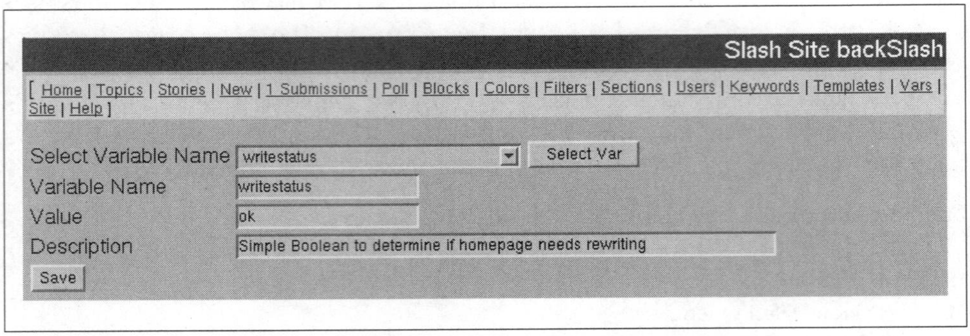

Figure 3-3. The Variables interface, used to edit configuration variables

All of the available variables are listed in the Select Variable Name menu. To edit or to view a specific variable, select its name from the menu and click the Select Var button. The other form fields will be filled in when the page refreshes. The Variable Name and Value boxes behave almost as expected. If you change the value and click Save, the database will be updated with the new value. If you type a new name in the Name box, a new variable will be created. If you select an existing variable and change its name, a new variable will be created, and the old variable will maintain its current value. New values will take effect within the system when Apache is restarted.

The Description field has no effect on site or variable behavior. It is simply descriptive and can be edited at any time. In case of emergency or forgetfulness, it's best to keep the descriptions up-to-date.

Care and Feeding of Configuration Variables

Slash stores all configuration data in the database as text and relies on Perl to convert values to numbers or boolean values when appropriate. Variables that have yes-or-no effects, such as allow_anonymous, are treated as booleans. In Perl, anything that evaluates to 0 or the empty string ("") is considered "false". Everything else is considered "true", including the strings true and false. To avoid ambiguity, the default variables use the numbers 1 and 0 to indicate true and false, respectively.

In normal database applications, an unescaped single-quote character can break a SQL statement. That is, a slogan of "Scamizdat's Slash Server" would have to be entered as "Scamizdat\'s Slash Server." Since Version 2.0, Slash has automatically escaped all special database characters automatically.

Several configuration variables are populated during site installation. Most of these pertain to file paths. Modifying these within backSlash may render portions of the site unavailable, requiring access to the server and the database itself to correct the damage. These variables are:

absolutedir and basedomain

Used for creating external links to the site (as, for example, in the exported RDF headlines file, which is explained in detail in the section "Secrets of Headline Swapping: XML, RDF, and RSS" in Chapter 9).

basedir

The file path to the root of the server's document directory hierarchy (set by the site configuration file's `DocumentRoot` directive).

datadir

The file path to the site's home directory. By default, it contains the `basedir` (*datadir/htdocs*) and `logdir` (*datadir/logs*) directories for the site.

logdir

The file path to the directory containing the site's access and error logs.

rootdir

The base URI of the site (i.e., *//slashdot.org*).

siteid

The unique name of the site, used to distinguish between multiple Slash servers running on the same machine.

Other variables set by *install-slashsite* won't cripple the site if they are mishandled but can disable some site functions:

adminmail

The email address to which Slash sends site notices and status reports.

imagedir

The base URL for images that will be used with the site (including Topic icons, the site logo, the rounded corners of Story boxes, and so forth). Heavily trafficked sites can use a separate machine to offload image requests to a separate machine (or redirect them to a lightweight web server such as *thttpd* or *Tux*), which alleviates load on the *mod_perl* server. Users won't see any images if this is set inappropriately.

mailfrom

The email address used in the `From:` header of outgoing email sent by Slash (as in, for example, the nightly headline mailings). Many mail transfer agents bounce mail if this header contains an invalid domain name.

siteowner

> The name of the system account Slash uses to perform operating system–level operations.

smtp_server

> The fully qualified domain name or IP address of an SMTP server used to process outgoing mail. The default installation assumes that the machine running your Slash server ("localhost") is also running an SMTP-compliant mail transfer agent. If this isn't the case, change this variable to point to a valid server where you have permission to send mail. Ask first.

stats_report

> Configures where Slash will send its nightly usage statistics report, and with what Subject: header. Multiple addresses and subjects can be included. This variable will be parsed into a Perl hash; the value should be of the form:
>
> ```
> 'address1' => 'subject1',
> 'address2' => 'subject2'
> ```
>
> with each address/subject pair joined by => and divided by commas.

Several other values should be modified before opening the doors to your site. Many of these variables are used in exported RSS files and will identify your headlines on other sites. sitename and slogan are just as their names suggest. The default value for both, "Slash Site," is rather bland. Choose something snappy and informative ("Whelk World", "Everything whelkish!"). rdfimg points to the site logo. By default, this is a nice little "Site based on Slash" icon (found at */images/slashlogo.gif*). This can be an icon-sized version of the site logo if your site has a distinctive look or custom graphics.

Other Slash configuration variables are discussed as they come up in subsequent chapters. For example, the section "Moderation Configuration Variables" in Chapter 6 describes the variables that affect the site's comment posting, moderation, and meta-moderation mechanisms.

4

Editing and Updating Stories

No matter what Topics a weblog covers, it will always require fresh content. In Slash terms, these are Stories. Consequently, most Authors will spend their time in the Stories list. It is always available from *Stories* or the relative URI */admin.pl*. Authors can review submissions, edit published Stories, and even create new Stories (see the *New* link in the Admin menu).

The Stories List

The Stories list (Figure 4-1) is the default page of the Admin menu. It's like a big map in the war room, used to review and coordinate the current site activity. As you'd expect, it is full of data. Most of the activity is centered around reading or editing Stories; an Author may decide to fix a typo in a Story title or introduction, or the administrator might decide to browse a Story that's attracted an unusual number of comments or page reads.

Stories appear on the list in reverse chronological order—newest first, grouped by day of publication. The horizontal columns on the page are unlabeled, but they are relatively straightforward. The leftmost column holds the Story number, with no special meaning outside of the Stories list. The number is a link to the Edit Story page, used to update a Story. The Story title is a link to the normal Story display page, as seen by users. The next three columns show the credited Author, the Story Topic, and the Story Section, respectively. Only the Section is linked, and it leads to the Section homepage.

The next two columns are numeric. The first is the number of page views, and the second is the current number of posted comments, if any. The number of views should exceed the number of comments because users must normally view the page before posting a comment. Not every reader will feel the need to comment,

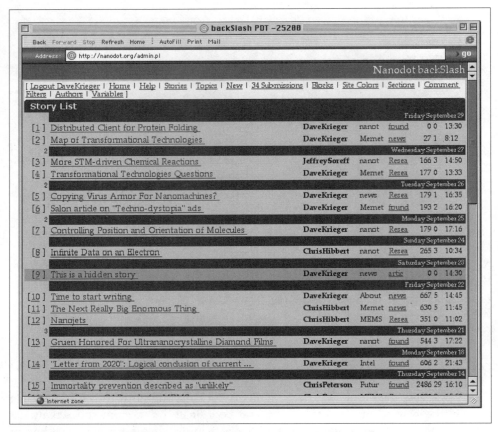

Figure 4-1. The Stories list (Stories set to Never Display are highlighted)

though Stories comparing operating systems or starship captains may lead you to believe otherwise.

The final column shows the official Story posting time. This, like the Author field, can be misleading. The time does not necessarily reflect the point at which the Story was accepted, nor does it take into account the possibility that another Author has edited the Story. It simply lists the time when Slash made the Story available to the public. See the section "The Edit Story Form" later in this chapter for a description of this trickery.

Within the Stories list, titles will be truncated to 50 characters plus an ellipsis (. . .). The Topic and Section columns will show only the first five characters. This affects only the display in the Stories list; it has no effect on the actual Story as stored in the database or displayed elsewhere. Keep these restrictions in mind when choosing Topic and Section names. "ConcertCalendar" and "ConcertReviews" will be visually indistinguishable Topics in the Stories list.

Besides its immediate pragmatic utility, the list is a helpful review of the Stories published by other Authors (or your own Stories, if you've forgotten everything after a marathon coding session). Is one Author posting all of the Stories this week? Has an infrequent Author posted a new Story generating a lot of interest? Are several Stories clustered around a single Topic? (This will frequently be the case when a major Topic event takes place, such as a technology conference or basketball playoffs, depending on the site. Some major events, such as a war, may trump normal coverage on any Slash site.)

The Edit Story Form

Most of the daily work of a site takes place in the Edit Story form. It provides several controls to modify Story attributes and edit or preview Story content. This is the most complex part of the backSlash interface, yet it is easy to learn and convenient to use.

There are five ways to access the Edit Story form. Story numbers in the Stories list lead there. Logged-in Authors will see an *Edit* link following each Story on the homepage (see Figure 4-2, left) and an *Editor* link in the Author box at the top right of each Story's individual page (see Figure 4-2, right). Previewing a user submission from the Submissions list (discussed in the section "The Submissions List" in Chapter 5) displays the submission in the form. Finally, clicking on the *New* link in the Admin menu brings up an empty Edit Story form.

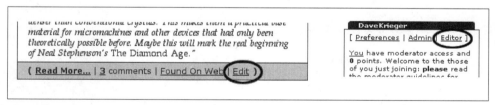

Figure 4-2. Links to the Edit Story page for a given Story

At the top of the form, the Story Preview shows the basic Story information: the Intro copy, the Extended copy (if present), and the Related Links box. When first displaying a Story, the Preview will show the Story as it exists in the database (see Figure 4-3). New Stories, of course, have no Preview. Any changes made and previewed will update only the Preview. The database is updated only when an Author uses either the Update or the Save button.

The Related Links box is a little more sophisticated. Any time the Story is previewed or saved, Slash looks for keywords defined in the `related_links` database table. This table associates words with HTML links. For example, if the word "slash" occurs in the Story (and not as part of another word), a related link to the Slashcode site will be created. Some sites have used this to generate advertising

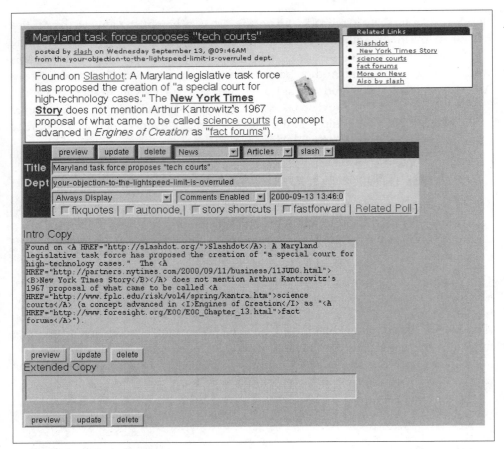

Figure 4-3. The Edit Story form

revenue in a subtle Google-esque scheme. These can be edited through the *Key-words* link on the Admin menu.

Given the number of ways a long Story can be lost (from network errors to browser crashes to well-meaning acquaintances trying to check their webmail), it's a good idea to have a backup ready. Many experienced Authors write and save their Stories with a text editor, pasting them into the web forms only as necessary. A little paranoia will serve you well.

The most vital elements of the Edit Story page are the Intro Copy and Extended Copy text boxes. The introduction appears on the sites homepage and is necessarily brief. Extended copy can go into more detail, expanding on a submission, or even containing the whole article in the case of an exclusive Story. Users can skip a Story if they don't like the introduction, without having to scroll past paragraphs of extended copy.

The Intro block appears on the main and Section homepages as well as on the Story's own page. It should give the user enough information to decide whether to read the Story or its comments. The Extended block appears only on the Story's own page and should contain the bulk of the content of long Stories. This arrangement fits the "inverted pyramid" style of journalistic writing, shifting the most significant information toward the beginning of the Story. The background information and less significant details comprise the remainder.

Unlike the text box on the Post Comment page (described in the section "Posting Comments" in Chapter 6), the text boxes on the Edit Story page do not automatically transform their contents. Optional transformations are available with checkboxes on the Edit Story page, however. The system assumes Authors will provide well-formed HTML. Make a habit of previewing a Story and testing all of its links before publishing it. (Note that Slash 2.2 has added an *ispell* compatibility mode. If the *ispell* program exists and points to an *ispell* binary, the Edit Story page will include a list of potentially misspelled words.)

Frequently, Slash Stories exist merely to point to interesting links elsewhere on the Web. In this case, the Intro Copy may contain all of the necessary Story information, leaving the Extended Copy blank. If most stories follow this pattern, readers may not realize that longer Stories will contain Extended Copy. As a visual cue, Slash will change the *Read More* link attached to the Story to read *xxx bytes in body*. This link leads to a page with no comments, only the Intro and Extended Copy.

For Author convenience, the Preview, Delete, and Save/Update buttons appear in the block of editing controls beneath the Preview Area and also follow both Copy boxes. Each button behaves identically in each location. The Preview button displays the Story as edited without modifying the database. The Update button (or Save button, for a new Story) saves the current contents of the form to the database. Just to the right of the first occurrence of these buttons are pop-up menus used to select Topic, Section, and Author, respectively. These behave as you'd expect, for the most part.

The Delete button appears only for Stories that have information saved in the database. Instead of purging the data immediately, Slash queues the Story for deletion and returns the Author to the Stories list. There will be a status message at the top of the list saying, "*story_id* will probably be deleted in *n* seconds," in which "*n* seconds" is approximate until the *slashd* daemon next updates the database. At that point, the Story and all attached comments will be permanently deleted. If an Author deletes a Story accidentally, he has until the next update to rescue it by editing the Story again then clicking the Update button. This will save the Story to the database and remove it from the deletion queue. Deletion is irreversible, so institute a good backup policy.

One potentially confusing aspect of Slash's Author attribution scheme is that the Author credited with a given Story is not necessarily the Author who edited it last. This can prevent unnecessary confusion—if Ben spots a misspelling in one of Jerry's Stories, he can correct it silently. However, it also enables Authors to put words in each other's mouths. Another option is to encourage the practice of marking updates (see the section "Original Content Versus Linked Stories" in Chapter 8).

Another way to prepare a Story in advance is to set its Display status to *Never Display* in the Edit Story form. These hidden Stories are highlighted in the Stories list (see Story #9 in Figure 4-1). Authors can maintain a reserve list of Stories to be published on slow news days. Be sure to set the date and time for these canned Stories far in advance so they don't age off of the Stories list and become lost in the database. The Stories list displays 40 Stories at a time, with a link to the next page of 40 Stories and an indicator of how many more Stories the database holds.

Story Fields

As described in the section "Slash User Preferences" in Chapter 1, Topics and Sections help Authors categorize and group Stories. In general, the administrator should define Topics in terms of the kinds of Stories covered on the site and define Sections in terms of the kinds of Stories published. Foresight Institute's Slash site Nanodot has Topics for "Robotics," "Machine Intelligence," and "Nanotechnology," with Sections including "Research," "Reviews," and "Questions for Nanodot Users." A Story on a newly released bit of robotics research and a review of Hans Moravec's newest book might both have the "Robotics" Topic, but the former would be in the "Research" Section and the latter in "Reviews." Chapter 7 discusses other schemes for managing Topics and Sections.

Assign a Topic and Section to a Story with the two pop-up menus under the Story Preview Section of the Edit Story page. Slash allows users to limit searches by Topic or Section or to list all Stories assigned to each Topic or Section. Assigning a Story to "All Topics" means the Story will be displayed in any search no matter which Topic the user selects. Note that if you wish to use a Topic available only in certain Sections, you must first assign the Story to the appropriate Section, hit the Preview button, and then select the appropriate Topic. Otherwise, Slash will display only the available Topics for the default Section.

As described earlier in this section, any Author can receive the credit for a Story. The third menu at the top of the metadata widget lists all active Authors, with the current Author's nickname as the default selection.

The text fields for a Story's Title and Department live beneath the pop-up menus. Unlike the corresponding Subject field on the Submit Story page for users (described in the section "The Submit Story Page" in Chapter 5), Authors may put HTML tags in the Title. This can occasionally be useful (if Prince changes his name back to *http://www.NPGonlineLTD.com/images/symbol/paisley-news-symbol-1.gif*, for instance). Most of the time, it will probably be annoying.

The Dept. field pays homage to the humorous taglines accompanying some older Dvorak articles. (Some wags also see connections to *Mad* magazine. *Mad*'s report on the new "sport" of "43-Man Squamish," for example, came from the *There's-a-soccer-born-every-minute* dept. Rob "CmdrTaco" Malda denies this.) The contents of this field will appear beneath the byline of the Story. Slash replaces spaces with hyphens so that "hackin' slash" will appear as "From the hackin'-slash dept." This is a good place for some go-for-the-jugular wit, if your audience will appreciate it and your Authors have the stamina. Otherwise, it can be disabled by setting the use_dept configuration variable to a false value.

The first pop-up menu under the Dept. field provides a choice of three different display modes for each Story. The default mode is *Always Display*. Stories with this setting will first appear on the homepage, move onto the Older Stuff list with age, and will also appear on the appropriate Section page. The *Never Display* setting will prevent the Story from being listed anywhere on the site. (Any user who knows or who can guess the Story ID, which forms the URL, can still reach the Story.) As mentioned earlier, *Never Display* allows Authors to queue Stories for future publishing. The third display mode, *Only Display Within Section*, publishes a Story only on the appropriate Section's homepage. It will not appear on the site homepage or Older Stuff list.

Administrators can control the ability of users to post and view comments on a Story-by-Story basis with the Comment Settings pop-up menu. The default setting, *Comments Enabled*, allows users to post comments that will be visible to other users. This gives the site a sort of community newspaper, Letters-to-the-Editor feel. The *Comments Disabled* setting prevents comments from being displayed with or added to the Story. Previously posted comments remain in the database but will no longer be viewable. Finally, the *Read-Only* setting prevents new comments from being added while displaying all previously entered comments. Chapter 6 covers the comment and moderation systems in detail.

As shown in Figure 4-1, Stories can be queued to appear automatically at a future date and time. The Date/Time field controls the official publication timestamp of the Story, which in turn controls its placement in chronological lists. All times displayed here will be in the GMT time zone because that is how they are stored in

the database. Setting this field to a time in the future will suppress the Story until
that time, after which it will appear on the homepage and in chronological lists as
usual. This field accepts dates and times only in the format *YYYY-MM-DD HH:MM:SS*,
e.g., `2001-04-01 14:30:00`. Entering the date and time in any other format will
have unpredictable results. The Fastforward option will automatically update the
Story to the current date and time, according to the database, when checked. This
option appears only for Stories that have already been saved to the database. It
can update a queued Story (saved as *Never Display*) for immediate publishing.

Extra Story-Editing Features

In an effort to make the lives of Authors easier, Slash includes several convenient
features to enhance or fix Stories. These features are rarely used in practice, but
when they're needed, they're amazingly handy.

Correcting eight-bit quotation marks

Some web browsers, when submitting an HTML form, send incompatible characters in place of standard quote marks. On other platforms, these will appear as
question marks. The Fixquotes checkbox enables a tool to correct this. If checked,
when a Story is previewed, all question marks in the Intro or Extended text fields
located between alphanumeric characters will be replaced by the plain ASCII single-quote character (').* This does not affect question marks bordered by a space,
as at the end of a question. This operation takes place only during a
preview. Be careful, because Fixquotes can affect necessary and proper question
marks, such as those within a URL query string (e.g., *http://www.google.com/
search?q=Paulette+Cooper*). In practice, this is rarely used.

Linking to Everything2

Blockstackers Intergalactic, Slashdot's original parent company, also created a col-
laborative web-based information management system called Everything
(*http://everydevel.com/*). The public Everything2 server (*http://www.everything2.
com/*) takes the form of a publicly edited encyclopedia. The Autonode checkbox
helps Authors to create links to Everything2 nodes by name. With this box
checked, when previewing a Story, backSlash will create Everything links from any

---

* The Perl regular expression `s/([0-9a-z])\?([0-9a-z])/$1'$2/gi` performs this substitution.
  Regexes describe and match patterns in a marvelously expressive and compact way. To learn more
  about these mysterious and powerful incantations, see *Mastering Regular Expressions* by Jeffrey E. F.
  Friedl (O'Reilly). There's a brief introduction in Chapter 6 of this book as well.

text in the Intro or Extended text fields enclosed by square brackets. This will produce links in the form of superscripted citation marks following the bracketed text. For example, the text:

```
the galactic overlord [Xenu]
```

will be replaced by:

```
the galactic overlord Xenu<SUP><A
HREF="http://www.everything2.com/index.pl?node=Xenu">?</A></SUP>
```

which will display in a browser as:

the galactic overlord Xenu[?]

Like Fixquotes, Autonode takes effect only during a Preview. After verifying the links, Authors can use Save or Update to keep the results.

Linking Stories to polls

Another popular Slash feature is the polling mechanism. While these polls are too insecure for serious uses (see the section "Managing User Polls" in Chapter 9), they can be lots of fun. Slash provides a convenient way to associate a poll with a specific Story. If the Story has been saved to the database, a *Related Poll* link will appear on the Edit Story page. Clicking this link will launch the New Poll screen with the Story ID already in place. Attaching a poll to a Story provides a somewhat quantitative measure of reader reaction to the Story, nicely complementing the more qualitative comments and moderation system. Even a poll stuffed by a scripted bot indicates, at least, that someone cared about the outcome.

Story shortcuts

The Edit Story text fields support several pseudo-HTML tags to make repeated constructs much easier to type. These can be found in the `Slash::DB::MySQL::autoURL` function and are called whenever a Story is edited. The current working tags are:

`<date>`
> Adds the current date

`<disclaimer:`*company name*`>`
> Adds a link to */about.shtml#disclaimer*, noting that the Author owns shares in *company name*

`<author>`

Adds a link to the current Author's homepage, using his initials as the link title

`<update>`

Adds an update notice from the current Author at the current time

Gotchas

A weakness of server-based web software is that it depends on user web browsers to comply with established standards.* Many web application developers have adopted a conservative strategy, requiring only the simplest common browser features. This attitude is particularly prevalent in the open source software community, since new browser features generally arrive first in proprietary forms, confined to particular makes of browsers on particular platforms. (For example, Javascript was initially an exclusive feature of Netscape browsers. Java support on the Macintosh has typically lagged behind that of other operating systems). Proprietary plugins (such as Flash) may never be fully available to all client platforms.

To date, Slash requires no special browser features aside from HTTP/1.1,† HTML 3.2, and RFC-2109-compliant browser cookies. Individual site administrators can configure their page layouts using more advanced HTML features, but Slash itself requires only the ability to accept cookies (used for user and Author authentication) and to submit HTML forms. Unfortunately, even these minimum requirements can be problematic, sometimes in fairly recent browsers.

Instead of merely redrawing the page, all but the latest versions of Netscape irritatingly reload the page from the server when the user resizes the browser window. If the page happens to contain an HTML form, it will probably lose the content.

Because backSlash requires a preview before committing a Story to the database, Authors will usually have the opportunity to spot these errors before publishing a Story. The potential for mishaps exists, though, so preview your Stories diligently.

---

* Browser manufacturers have begun to take standards compliance seriously. The Web Standards Project (*http://www.webstandards.org/*) has served as an organized voice of webmasters and web software developers to lobby Microsoft and AOL/Netscape to make their browsers more standards-compliant.

† The Virtual Host features, enabled by default in Slash 2.2, require user agents to send the Host: header. Some HTTP/1.0 clients may send this header for forward-compatibility purposes. Most web browsers in widespread use will work here.

5

Reviewing and Approving Submissions

A dedicated Author with a singular vision (and plenty of spare time) can search the Internet for worthwhile and informative ideas. However, a typical Slash site harnesses the powers of its userbase to find and recommend potential Stories. This can relieve the Authors from the often tedious task of continually scaring up fresh Stories, moving them to an editorial role. Slash provides several tools that enable Authors to filter, review, and polish user submissions into publishable gems.

The Submit Story Page

Users submit Stories via the Submit Story page, available almost everywhere through the *Submit Story* link. The Submit Story page presents a simplified version of the Edit Story page (see Figure 5-1). Its relative URL is */submit.pl*. When a logged-in user accesses the page, Slash fills in some form values from the user's profile information. Otherwise, the form will contain generic Anonymous User information. In either case, users can edit or delete these values before submitting the form—even logged-in users can submit a Story anonymously. (As anyone who's seen *All The President's Men* can attest, all the best Stories require anonymity).[*]

A logged-in user will see a summary of his submissions (if any) at the top of the page. This information includes the date and time, Story subject, Section and Topic, and outcome (whether the Story is pending, was rejected, or was accepted and published) for each submission. The site administrator can control the frequency with which logged-in users can submit Stories with two configuration

---

[*] Setting the `allow_anonymous` variable to 0 prevents Anonymous Users from posting comments on published Stories but doesn't affect the submission of Stories. See the section "Modifying Configuration Variables" in Chapter 3 for a description of how to set Slash configuration variables.

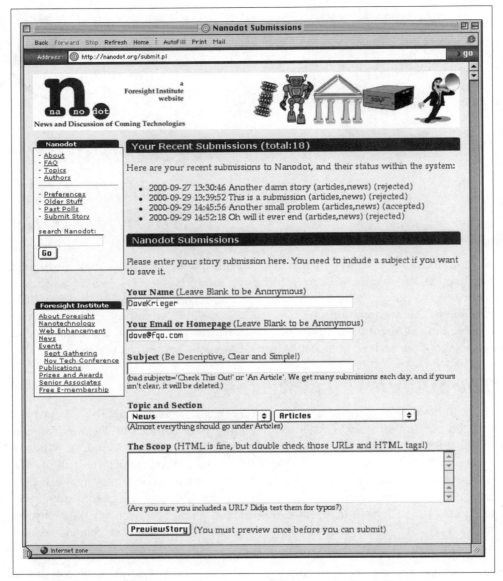

Figure 5-1. The Submit Story page presents a simplified version of the Edit Story page

variables. A user can submit no more than `max_submissions_allowed` per day. They must be at least `submission_speed_limit` seconds apart.

As with the Edit Story page, the Story's text entry field comprises the meat of the Submit Story page. Jocularly labeled The Scoop, it accepts arbitrary HTML. In the hope of ensuring at least moderately functional HTML, users must preview a submission at least once before they can submit it. The preview appears beneath the

Topic and Section menus and above the main text entry field. It reflects the changes Slash will make to the Story, placing the text of the submission in italics inside double quotation marks, attributed to the submitter:

> Billy Miles writes, *"As a multiple abductee, I must protest . . . "*

Users can revise or preview a submission multiple times before finally clicking the SubmitStory button to send it to the queue.

The Submissions List

Logged-in Authors will see a link in the Admin menu labeled *n Submissions*, in which n is the current number of user submissions in the queue. Clicking the link leads to the Submissions list (relative URL */submit.pl?op=list*). Similar in format to the Stories List, it summarizes the queued submissions, listing the oldest Stories first. This is the Slash version of a slush pile.

Slashdot, the mothership of Slash sites, receives several hundred user submissions per day. When a news story particularly dear to the hearts of its readers breaks, the queue may receive dozens of near-identical submissions. The Submissions list has several features intended to help Authors cope with this situation. It shows lots of information, so a wide browser window is necessary.

The table at the top of the page summarizes the distribution of current submissions across site Sections (see Figure 5-2). Only those Sections with queued submissions will appear. Clicking on either a name or a number will lead to a trimmed-down version of the list, showing only the submissions for that Section. This can quickly break a large list into manageable chunks. The *Submissions* link found on every Section's homepage also leads to the single-Section view of the Submissions list.

The Submissions list displays the date, time, and subject of each submission, along with the nickname and email address given by the submitter. The subject is a link leading to the Review Submission page (described in the next section). A set of controls accompany each Story in the list. These allow rapid handling of the queue. The entire list is a single HTML form. Authors can choose an action for each submission in the queue, performing them all by clicking the Update button.

Managing Submissions

On active sites that receive many user submissions, most will be deleted. The subject alone may reveal that the submission duplicates the important Quake IV news already published. The Delete box is an unlabeled checkbox following each entry. All submissions with this box checked will be removed from the queue when the Author clicks the Update button. Unlike the Delete button on the Edit Story page,

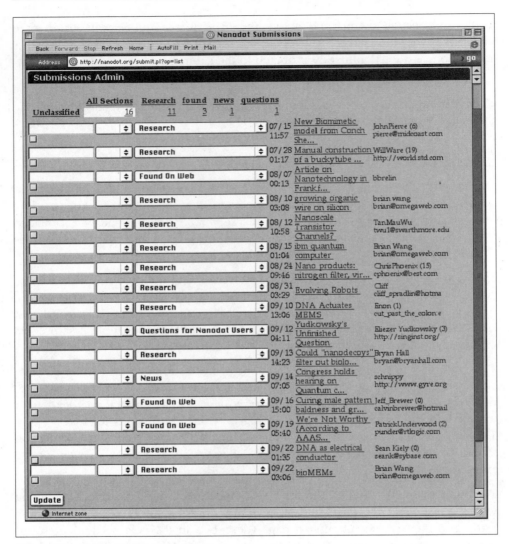

Figure 5-2. The Submissions list

there is no grace period. Deleted Stories are gone for good (barring black magic), so exercise caution.

The unlabeled Comment text box allows Authors to annotate submissions. These comments might be, "Let's save this one for Monday," say, or "Your call, Bob." Comments appear in the same text boxes on subsequent viewings and are available to any Author who previews the submission for publication. (See the section "The Review Submission Page" later in this chapter).

To reassign a submission to a different Section, simply choose from the Section pop-up menu for each submission and click Update.

The first pop-up menu in each row allows Authors to move submissions off of the main list without deleting them. Its default value is blank. The other options are *Hold* and *Quik. Hold* "tables" a submission, in the parliamentary sense, keeping it around but out of the way. Held submissions do not appear in the main queue. Instead, they are listed in a special Hold queue (as well as in the appropriate Section queue.) The summary table at the top of the Submissions list shows how many submissions are currently on hold (see Figure 5-3). To view held Stories, click on any of the numbers in the *Hold* row.

	All Sections	Research	found	news	questions
Unclassified	12	8	0	2	2
Hold	1	0	1	0	0
Quik	4	3	1	0	0

Figure 5-3. The summary table at the top of the Submissions list shows how many submissions have been assigned Hold or Quik status

Grouping Submissions with "Quickies"

The *Quik* selection in the first pop-up menu invokes Slash's Quickies mechanism. This combines multiple submissions (too good to throw away, too insubstantial to stand on their own) into a single omnibus entry. All entries marked as Quik move to a third separate Submissions queue also appearing in the summary table (see Figure 5-3). As with the Unclassified and Hold views, clicking on the *Quik* link displays all submissions in this state. Clicking on a number in the row displays all Quickie submissions for a given section.

To combine the current crop of Quickies into a single submission, click the Gen-Quickies button at the bottom of any Quik submission. This creates a new submission with the subject "Generated Quickies". Its text contains the chronologically concatenated text from each current Quickie submission. This gathers Quickies regardless of their assigned Section and does not delete the original submissions. They can be deleted manually, if so desired. This conservative policy helps to prevent accidental deletions from another Author's section.

The Generated Quickies entry will appear in the main Submissions list under the default Section ("Articles", unless the administrator has changed it). Clicking on the subject of a Quickies entry (or any other submission) brings up the Review Submission page. Enjoy; with so many links, a Quickies Story can get messy.

The site administrator can choose to make a version of the Submissions list available to the public by modifying the `submiss_view` configuration variable. If `submiss_view` is set to true, a link to the Submissions list will be appear at the top of the Submit Story page, labeled *View Current Pending Submissions*. The public version of the Submissions list provides no HTML controls. The subject of each Story links to a simple preview resembling the preview Authors see on the Review Submission page. The nature of the site will determine whether this is necessary. (Slashdot receives so many submissions that duplicates and spam make this list less than interesting to most readers.)

The Review Submission Page

The final stop before a submission becomes a Story, the Review Submission page allows an Author to preview the text entered by a user. This page also displays any comments on the Story entered from the Submissions List page (see Figure 5-4). Slash automatically modifies the submission, italicizing the user's text and placing it inside double quotes. It also creates a default attribution at the beginning of the entry from the provided username and web or email address. Slash will detect several types of addresses, constructing a URL with the appropriate protocol: *mailto:* for email addresses, *http:* for web pages, and so on.

The Delete Submission button instantly and irreversibly deletes a submission. Click responsibly. The Title and Dept. fields, as well as the Topic and Section pop-up menus, behave identically as their counterparts on the Edit Story page. The Preview button will display the submission in the Edit Story form (described in the section "The Edit Story Form" in Chapter 4). A submission must be reviewed/previewed before it can be posted.

Editing User Submissions

Authors can winnow out off-topic or duplicate Stories from the Submissions list, but the Review Submission page provides the opportunity to review Stories in depth. A typical submission is built around a URL pointing elsewhere on the Web. If the user has included a well-formed <A HREF> tag, the preview will contain a working link to the destination. To validate and verify the link, use the Open Link in New Window command found in many web browsers.

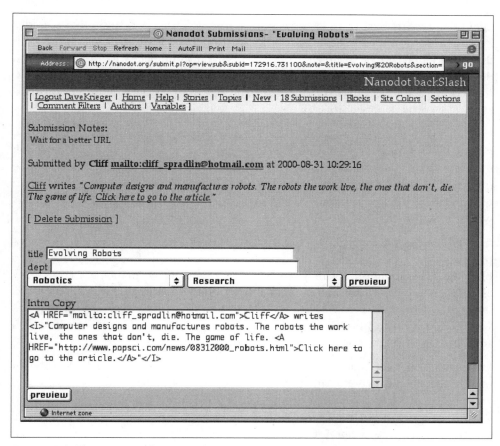

Figure 5-4. The Review Submission page, showing a note added using the Comment text box on the Submissions List page

 Viewing the destination link will quickly verify if the link is well-formed, whether the page exists, and if the page is actually relevant to the site. Spammers and practical jokers are everywhere, and some consider it the height of comedy to post relevant-looking Stories with URLs to commercial, embarrassing, or irrelevant pages.

If the URL does point to something worth seeing, make sure that it will continue to do so. For example, is the link target the homepage of another site? Many news-related web sites display stories on the main homepage or on a Section page, aging them to archival URLs, as new stories arise. (Newspapers and other weblogs frequenty use this technique.) Users who don't realize this may submit Stories with the homepage URL. If a linked page seems totally unrelated to the submission description, perhaps the destination Story has already moved to an archival link. It's worth looking around for a permanent URL to salvage a good submission. Many sites provide keyword searches to find archived Stories.

Even if the URL is relevant to the Story, it may represent a hidden agenda on the part of the submitter. For example, a CD or book review will often include a link to the reviewed item on a major online retailer. The submitted URL may include query information for the retail site's Associate or Affiliate program. This would give the reviewer (or a friend) a kickback from any items purchased by readers who follow the link.

It may be appropriate to allow book reviewers to do this—it gives them an incentive to submit reviews, but it should be done only with the site administrator's blessing. (The administrator may want to use a site-specific participant code, after all.) Other "sneaky URLs" include those that credit the submitter with an ad click-through or generate a poll or survey vote when followed. Also beware of URLs with numbers instead of domain names, session-tracking parameters, or embedded "@" symbols. If it looks suspicious, be careful.

Frequently, user-submitted URLs point to items on other weblogs or sites that merely link to the genuine article. Readers will (silently) bless Authors who provide a direct URL to the primary source. It is good form, though, to give credit to the other site where the user found the story: "Found on *Slashdot*: Advance screenshots are now online for *Leisure Suit Larry: Team Fortress . . .* ".

A good submission may motivate an Author to seek out additional URLs. For example, submissions to Nanodot frequently point to press releases about recent research. Adding links to the appropriate research department or to the home-pages of the researchers, or to the research project page, university or company homepage (et cetera) can really improve the Story.

Users will often use the URL itself as the text of the link:

```
Prof. Kent also has a faculty page online at
<A HREF="http://www.ualberta.ca/~socweb/people/faculty/kent.html"
>http://www.ualberta.ca/~socweb/people/faculty/kent.html</A>.
```

Most web browsers will not wrap a long URL. This can break page layout. It's more visually appealing to use a description of the content as the text of the link instead:

```
Prof. Kent also has a
<A HREF="http://www.ualberta.ca/~socweb/people/faculty/kent.html"
>faculty page online</A>.
```

Users can still find the entire URL via the browser Status Bar or by using the Copy Link option.

In a Story with multiple URLs, consider highlighting the most important link with the <B> (boldface) HTML tag:

```
<A HREF="http://www.xenu.com/"><B>Operation Clambake</B></A>
```

Longer Stories and User Essays

If the submission includes an essay by the user, the Author should separate it into Intro and Extended Copy components on the Edit Story page. Since both blocks display on the Story page, it's unnecessary to duplicate content between them. If the first paragraph of the essay is sufficiently descriptive and represents the overall content, move it into Intro Copy. Otherwise, move the entire submission into Extended Copy, and write a more suitable introduction. (This could be completely original, a different paragraph, or even selected quotes from the essay.)

From the days of Usenet over UUCP, proper attribution of text and ideas has been a fundamental component of netiquette. Slashdot (the Mother Country) started the convention that Authors use quotation marks and italics to distinguish their own words from those of the attributed user within a Story Intro. Follow the principle of "YOYOW" (You Own Your Own Words) when adding an editorial comment. Don't put words in the submitter's mouth:

posted by RedBaron on Monday February 12, @10:14AM

SopwithCamel writes, *"The spec for the LSMFT v0.9 protocol has just been posted to the W3C site."* [LSMFT has been vaporware since it was announced. Without any reference implementations, this turkey will never fly. — rb]

If the user either didn't know HTML or was in too much of a hurry to whip the submission into shape before leaving work, an Author will need to polish the formatting. Submitters may use ASCII text-formatting conventions used in email or Usenet. These are easily translated into HTML:

- Blank lines indicate paragraph breaks and call for <P> tags. This one change will do the most to preserve readability; HTML text without <P> tags runs together into one long paragraph. The *Plain Old Text* filter setting of the Post Comment page (see the section "Posting Comments" in Chapter 6) performs this substitution automatically for comment posters.

- Plus signs or asterisks at the beginning of lines indicate bullet points; replace each one with <LI> and wrap the list in <UL></UL> tags.

- Underscores or asterisks surrounding words within text indicate emphasis; replace them with <I></I> or <B></B> tag pairs.

Beyond these merely mechanical recommendations, Authors must take into account the content and tone of the submission in relation to the site as a whole. The section "Setting the Tone" in Chapter 8 discusses this subject in greater detail.

6

Comments, Filters, and Content Moderation

The comment and moderation systems make Slash a tool for community discussion instead of simply a content management system. This chapter discusses how the processes of posting and viewing comments works for users, how to forbid certain types of comments with filters, and how the moderation system encourages a self-policing user community.

A Slash comment can be attached to a Story, to another comment (its *parent*, in Slash terminology), or to a specially created discussion SID. Parented comments lead to a branching discussion tree similar to those that occur in Usenet newsgroups or mailing lists. Slash regularly distributes a passel of *moderation points* to its users. These can be used to raise or lower the *moderation score* of comments posted by other users. Each user has an individual *karma score*. Moderation performed on a user comment affects that user's karma. Users can also earn karma by submitting a Story that gets published. High karma grants other user privileges, such as posting comments at a higher initial score.

Comments that meet with the approval of a significant cross-section of the site's users will acquire high scores.* Users can choose to filter and rank the comments on a particular Story. Slash provides a minimum *threshold score*; comments below this value will be suppressed unless specifically requested. The remaining comments can be sorted by their score or age and can be threaded to retain the branching structure of the discussion.

---

* In theory, that is. At its heart, moderation is very much an individual activity. Over time, the moderation system tends to normalize the available pool of moderators, but it's not an exact science.

Viewing Comments

A block of HTML controls beneath the main text of every Story page allows users to control their comment view (see Figure 6-1). The pop-up menus govern viewing preferences, and the Change button will redisplay the Story with the new view. If the Save checkbox is checked, the new settings will be retained as the default view of all subsequent Stories. Otherwise, the new settings will apply only to the current Story.

Figure 6-1. Controls to change the display of Slash comments follow the Story's main text

The Threshold pop-up controls minimum score (from –1 to 5) for comments to be displayed. It also lists the number of comments currently at or above each value:

```
-1: 33 comments
 0: 33 comments
```

```
1: 32 comments
2: 12 comments
3:  8 comments
4:  4 comments
5:  1 comments
```

Comment scores never go beneath the minimum value, so a threshold setting of −1 will display all comments. Comments from logged-in users start with a moderation score of 1. A threshold setting of 1 will display all regular comments except those that have been explicitly downgraded. Because the availability of moderation points depends on the level of site activity, it may be rare for a comment to reach a score of 4 or 5. On Slashdot, the noisiest and busiest Slash site in existence, a threshold of 1 or 2 captures most of the conversation in sufficient detail.

The threshold setting also affects the view of the site and Section homepages. When a registered user views one of those pages, the Story summaries will display the total number of comments and the number of comments at the user's current threshold (see Figure 6-2). When viewing a Story, the comments listing will include HTML links of the form *n replies beneath your current threshold*, in which n is the number of comments suppressed due to low scores. Clicking on these links will display the comment in all its glory. (Setting the *hard thresholds* in User Settings will prevent this, as if low-rated comments did not even exist.)

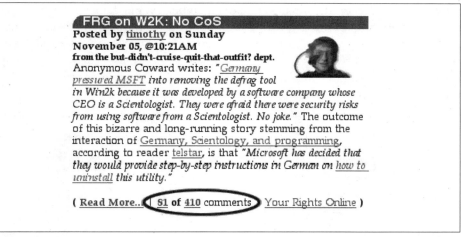

Figure 6-2. The number of comments on each Story and the number of comments at the current Threshold setting

Comments Settings

The Display Mode pop-up menu has four possible settings:

No Comments
> Suppresses the display of comments entirely.

Nested
> Displays child comments indented underneath their parent comments.

Threaded
> Displays only top-level comments in full, with HTML links to their child comments at or above the current threshold. The text of each link is the subject of the linked comment.

Flat
> Ignores parent-child relationships, listing all threshold-satisfying comments in a single flat list.

The Sort pop-up menu controls the order in which comment families (or individual comments, in Flat mode) appear. *Oldest First* and *Newest First* display comment families (top-level comments and their children) in forward or reverse chronological order, respectively, according to the timestamp of the topmost parent comment. *Highest Scores First* displays comment families in descending order by the moderation score of the highest-ranked member of the family. For example, a comment family with a top-level parent comment scored at 3 but with a child of score 5 will appear earlier in the listing than a family whose highest moderation score is 4. (No "Lowest Scores First" option exists, for some reason.) Choosing an option with the extra (*Ignore Threads*) option will override the Display Mode setting. Figure 6-3 demonstrates these concepts visually.

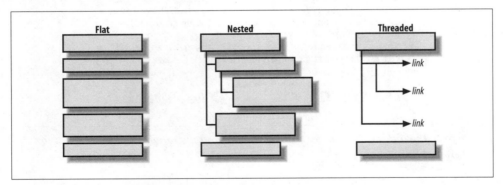

Figure 6-3. The three Comment display modes

Posting Comments

Adjacent to the view controls, the Reply button allows users to post a top-level comment on the Story. Furthermore, each displayed comment contains a *Reply To This* link. Both bring up the Post Comment form (see Figure 6-4), which provides a field for the subject heading and a field for comment text. The form will display the parent comment, if any, above the form. This makes it convenient to copy text to quote in a reply.

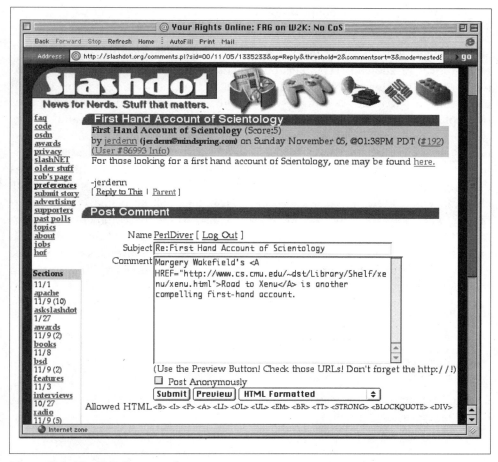

Figure 6-4. The Post Comment form

Slash automatically restricts the available HTML tags in comments to a set defined by site administrators. This helps to prevent mischievous users from breaking the page's layout by including a huge image or by adding unbalanced `</TD>` or `</TABLE>` tags. The list of allowed HTML tags can be set in the `approvedtags` site variable and will display just beneath the Post Comment form.

Another site variable, `allow_anonymous`, controls whether non-logged-in users can post comments. Even so, the Post Anonymously checkbox lets logged-in users post as "Anonymous User" (the generic user pseudonym) without having to log out. If anonymous commenting has been disallowed, non-logged-in users will get a "Sorry" message after clicking a Reply button or following a *Reply to This* link.

Slash provides four possible filters for comment text. The default, *HTML Formatted*, removes disallowed HTML tags but makes no other changes to the submitted text.* *Plain Old Text* removes disallowed HTML tags, converting line breaks and blank lines to `<BR>` and `<P>` tags. It tries to preserve leading indenting and spaces by replacing Tab characters with the HTML entity for non-breaking spaces (` `). *Code* mode handles comments made up of programming code. Such text usually contains special characters that would render the code unreadable if interpreted as HTML. This type does everything *Plain Old Text* does and also replaces the ampersand (`&`) and angle bracket (`< >`) characters with their respective HTML character entities (`&amp;`, `&lt;`, and `&gt;`). HTML tags will be displayed, not interpreted, when the comment is rendered. *Code* also wraps the comment text inside the HTML `<CODE></CODE>` tags. Generally, web browsers render such text with a monospaced font. *Extrans (html tags to text)* makes the same changes as *Code* except for wrapping the comment in `<CODE>` tags. The comment will be appear in the normal font.

If the following HTML was submitted as the comment text:

```
I <B>heartily</B> recommend that you visit
this web site:
<A HREF="http://www.xenu.net/">Operation
Clambake</A>.
```

it would be stored in the database and presented a web browser, for each of the comment types, as:

---

* Note that whitespace is not significant in HTML. Blank lines, line breaks, and multiple spaces will display as a single space. While Slash preserves the whitespace, standards-compliant web browsers ignore it when rendering a comment.

HTML Formatted

Stored as:	
| | ```
I <B>heartily</B> recommend that you visit
this web site:
<A HREF="http://www.xenu.net/">Operation
Clambake</A>.
``` |
| Rendered as: | I heartily recommend that you visit this web site: *Operation Clambake* . |

Plain Old Text

Stored as:	
| | ```
I <B>heartily</B> recommend that you visit
<BR>this web site:
<BR><A HREF="http://www.xenu.net/">Operation
<BR>Clambake</A>.<BR>
``` |
| Rendered as: | I heartily recommend that you visit
this web site:
Operation
Clambake. |

Code

Stored as:	
| | ```
<CODE>I &lt;B&gt;heartily&lt;/B&gt; recommend that you visit
<BR>this web site:
<BR>&lt;A HREF="http://www.xenu.net/"&gt;Operation
<BR>Clambake&lt;/A&gt;.</CODE><BR><BR>
``` |
| Rendered as: | ```
I <B>heartily</B> recommend that you visit
this web site:
<A HREF="http://www.xenu.net/">Operation
Clambake</A>.
``` |

Extrans (html tags to text)

Stored as:	
| | ```
I &lt;B&gt;heartily&lt;/B&gt; recommend that you visit
<BR>this web site:
<BR>&lt;A HREF="http://www.xenu.net/"&gt;Operation
<BR>Clambake&lt;/A&gt;.<BR><BR>
``` |
| Rendered as: | I <B>heartily</B> recommend that you visit
this web site:
<A HREF="http://www.xenu.net/">Operation
Clambake</A>. |
```

Table 6-1 summarizes the differences between the comment modes.

Table 6-1. Features of comment-posting modes

	HTML Formatted	Plain Old Text	Code	Extrans (html to text)
Preserves line breaks	No	Yes	Yes	Yes
HTML Tags	Rendered	Rendered	Shown	Shown
Typeface	Page font	Page font	Monospaced	Page font

Like the Submit Story and Edit Story pages, the Post Comment page provides a Preview button for users to catch mistakes before committing a post to the ages. Slash will add a user signature to the preview if the user has defined one in user preferences (as shown way back in Figure 1-8).

Once a user has posted a comment, she cannot delete or modify it. Sufficiently privileged Authors can delete user comments (see the section "Comment Moderation" later in this chapter) but not modify them. Modifying a user comment requires direct access to the underlying database, as described in Appendix B. This is so fraught with peril as to be almost useless. Consider posted comments to be written in stone. It's possible to smash them, but fixing a typo (chisel-o?) is quite involved.

Comment Filters

When Slashdot first implemented user comments, a curious phenomenon developed. A small portion of the userbase developed a strong competition to post the first comment on a fresh Story. This lead to a significant volume of "Me first!" comments instantly attached to Stories, adding little to the quality of discussion. They were followed by users who thought it the height of hilarity to post ASCII art, breaking the site's layout. First posters were noisy, but ASCII "artists" were annoying. Soon, comment filters were born.

The Comment Filters List

A Slash comment filter has two parts: the *behavior* detected by a pattern match and a *quantitative level* of that behavior to tolerate. For example, if half or more of a comment consists of non-alphanumeric characters, it may be an ASCII drawing instead of a thoughtful discussion. (It may also be a regular expression.) A Slash site functioning as a church newsletter may wish to suppress excess occurrences of certain colorful Anglo-Saxon monosyllables.

Each filter contains a regular expression that defines and measures the behavior component. Additionally, two numeric fields set the limits on its occurrence: a *ratio* (how much of the behavior is permitted) and a *threshold number* of occurrences (how many times is it permitted). This allows a filter to block posts either by frequency of behavior or by the number incidents of the behavior. For example, any post that uses the words "Nazi" or "Hitler" more than once could be disallowed on the grounds of "Godwin's Law."*

Clicking on the *Comment Filters* link in the Admin menu brings up the Comment Filters page, which lists all current filters in a tabular format (see Figure 6-5). Each filter has a unique Filter ID; clicking on the number brings up the Edit Filter page for that filter. The Regex column shows the regular expression describing the filtered behavior. The Modifier column allows optional features of Perl regular expressions: g means "look for multiple matches," while i means "ignore upper/lowercase differences in potential matches." (Perl provides other match modifiers; Slash ignores the rest.)

The Field indicates which field of the comment form to search. This will most commonly be either postersubj (the subject of the comment) or postercomment (the text of the comment).

Ratio sets the maximum fraction of the total length which the Regex can match without the comment being rejected. The Minimum Match field sets the number of times the Regex can occur in the field before it is rejected. These fields are exclusive—each filter can use either the Regex or the Minimum Match field, but not both. If both fields are zero, the comment is rejected if it matches Regex at all.

Minimum Length and Maximum Length, when provided, set bounds on the length of the searched field to which the filter will apply. The field must be within the range of these values, or Slash will skip the filter for that comment. If either field is zero, then the filter will be applied regardless of the length of the searched field.

Finally, Error Message contains the text presented to the user when Slash rejects a comment triggering the filter.

Regular Expressions

Comment filters use Perl's incredibly powerful regular expression parser. Regular expressions are a concise and powerful vocabulary for describing patterns in text, allowing matches and substutitions on matches. This section will only touch on the rudiments of regular expressions. For a fuller treatment, consult *perldoc perlre* in

---

* "As a Usenet discussion grows longer, the probability of a comparison involving Nazis or Hitler approaches one." (See the Jargon File, *http://www.jargon.net/jargonfile/g/GodwinsLaw.html.*) The first person to trigger the Law automatically loses the argument, and the thread is over. This is one place where Slash is measurably superior to standard editorial pages.

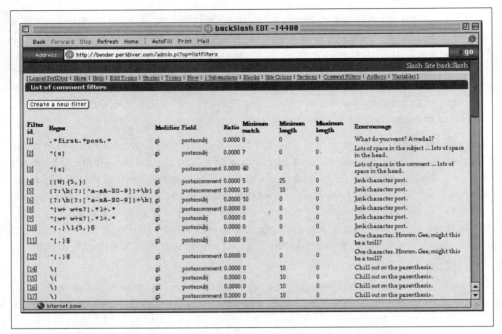

Figure 6-5. The Comment Filters page; click on the filter number to edit that filter

the standard Perl documentation. *Mastering Regular Expressions* by Jeffrey E. F. Friedl (O'Reilly) is also excellent. (In Perl circles, it is known as the "Hip Owl" book.)

Regular expressions look like gibberish to the uninitiated, but with practice they are easy to read and create. The simplest kind of regex simply matches an exact substring. For example, the regex Tom will match if the exact string "Tom" occurs anywhere in the source string. Postive matches will include "Tomahawk" and "Uncle Tom", while "atom" will fail. With the i modifier, the regex will match regardless of letter case; "TOM", "tOM", and "tom" will all match Tom.

The pipe (|) character separates alternative matches. These alternations are frequently grouped in parentheses to clarify the start and end of the alternation.* The regex (Tom|Dick|Harry) will match if the searched string contains any one of those three names. It translates to "match Tom or Dick or Harry."

The parentheses and pipe are both *metacharacters*, with special meanings in regular expressions. To search for a literal metacharacter, escape it by prepending a backslash character (\). Thus, the regex \(will match on any left parenthesis in the searched string, and \\ will match the backslash itself.

---

* Parentheses have other purposes, as well. Again, read *perldoc perlre*. It will eventually make sense.

Square brackets ([ ]) are also metacharacters. They mark a *character class*, a set of alternative one-character strings. For example, i|o|a is functionally equivalent to [ioa]. This means that (tim|tom|tam) could be reduced to either (t(i|o|a)m) or (t[ioa]m). Inside a character class, the hyphen (–) defines a range of characters. For example, [a-z] matches against any one lowercase alphabetic character; [a-zA-Z] matches against any letter, regardless of case; and [a-zA-Z0-9] matches against any single alphanumeric character.

A character class can be negated by placing a caret (^) as the first character inside the brackets. The class [^a-zA-Z0-9] will match any one character *except* for a letter or a number. To include the caret in a class, place it anywhere except in the first position. For example, [()^] will match the left or right parenthesis or the caret.

Perl provides several predefined character classes suitable for Slash comment filters. Each class (or *metasymbol*) consists of a backslash followed by a letter. For example, \w (think "word") is the same as [a-zA-Z0-9_], while \W matches [^a-zA-Z0-9_] (the exact opposite). Similarly, \s matches any whitespace character (Space, Tab, Backspace, Newline, and Carriage Return), and \S matches any non-whitespace character.

Regular Expression Metacharacters

Perl also includes metasymbols for single characters that would otherwise be hard to represent. The \t symbol matches the Tab character, while \b matches a Backspace. The period (.) is a special metasymbol, matching any single character (except, normally, a Newline). Thus, T.m will match "Tom", "Tim", "T5m", or "T m". Use \. to match a literal period.

Other metacharacters quantify how many times the preceding character or grouping should occur. The asterisk (*) means "match this item if it occurs *zero or more* times." For example, Har*y will match "Harry", "Hary", "Harrrrry", or "Hay".* (Tom|Dick|Harry)* will match "Tom", "Dick", "TomDick", "HarryHarryTom-TomDick", or the empty string ("").

The plus sign (+) means "match *at least one* occurrence." Har+y will match "Harry", "Hary", or "Harrrrry", but not "Hay", and (Tom|Dick|Harry)+ will not match the empty string.

Finally, the caret (^) and dollar sign ($) metacharacters specify that the pattern must occur at the beginning or at the end of the matched string, respectively. ^Once\s+ means the string must begin with "Once" followed by whitespace, while

---

* This is a common gotcha with the asterisk. There are exactly zero r characters between the a and the y.

end\.$ means the string must end with "end." (Note the escaped period). To match ^[a-z]+$ the string must consist of one or more lowercase letters, with no other characters present. ^.*$ will match any string, including the empty string.

This only scratches the surface of regular expressions, but these basics will suffice for most Slash comment filters. As an example, consider the "first post" epidemic mentioned earlier. The first comment filter in a default installation of Slash is defined as follows:

Field name	Value
Regex	.*first.*post.*
Modifier	gi
Field	postersubj
Ratio	0.0000
Minimum match	0
Minimum length	0
Maximum length	0
Error message	What do you want? A medal?

This catches any comment with "first" anywhere in its subject and "post" anywhere after that. .* matches any sequence of zero or more characters, so this matches if "first" occurs in the subject and if "post" follows anywhere in the string. They may even run together as "firstpost". This, unfortunately, will also flag potentially legitimate subjects such as "my first Farrah Fawcett poster," but few "first posters" remember those days.

The default installation contains a filter to suppress ASCII diagrams:

Field name	Value
Regex	[^a-zA-Z0-9]
Modifier	gi
Field	postercomment
Ratio	0.6000
Minimum match	0
Minimum length	0
Maximum length	10
Error message	Ascii Art. How creative. Not here though.

This filter stop comments longer than 10 characters in which more than 60% of those characters are non-alphanumeric. Another filter catches users who've accidentally left the Caps Lock key engaged:

Field name	Value
Regex	[^a-z]
Modifier	g
Field	postercomment
Ratio	0.5000
Minimum match	0
Minimum length	2
Maximum length	0
Error message	PLEASE DON'T USE SO MANY CAPS. USING CAPS IS LIKE YELLING!

This is intended to flag subjects over two characters in length, in which half or more characters are not lowercase letters or numbers. In practice, this is a troublesome filter. See the section "The Content Filter Cold War" in Chapter 8 for more.

Comment Moderation

The Slash moderation system exists to raise the quality of discussion as perceived by the userbase at large. It uses positive feedback to encourage constructive participation and negative feedback to discourage noise and flames. The system is designed to distribute power widely throughout the userbase, while tending to concentrate this power in the hands of those who use it in a socially desirable fashion.

Evaluative power exists in the form of moderation points. A user can spend points to raise or lower the moderation scores of individual comments. Any logged-in Slash user may become eligible to moderate and may find herself awarded points at any time. (See the sidebar "Mommy, Where Do Moderation Points Come From?"). These points will decay over time to encourage active use of the moderation system and discourage point hoarding.

A special moderation Slashbox will appear on Story pages when a user has moderation points (see Figure 6-6). A pop-up menu will also follow each posted comment, accompanied by a Moderate button at the very end of the page. To moderate a comment, choose an evaluation from the pop-up menu following the Moderate button.

Types of Comment Moderations

The moderation system predefines 11 different ways of evaluating a comment. *Normal* (the default) leaves the comment's moderation score unchanged. *Offtopic, Flamebait, Troll, Redundant,* and *Overrated* are negative evaluations. They deduct one point from the comment's score. The remaining labels (*Insightful, Interesting, Informative, Funny,* and *Underrated*) are positive and increase the comment's score by one point. Attempting to moderate a comment past either limit will

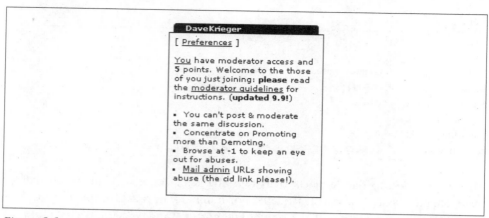

Figure 6-6. A special Slashbox showing available moderation points

consume a moderation point with no visible effect. Also, the *Underrated* evaluation will affect only comments scored at 1 or less. Similarly, *Overrated* is limited to comments with a score of 0 or higher. A comment already at –1 cannot be marked overrated.

Two configuration variables control the moderation labels. The badreasons variable contains the number of negative moderation labels. reasons is a comma-separated list of all of the allowed moderation labels. The first reason is always *Normal.* If badreasons is 4, the next four reasons will cause a comment to lose a point. The final two reasons are special; they do not appear in meta-moderation. Suppose reasons held bad1, bad2, bad3, bad4, good1, good2, good3, special1, and special2, and badreasons was set to 4. The first four labels, bad1 through bad4, cause a comment to lose a point. good1 through good3 cause a comment to gain a point. The penultimate label, special1, deducts a point from the comment, and the final label, special2, adds a point. Neither of the special labels are available for meta-moderation.

If a user attempts to use more moderation points than she has available, the system will use only the available number of points, ignoring the rest of her choices. Slash may not process the moderations according to the visible display order, due to variations in nesting and sorting. A better practice is to choose exactly the correct number of comment moderations to make. (On high-traffic sites, it may be better yet to open each moderatable comment in a new browser window to perform the moderation. This can save points, especially if one user flags a post for moderation, reads the rest of a long Story, and another moderator handles the post before the first finally hits the Moderate button.

Slash also prohibits users from moderating comments attached to a Story to which they have themselves posted comments. If the user has previously posted a comment, the Story will not display the moderation menus. If the user has moderated a Story and subsequently posts a comment, Slash will undo the moderations. This prevents a user from unduly moderating a discussion in which he also participates. Unintentionally, it also allows a user to correct a mistaken moderation by posting a follow-up comment. Slash does not refund used moderation points, however.

Gaining Moderator Access

To be eligible for moderation, a user must meet the following criteria:

Be logged in

> Accountability requires that each moderator have a stable, if pseudonymous, identity. Anonymous Users cannot moderate.

Use the site regularly

> Slash tracks coarse-grained access statistics for each visitor—how many Story pages has Joe Doakes viewed this week? The system chooses moderators from near the median, eschewing both compulsive reloaders and occasional surfers.

Use the site for a while

> The system also excludes the newest accounts. This tends to prevent cheaters from starting new accounts only to gain moderator access. It also encourages new users to participate in the community for a while before attempting to guide it.

Choose to help moderate

> As discussed in the section "Slash User Preferences" in Chapter 1, a User Preferences checkbox allows each user to opt out of participating in contente moderation.

Possess good karma

> What goes around comes around. Slash knows who's been bad or good (so be good, for goodness' sake). Karma reflects the sum total of moderations performed on a user's comment. This tends to represent the user community's collective opinion of user contributions. A user with negative karma cannot moderate.

The *moderatord* task doles out moderation points at regular intervals, based on the level of posting activity. It bestows these points to a subset of eligible moderators, who must use them or lose them. The shelf life of moderation points is controlled by the `stir` configuration variable and has a default of three days.

Mommy, Where Do Moderation Points Come From?

The algorithms used to generate and distribute moderation points are rather complicated. The *moderatord* task gives "tokens" to users. These tokens accumulate over time and do not decay. When an individual user's tokens reach a specific level, *moderatord* converts them to moderation points. Moderation points expire over time.

When the *moderatord* task runs, it first determines the number of new comments posted since it last ran. (The site variable lastComments holds the previous value, and totalComments holds the current value). It multiplies this number by the value of tokenspercomment. The task then adds the number of moderation points that have expired without being used, recycling them. Finally, *moderatord* multiplies the total by the value of tokenspercomment to determine the number of tokens to distribute.

Next, the task identifies the pool of available moderators. It applies the criteria already discussed, then drops everyone at the low or high ends of the pool, according to the m1_pointgrant_start and m1_pointgrant_end ratios. This is intended to select a very average group of users as moderators. *moderatord* then distributes one token at a time to a random eligible moderator until all tokens have been distributed.

Finally, each user whose current number of tokens has reached the maxtokens threshold will have the tokens converted to moderation points. *moderatord* divides maxtokens by tokensperpoint, adding the result to the user's available moderation points. It also subtracts maxtokens from the user's current number of tokens. Finally, it records the date so that tokens can expire if they aren't used within stir days.

Instant Karma

The visible final product of moderation is the karma rating of each user. High karma carries some privileges. For example, users with karma above a threshold value (the goodkarma configuration variable) have the option of adding a one-point bonus to their initial comment-posting scores. By default, registered users post at a score of 1. The good karma bonus can bump the value up to 2. Beyond that, karma is little more than a gold star—fun for a 5-year-old, but an insubstantial reward for a 25-year-old.

The moderation system attempts to encourage comments that meet a community standard for quality, discourage noise, and distribute the responsibility and power of moderation as widely as possible. (Both "quality" and "noise" are subjective and will be different for each Slash site's community. This corresponds nicely with real life, in which community standards of of "obscenity" and "artistic merit" vary. Some people even like boy bands.) To check potential abuses of power even further, Slash includes a second level of *meta-moderation* (or "M2") to moderate the moderation process ("M1").*

Meta-Moderation

Every logged-in user with zero or positive karma can participate in meta-moderation daily. A link on the homepage (*Have you meta-moderated today?*) leads to the meta-moderation page. This page displays a set of 10 recently moderated and randomly chosen comments, with the moderation judgment under consideration (*Insightful, Offtopic*, etc.) beneath each comment. Three radio buttons allow the meta-moderator to consider each moderation as fair, unfair, or neutral (see Figure 6-7). Each meta-moderation ranks the moderation of the comment, not the comment itself. Thus, a comment may appear more than once with different or identical moderation labels.

Meta-moderation rewards fair moderators and penalizes unfair ones by adjusting their karma. Meta-moderators can earn karma for meta-moderating, but the bonus is too small to earn the +1 posting bonus. Meta-moderators can also be penalized for abusing the M2 system by rating too many moderations as unfair.

Authors and Moderation

Site Authors may have a different view of the moderation system. If the configuration variable `authors_unlimited` is true, Authors have a bottomless bag of moderation points. When a logged-in Author views a Story page, she will see the moderation Slashbox with "0 moderation points" (as seen in Figure 4-2). The standard moderation pop-up menus follow each comment, allowing her to moderate any or all of the posted comments. Authors are also not prohibited from commenting on and moderating the same Story.

Authors also have the ability to delete posted user comments. Beneath each comment and following the moderation pop-up menu, Authors see an unlabelled checkbox. If checked, the comment and its replies will be removed from the database when the user clicks the Moderate button. There is no grace period and

---

* Qui custodiet ipses custodes? Meta-custodes (maximi custodes)?

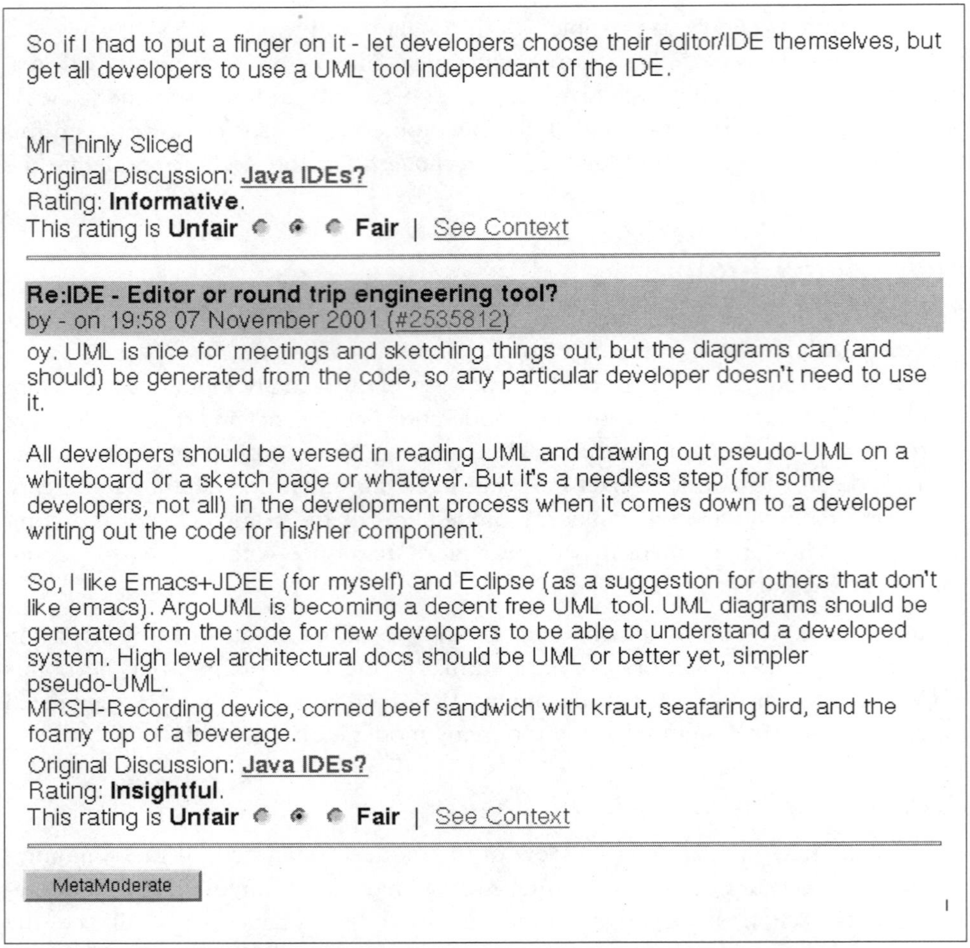

So if I had to put a finger on it - let developers choose their editor/IDE themselves, but get all developers to use a UML tool independant of the IDE.

Mr Thinly Sliced
Original Discussion: **Java IDEs?**
Rating: **Informative**.
This rating is **Unfair** ◌ ◉ ◌ **Fair** | See Context

Re:IDE - Editor or round trip engineering tool?
by - on 19:58 07 November 2001 (#2535812)

oy. UML is nice for meetings and sketching things out, but the diagrams can (and should) be generated from the code, so any particular developer doesn't need to use it.

All developers should be versed in reading UML and drawing out pseudo-UML on a whiteboard or a sketch page or whatever. But it's a needless step (for some developers, not all) in the development process when it comes down to a developer writing out the code for his/her component.

So, I like Emacs+JDEE (for myself) and Eclipse (as a suggestion for others that don't like emacs). ArgoUML is becoming a decent free UML tool. UML diagrams should be generated from the code for new developers to be able to understand a developed system. High level architectural docs should be UML or better yet, simpler pseudo-UML.
MRSH-Recording device, corned beef sandwich with kraut, seafaring bird, and the foamy top of a beverage.
Original Discussion: **Java IDEs?**
Rating: **Insightful**.
This rating is **Unfair** ◌ ◉ ◌ **Fair** | See Context

MetaModerate

Figure 6-7. The meta-moderation (M2) interface

no Undo option. In Slash 1.x, there were no visual cues or explanations of this checkbox, which lead to accidental deletions. Modern versions of the software have added a warning next to the Moderate button, noting that all checked comments will be deleted. Proceed with caution.

Moderation Configuration Variables

More of Slash's configuration variables deal with moderation and meta-moderation than with any other aspect of the system. Site administrators have considerable power to fine-tune the moderation system by tweaking these variables.

Variables Governing User Karma and Comment Scores

The following variables control user karma levels and comment posting scores:

goodkarma and badkarma

Define levels at which karmic consequences occur. A user with karma below badkarma will experience a penalty of −1 on any new comments. She will not receive the +1-point boost for logging in and will post with a default score of 0 until her karma rises. A user with karma greater than goodkarma will receive the option of posting new comments with a +1 bonus. These comments will start with an initial moderation score of 2 instead of 1. The default value of badkarma is −10, and the default value of goodkarma is 25.

maxkarma and minkarma

Set the upper and lower bounds on karma values. The default range is −25 to 50.

comment_minscore and comment_maxscore

Define the lower and upper limits of comment scores, respectively. Slash ignores all attempts to moderate a comment past these bounds. The default range is −1 to 5.

submission_bonus

The number of karma points a user gains each time one of his Story submissions is published. The default is 3.

down_moderations

Limits the number of downward moderations an IP address or user ID can accumulate within a three-day period. Users who exceed this will be prevented from posting new comments. When a user attempts to post a comment, Slash calculates the *net* moderation (total upward moderations minus total downward moderations) received by posts from the user's current IP address and by posts from the current user's user ID. If either result is less than or equal to down_moderations, Slash will reject the comment with an error message. This tends to squelch new comments from users who have reaped a large negative reaction. The default value is –6.

Variables Governing Tokens and Moderation Points

Several configuration variables regulate the availability of moderation tokens, the conversion of tokens to moderation points, and the distribution of points to potential moderators:

tokenspercomment

Determines how many tokens will be fed into the moderation system for each posted comment. Increasing this value increases the number of available moderation points. The default is 6.

maxtokens

The threshold at which a user's available tokens will be converted into moderation points. This must be evenly divisible by tokensperpoint, or some tokens will be lost in rounding. If this is less than tokensperpoint, no moderation points will ever be generated. If maxtokens is greater than the product of maxpoints and tokensperpoint, any moderation points generated from the difference will be discarded. The default value, 40, is exactly equal to the product of the default values of maxpoints and tokensperpoint.

tokensperpoint

The exchange rate for turning tokens into moderation points. Reducing this value increases the total number of moderation points that will be generated because a moderation point will cost less tokens. The default value is 8.

maxpoints

The maximum number of moderation points a user can hold. Slash discards any points awarded beyond this threshold. The default value is 5.

stir

The lifetime, in days, of an awarded moderation point. If a user does not use all his points within stir days, they will expire and be converted into tokens for redistribution. The default is 3.

authors_unlimited

As previously mentioned, controls whether site Authors have unlimited moderation powers. By default, this feature is enabled (with a default value of 1). If disabled, Authors must earn their moderation points like everyone else.

Meta-Moderation Configuration Variables

Variables with names beginning with m2_ deal with the meta-moderation system:

m2_comments

Determines how many moderations a meta-moderator can evaluate at once. The default value is 10.

m2_bonus

Sets the amount of karma a user earns for participating in meta-moderation. This is subject to the effects of m2_mincheck, m2_toomanyunfair, m2_maxunfair, and m2_maxbonus. The default value is 1.

m2_toomanyunfair and m2_maxunfair

Limit the number of unfair judgments allowed in meta-moderation. If the ratio of unfair judgments exceeds m2_toomanyunfair, Slash ignores the M2 operation. The karma of the original moderators will be unaffected, and the meta-moderator earns no m2_bonus. If the ratio exceeds m2_maxunfair, the meta-moderator not only earns no bonus, but suffers a karma penalty of m2_penalty (–1 by default). If m2_toomanyunfair is greater than m2_maxunfair, no penalty will ever occur. The default value of m2_toomanyunfair is 0.3, and the default value of m2_maxunfair is 0.5. Both variables are ignored if the total number of meta-moderations submitted is less than m2_mincheck (with a default value of 3).

m2_penalty

The number of points deducted from a meta-moderator's karma for marking too many moderations as unfair. The default is 1.

m2_mincheck

The minimum number of meta-moderations a user can submit before Slash checks to see if too many moderations have been marked as unfair. The default is 3, or a third of m2_comments.

m2_maxbonus

Limits the amount of karma a user may earn through meta-moderation. Users with karma at or above this value will earn no bonus for meta-moderating. This prevents users from gaining the +1 bonus, as long as m2_maxbonus is less than goodkarma. The default value is 12.

m2_userpercentage

Governs the available pool of meta-moderators. The value of this field is a decimal; users with user IDs greater than m2_userpercentage multiplied by the highest current user ID are ineligible for meta-moderation. The default value is 0.9. If there are 3,000 registered users, only those with user IDs below 2,700 can meta-moderate. This helps foil the strategy of registering new user accounts en masse to distort the meta-moderation system.

7

Managing Topics and Sections

Any identifiable net community has at least one common interest, and individual members have their own unique likes and needs. Slash provides several tools by which users can adapt site presentation to their liking. To achieve this, site Authors and administrators have to provide sufficient metainformation. One such category is the classification of Stories into Topics and Sections. As mentioned in the section "Slash User Preferences" in Chapter 1, this allows users to view or exclude Stories by category.

The site theme will govern the necessary Topics and Sections. The default Slash theme includes three Sections (Articles, Features, and Slash) and four Topics (Slash, Slashdot, News, and Linux). This chapter explains how and why to replace or to supplement the default categories.

Managing Topics

The *Topics* link appears in the Admin menu for Authors with a seclev of 10,000. It links to the Topics Editor page (see Figure 7-1). A pop-up menu at the top of the form lists the currently defined Topics by name. Choose any Topic and click Select Topic to edit it. This will reload the same page with the Topic information, including the currently selected Topic image.

Topic Attributes

Slash automatically assigns Topics unique identifiers, used internally. These values are not appropriate for display purposes, so the Short Name field is used in all menus where Authors can select a Topic. These names should be short and unique within the first five characters, as discussed in the section "The Stories List" in Chapter 4. The Alt Text field is similar. Its contents appear in the ALT attribute of

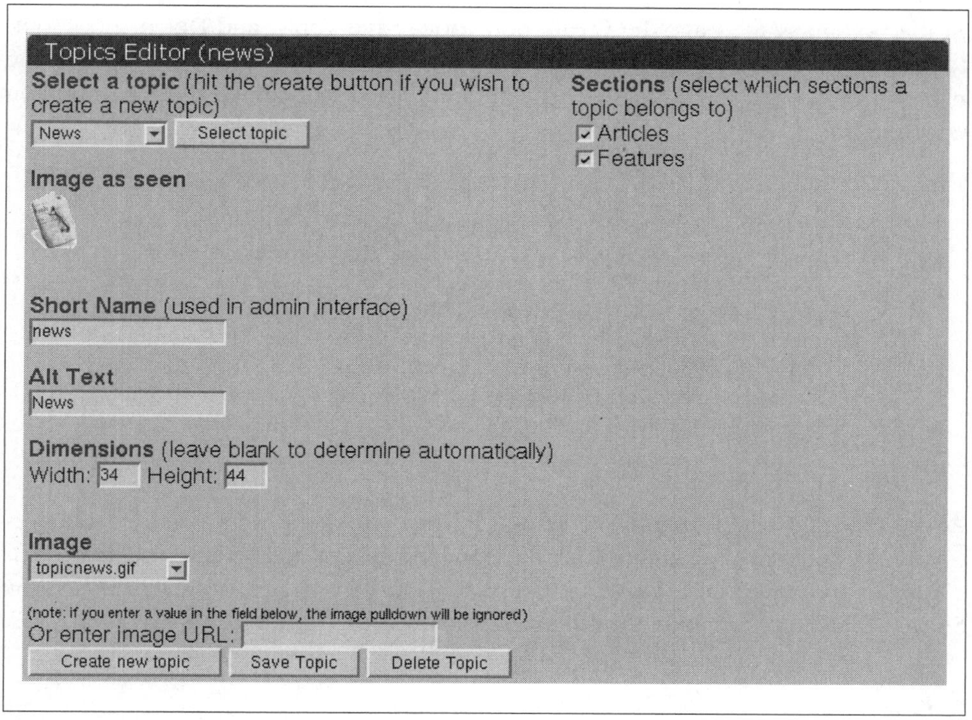

Figure 7-1. The Topics Editor page

the <IMG> tag used to display Topic images. This is helpful for users with text or aural browsers. There is no five-character limit for Alt Text, so feel free to be as descriptive as necessary. (For example, a Topic with a Short Name of "cats" could have Alt Text of "The antics of Ashley, Hannah, Grumpy, and Mars.")

The Image pop-up menu allows you to choose an image file to use as the Topic icon. Based on the selected image, Slash will automatically fill in the pixel Width and Height fields. These values are also used in the <IMG> tag used to display the icon. Manually providing "incorrect" attributes will force some browsers to scale or distort the image when displayed. This can be exploited to achieve some interesting visual effects, but it's usually safe to let Slash handle this automatically.

The Image menu is populated with the names of files found in the *images/topics* subdirectory beneath the directory listed in the `basedir` configuration variable. Slash scans this directory for files with extensions of *.gif, .png,* and *.jpg* every time it builds the Image pop-up menu. Alternately, entering a URL into the image URL field will override anything selected from the Image menu. Slash will not automatically fill in the Dimensions. This is just as well because it's rude to link to images on someone else's site without permission. This field is best used for images residing on another web server under your control.

At the bottom of the page the Create new topic, Save Topic, and Delete Topic buttons do just as they imply. Note that creating new Topics will not change the name in the Select Topic menu. This can be a little disconcerting the first time you encounter it.

 Deleting a Topic is a two-step process. First, choose the Topic name in the top pop-up menu and click Select Topic to reload the page. After it refreshes, click the Delete Topic button. The currently displayed Topic will be deleted, not the Topic selected in the name menu. Beware that there is no grace period for deletion. Deleting a Topic does not delete Stories assigned to the Topic. Until they are assigned a new Topic (from the Edit Story page), they will display a browser's "missing image" symbol as their Topic icon.

At the top right of this menu, the Sections menu lists all currently defined site Sections. A Topic can be assigned to as many or as few Sections as needed. This allows finer-grained customization. Simply check the box next to the name of any Section that should include the current Topic.

Choosing Topics and Icons

As the administrator, you should have some idea of your site's focus. For example, Barrapunto covers Free Software in Spanish, while use Perl handles all sorts of Perl news. Though it has roots in Slashdot, Slash itself is content-neutral and can serve a community built around just about anything. The Slashcode web site (*http://slashcode.com/sites.shtml*) lists dozens of known sites, including those devoted to Christianity, freedom, jazz, drug policy, sports, media, sex, and local community resources. The site theme should direct you to choosing appropriate Topics.

Though your theme can be anything imaginable (and quite possibly, something the Slashteam would *never* have imagined), several guidelines apply:

Choose Topics that cover the subject matter without overlapping

> If a Story can fit within two Topics equally well (perhaps in both "Politics" and "Free Speech"), Authors will have trouble classifying it, and users won't know where to find it. Consistency is important. If you need overlapping Topics, consider creating some guidelines to clarify what the Authors should do in a similar situation.

A "Miscellaneous" Topic is a good investment because it can catch the few Stories that fall through the gaps. If more and more Stories fall under this catchall, it's a sign that you need to add Topics. Review these orphans for inspiration.

Revise the Topic scheme occasionally

The theme and tone of a site will evolve along with the community it serves. Topics need to grow and change as well. If a single Topic holds a large chunk of the Stories, divide it into more narrowly defined Topics and reclassify the Stories. The more accurate and clear your phyla, the easier users can fine-tune their preferences and reading habits. An hour of your time spent making things more convenient for thousands of users is a good investment.

Don't worry about underused Topics

A Topic used once in a blue moon costs little more than screen real estate on the Topics and user preferences pages. An unused Topic rarely intrudes on users. If it's truly distinct from other Topics, keep it around. On the other hand, if the Topics pop-up menu becomes unwieldy, consider merging little-used but related Topics.

Respect the IP of others

Trademark and copyright are sensitive topics these days, with the Digital Millennium Copyright Act skulking turgidly. Using a company's logo, trademarks, or copyrighted data without permission can leave you open to legal action. The likelihood increases if your site is critical of or offensive to the copyright owner. Investing in inexpensive or free clip-art, or having custom icons made specifically for your site, is much safer and wiser.*

Consider textual icons

A site with abstract, specialized, or obscure content may have trouble finding or even creating appropriate Topic icons. For example, Nanodot Topics include "Nanoscale Bulk Technologies" and "Abuse of Advanced Technology"—not readily illustrable concepts. Users may not immediately realize that a pogo stick–riding robot represents "Runaway Artificial Intelligence." Including the Alt Text in the icons can help to eliminate confusion. Text-only icons require still less time, effort, and creativity. They also might inspire equal parts creativity and pity in a dedicated user with actual artistic talent and the time to donate better icons.

---

* A Slash-specific project is discussed at *http://slashcode.com/article.pl?sid=01/11/07/0822243*.

Managing Sections

The *Sections* link in the Admin menu leads to a page listing the defined Sections
(*/sections.pl*). Each Section name is a link to the Edit Section page (see Figure 7-2)
for that Section. This page resembles the Topics Editor. At the top, three links lead
to pages of more information about the Section. *Stories* lists Stories assigned to the
Section. *Submissions* shows user submissions assigned to the Section. *Preview*
shows the Section's homepage (*/index.pl?section=sectionname*), though it does not
take into account unsaved changes. All Topics assigned to the Section appear in a
list on the right side of the page.

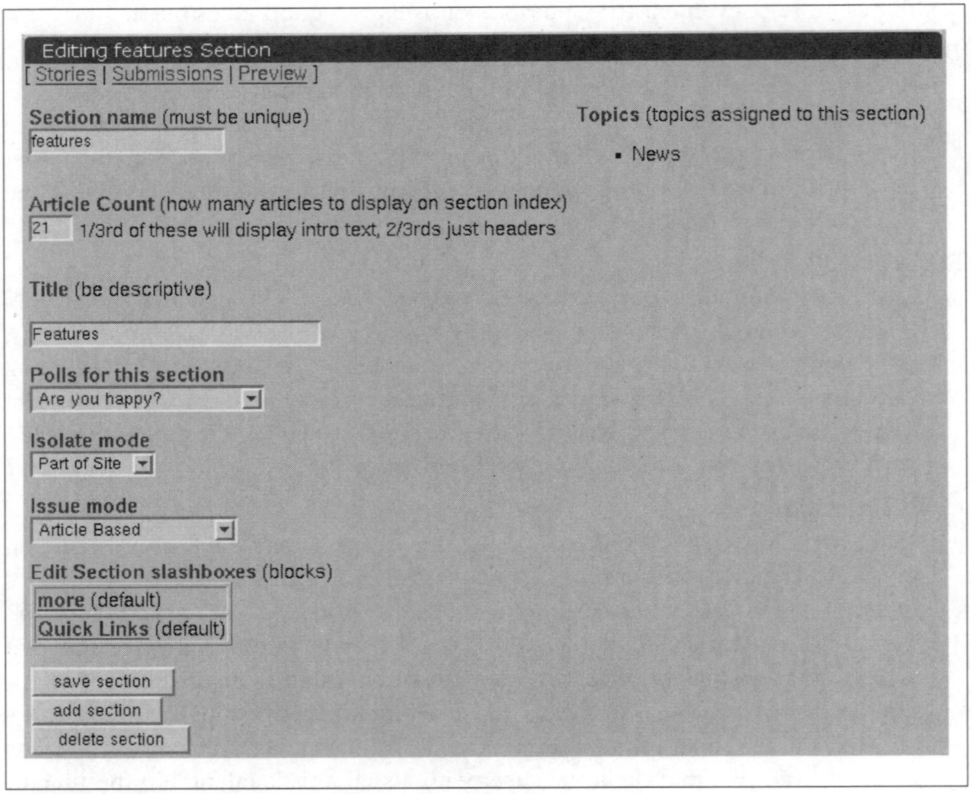

Figure 7-2. The Edit Section page

The Section name and Title fields correspond to the Short Name and Alt Text
fields of the Topic Editor. The Section name ties Stories to Sections within the
database (and must be unique), while the title appears in lists, pop-up menus, and

other interface elements. The Section name should not contain spaces. Slash automatically strips out all characters besides alphanumerics and the dash symbol.*

The Article Count field controls how many Stories will appear on the Section's homepage at any given time. As with Maximum Stories (in user preferences), one third of the Article Count number Stories will appear as titles and introductions in the central columns. The remainder will display as titles alone in Older Stuff. Additionally, each Section can display a different poll on its homepage. The polls for this Section's pop-up menu change the active poll.

Issue mode treats Stories more like a magazine than a news site. Stories can be grouped by date. Instead of (or in addition to) appearing in a strict chronological order, issue mode collects all of the Stories from one day in a convenient format. This is little used on most sites, probably because it is not well-documented (but Slashdot uses it).

The three available options govern how Slash will handle Stories within this Section. `Article Based` is the default behavior. There are no apparent breaks within the Story or headline lists. `Issue Based` treats each issue as a separate entity, adding a *Yesterday's Edition* link, pointing at the previous issue. Finally, `Both Issue and Article` is a combination of the two. There are no apparent breaks, but individual issues are accessible.

Unless you have a large volume of Stories (such as at Newsforge or Linuxgram), pure issue mode is rarely worthwhile. The hybrid option can be convenient for a front page—it can allow users to catch up if they miss a day. However, given the relative confusion and inflexibility surrounding this feature, it is probably best to stay with the default.

Standalone Sections

Sections can be integrated with the rest of the site or can stand alone. Stories assigned to integrated Sections are allowed to appear on the site's homepage. Standalone Sections are not automatically linked from the homepage, and they do not appear in Section pop-up menus available to normal users (for example, on the Submit Story or Search pages). Also, Stories cannot move from a standalone Section to an integrated Section; the Edit Story page for Stories in a standalone Section has no Section pop-up menu.

Standalone Sections are essentially invitation-only portions of the site. Only those who know or can guess the appropriate URL can find them. (This makes them

---

* The actual regex is s/[^A-Za-z0-9\-]//g.

obscure, but not secure. Don't put anything there you wouldn't want your mother to see.) To create one, choose Standalone from the Isolate Mode pop-up menu. The default option, *Part of Site*, produces an integrated Section.

Extended Section Information

For the sake of future extensability, additional attributes can be attached to Sections. These will be translated into additional fields on the Story Edit page for Stories within that Section. For example, a "Book Reviews" Section might have additional parameters of ISBN and Publisher.

These extra parameters are stored in the section_extras table in the database. This table holds three important keys: section is the name of the Section to which the parameters apply, name is the displayed name of the parameter when it appears on the Edit Story page, and value is the name of the parameter that will be stored in the story_param table. According to the previous example, the Reviews Section would have two rows in section_extras:

```
mysql> select section, name, value from section_extras where section = 'reviews';
+-----------+-----------+-----------+
| section   | name      | value     |
+-----------+-----------+-----------+
| reviews   | ISBN      | isbn      |
+-----------+-----------+-----------+
| reviews   | Publisher | publisher |
+-----------+-----------+-----------+
2 rows in set (0.00 sec)
```

When editing a Story assigned to this Section, two additional fields will appear beneath Dept.: ISBN and Publisher (see the section "The Edit Story Form" in Chapter 4). All Stories in this Section will have entries in the story_param table with the values of these fields. A book review of Annie Dillard's *For the Time Being* might have entries such as:

```
mysql> select name, value from story_param where sid='01/09/08/143026';
+-----------+------------------+
| name      | value            |
+-----------+------------------+
| isbn      | 0-375-40380-9    |
| publisher | Alfred A. Knopf  |
+-----------+------------------+
2 rows in set (0.00 sec)
```

Unfortunately, there is no web interface for adding extra fields to a Section. It must be done via SQL commands. Watch the plugin repository on Slashcode for a solution to this.

Choosing Sections

Sections can be confusing to new Authors and administrators. What purpose do they serve? What's the difference between "Articles" and "Features"? As with many Slash features, they can do anything the administrator wants. Sections can provide a secondary means to categorize Stories. Within this context, there are at least two useful paradigms for designing Sections.

The first strategy is to define Sections at right angles to the Topics. This allows Sections to divide Stories along different dimensions than the Topics. For example, where a Topic describes what a Story is *about*, the Section might describe the *kind* of Story it is. A sports site might have individual teams or sports as its Topics, with Sections such as Interviews, Game Recaps, Opinions, News, and so forth. These can also be reversed, with a Section devoted to each team. Nanodot Topics tend to be particular areas of science and technology, while Sections are Story types: News, Opinion, Question, Research, Reviews, and so on.

The second option is to use Sections to contain related Topics. This can come in handy for sites with a wide range of Topics. A news site with Topics such as Global Warming, Vanishing Rainforests, and Biodiversity could group them together under an Environment Section. This would allow users and Authors to search for and review Stories under these Topics collectively.

These two approaches are not mutually exclusive. Both types of Sections can exist on the same site, though a Story can belong only to one Section. Since Sections classify Stories on a higher level than Topics, this is less important than choosing the appropriate Topic. Many Slash sites leave most Stories in the default Articles Section. Choosing the right Section is more a matter of taste and judgment than an exact science.

Be aware that Sections typically receive very few page views compared to the site's homepage. The numbers can vary by an order of magnitude. On a smaller site, a Story posted only to its Section may be dead. For larger sites, this feature is useful to build a small, dedicated community. Think of it as a nice, out of the way neighborhood park in the middle of a big city.

8

Managing a Slash Community

The physical and mechanical acts of running a Slash site are easy—the software handles most of the dirty work. Out go the Stories; in come the comments. Barring hardware failure and software glitches, everything will run smoothly until you add users. Perversely enough, the wide ranges of opinion and background that make community sites so attractive also make a diverse userbase occasionally frustrating. People are unpredictable. Without users, though, you might as well trade the server for a soapbox on the corner. Bandwidth is cheaper that way.

If there's a trick to building a successful site, it's simply to encourage users to participate in constructive ways. This philosophy underlies every editorial or administrative decision, from the Topics to cover to the Stories to run. It governs how Authors do their jobs and suggests how to treat users. Your site may never grow as large as Slashdot, but if you can encourage good discussion and handle the inevitable growing pains well, you will be successful.

How to Stifle a Community

The easiest way to build a community is to build a site that welcomes new users and rewards user participation. The site provides a service, whether information, entertainment, opinions, or some combination of the three. Visitors who find no special value will not return. Users who find the price—not necessarily financial—too high will leave.

Frequent users will also develop a sense of ownership in the site. They read Stories, submit Stories, post comments, and moderate. Without their participation, the site would not exist. Users will lose confidence if they perceive that the Authors are careless or that the administrators ignore user concerns. They will notice any discrepancies, such as disappearing comments, shiftily edited Story introductions, or mysterious site outages. Cultivate the habit of posting regular site updates.

Granted, the Internet has always attracted a certain class of people quick to propose conspiracies and flame from the comfort of their own homes. These users will rarely be satisfied. The trick is to keep their numbers as low as possible. A few disgruntled users can make a lot of trouble, but if they're severely outnumbered by fans and well-wishers, the site will operate much more smoothly.

The best way to strangle an existing site is to lose your perspective. Put less time into editing Stories. Ignore user suggestions and questions. Be critical and off-topic in Story introductions. Reject interesting submissions. Filter out email from users. If the Authors don't take the site seriously, why should the readers? Of course, caring too much is no solution either. Unless you're Scheherazade, your life doesn't depend on new Stories. At the end of the day, it's all just bits in a database.

A little common sense and integrity will solve more problems than any technological solution.

Setting the Tone

Two Slash sites may have the same theme, post the same Stories, and target the same audience. If both succeed, they will grow in different directions. One site may see little public discussion as its users treat it as a source, preferring other channels of communication. The other site might spawn hundreds of threads on semi-related tangents. The difference is the *tone* of the site, an unquantifiable quality that can only be identified experientially.*

While users add an element of the unknown, administrators have the biggest influence on the site. Authorship bestows the ability to publish (and to modify!) words on the homepage, words read by hundreds or thousands of people. These editorial decisions set the stage for subsequent discussions and future Stories.

Choosing Stories

Your site's biggest initial draw will be the published Stories. A sports site dedicated to American football, baseball, and basketball will attract few visitors if the latest Stories discuss the Super Bowl (late January) during the NBA playoffs (June). Likewise, a sudden barrage of links to curling and jai alai tournaments will likely confuse the dedicated readers. Some sites have very flexible Topics, with freewheeling discussions, while others follow a clearly defined, if narrow, path. Your site will

---

* Like the difference between a good garage band and a bad garage band, the only way to know is to listen.

evolve with new users and new Stories, finding its own niche. Be aware of these changes in direction and communicate them clearly. Use words, if necessary.

Before deciding which stories to publish, explore the purpose of the site. Does it exist to aggregate breaking news? Do the Authors regularly generate original content of their own opinions? Does the site produce new information? How formal should things be?

A site such as Newsforge (*http://newsforge.com/*) works much differently from Slashdot. While Slashdot is irreverent and full of opinions, Newsforge serves up straight news. Slashdot might post a handful of financial Stories every year, favoring news on the latest *Star Wars* movie, while Newsforge eschews entertainment in favor of press releases and analysis. Slashdot is half information, half entertainment. Newsforge is pure information.

Topics and tone

Having established the purpose of the site, select a few likely Topics (the section "Choosing Topics and Icons" in Chapter 7 gives several good guidelines.) As the site grows, the initial Topics will change. Some will prove excessively popular and will need to become more specialized. Others may receive little traffic. The available Topics provide a way for users to categorize their own submissions early.

Even the Topic Icons themselves can subtly shape the tone of discussions. A Slash site devoted to biotechnology might have a Topic dedicated to genetically engineered food. Proponents of genetic engineering could use an Icon showing golden wheat. Opponents might prefer a red X superimposed over an ear of corn. A neutral site may use an Icon with a test tube and a potato.

Don't forget to prune the default RSS blocks available for users. If your site has a specific theme, make the default Slashboxes applicable to the theme. A gaming site would not normally link to Perlmonks.org. Most sites fail to do this. The subtle touches make a site look professional.

Gauging user response

Some Stories will elicit a tremendous response. A piece of breaking news, the latest round in a long-running standoff, or a particularly controversial opinion can easily produce many times the normal number of comments. On the flip side, an exciting announcement may evoke yawns from all but a die-hard contingent. Be prepared for surprises.

If the site depends on users, adminstrators need to be aware of trends. Which Stories resonate with the readers? Which generate real discussion and which generate mere sound and fury? Armed with this knowledge, Authors can balance the published Stories, saving something interesting but unlikely to provoke much discussion for Quickies. (Resist the temptation to reword things to push hot buttons, such as "Microsoft Blames GPLd Quake for Columbine".)

Slash provides some general means to discover the most popular and active Stories. The Hall of Fame (*/hof.pl*) provides several lists. Most Active Stories lists the 10 Stories with the grestest number of comments. Most Visited Stories links to the top 10 most-read Stories. Most Active Poll Topics lists the 10 polls with the most votes.

If those statistics aren"t enough, the Slash database tables themselves contain finer-grained information. For example, the `story` table contains a hits field to track the number of users who have read the Story. A few simple SQL queries can unearth more information. (For more about the Slash tables, see Appendix B.)

The *kinds* of Stories published will attract a particular audience. Moreover, the tone of Stories and comments will bring out people on many sides of an issue, just as the old standby Usenet groups (such as `alt.atheism` and `alt.religion.scientology`, not to put too subtle a point on it) did. (Slashdot itself leans toward libertarianism, though its diverse readership makes generalizations difficult.) This seems to work best with controversial Topics, in which "controversy" depends on the site and readers. A site with little real debate might as well disable comment posting.

That's not to say that controversy for its own sake works, in a long-term sense. If the raging debate between Purple and Green Drazi always generates hundreds of comments, posting the latest breathless news, "Just In: Purple says Green Sucks!" might work the first few times. Eventually, clueful users will get the point— pageviews matter more than intelligent discourse. When something interesting happens, post it. Save rehashing the same old Story for Quickies or Story updates.

Occasionally, a Story will appear outside the scope of the site. The Authors must decide whether to post it. In general, if the subject relates to a regular site Topic, even tangentially, it's worth mentioning. To defer a flood of "Why does this matter?" from loyal readers, add an editorial comment. For example, a sports site reporting on new wireless receivers might ask, "Could this be used to call basketball plays?" Stories with very tenuous connections to normal site Topics will rarely be posted.

Posting Stories

Having chosen a Story for publication, the Author faces another set of questions. Is the introduction accurate? Is it fair? Does it summarize the Story well? Does it fit the tone of the site? Is it poorly spelled or misleading? Who takes responsibility for mistakes and corrections?

Creating good introductions

Introductions need to be concise, making a single, clear point. As with the lead paragraph of a newspaper story, they hook the reader. A good introduction will impel users to read further. Unlike newspapers, judicious hyperlinks can provide background information, if needed. For example, an introduction such as:

```
<a href="http://speakeasy.org/jlp/">jlp</a> writes, "Microsoft's newest
computer game targets a unique audience.  In the same vein as Flight Simulator,
<b><a href="http://www.microsoft.com/games/trainsim/default.asp">Train
Simulator</a></b> is expected to be a big hit."
```

The links allow users to visit jlp's homepage to find out who he is, to explore an earlier Story, and to see exactly what the main Story is. This provides background information not everyone will need.

With the basic introduction in place, Authors can add editorial comments if necessary. "Necessary," of course, requires a judgment call. Does the introduction stand on its own? Are there additional links to add? If the destination Story is an opinion (or requires an opinion), can and should the Author offer additional thoughts?

Again, these answers depend on the tone of the site. Two axioms must be kept in mind: be accurate and encourage good discussion. Regarding the former, Authors should never change the *intent* of a submission. Formatting changes are one thing, but even grammar and spelling modifications should be marked. (Some sites allow only formatting changes.) If an introduction needs a severe overhaul, give credit to the submitter, but mark the introduction as your own words. Even unpaid, pseudonymous authors deserve to be quoted fairly.

"Good discussion" is nebulously hard to quantify. A site devoted to the latest developments in particle physics may have the playful back-and-forth peer review bantering a pop-music fan site would eschew in favor of serious comparison of set lists. If an Author treats a Story flippantly, misunderstanding the information, a significant portion of the comments may take him to task. Though the meritocratic approach of allowing users in the know to post insightful analysis and corrections to articles can correct accidental misinformation, it's irresponsible to expect this to excuse an Author from doing a little research before posting a questionable Story. Besides that, some sites pride themselves on not tripping people's satire detectors.

Editing and updating introductions

A significant portion of site readers will never post comments on a Story. In fact, a sizable percentage of that chunk may not even *read* Story comments. While the warning *caveat emptor* applies, a demonstration of good faith on the part of the Authors can defuse charges of sloppiness. People will remember one mistake on the heels of 99 perfect posts, but reasonable people will accept an honest explanation.

When mistakes happen (not if!), correct them appropriately. Some Stories will need only an update notice added to the Intro Copy. The special <update> tag will automatically insert an update notice and the current date when the submission is previewed, turning:

```
... <update>  fixed a broken link.
```

into:

```
... <b>Update, (06 August 2001):</b>  fixed a broken link.
```

This suffices for smaller changes, such as fixing a formatting or spelling error, pointing to the previous Story in case duplicates, or adding a new source of information. Larger changes, such as a retraction or a sizable update, deserve their own Stories, perhaps with a link to the previous Story:

```
        <a href="http://domaintje.com/ann/">kudra</a> writes, "I don't
know where you got your information, but YAPC::Europe is <b>not</b>
a secret meeting of the Bavarian Illuminati. We're just Perl Hackers."  Oops,
our previous Story was wrong.  Apologies all around!
```

Occasionally, a submitter will make a mistake. It could be a simple grammatical error or a malformed HTML tag. Following the first principle mentioned earlier, any changes to the wording of a submission should be clearly marked. Unless submitters are aware that the Authors will edit submissions for clarity and grammar, even changing "teh" to "the" can be construed as misquoting the submitter. (Really picky sites might make liberal use of "[sic]", indicating that the original submission did not meet Strunk & White guidelines.)

The mistake might also be more serious—mistaking one entity for another, for example—or alleging something quite different from what the linked Story says. Authors will have to use their own judgment on these issues. By convention, submitter comments are italicized, while Author comments appear in a standard typeface. This distinguishes visually between the original submission and subsequent editorial comments. Authors have the opportunity to add a few words of explanation to guide Story discussion to more appropriate paths. Hair-trigger flamers might still blame you for words you didn't write, but they'll find something to complain about anyway.

Some submissions may be completely unworkable, consisting of little more than a link and a "this is interesting" note. It can be a gamble to wait for a better submission on the same subject. It's probably best to annotate the Story (see the section "Managing Submissions" in Chapter 5), resolving to write a better introduction if nothing more suitable arrives in time. In the new text, mention the original submitter and link to his address, if provided. This will give appropriate credit for finding a Story, encouraging readers to continue their contributions.

Metacomments: when the site itself becomes news

A dirty little secret of the news business is that the mere act of reporting has an effect on the Story in question. (Why else would people stage protests around the schedule of the camera crew?) In Slash terms, this means any site that claims to be a source of information will occasionally find itself a fit Topic for discussion. By channeling this, site administrators can gather good ideas and communicate with their users more effectively.

The most basic questions concern site operations. Who's in charge? What kind of software and hardware run the site? How do users submit stories, and how do Authors choose them? What is Moderation and how does it work? Some questions are practical in nature, such as arranging and requesting Slashboxes. Others are merely welcome curiosities, such as, "How can I send you money?" or, "Why was my comment moderated down?"

By default, Slash provides a *FAQ* page to address any and all frequently asked questions, located at the relative URL */faq.shtml.* A link is also available in the Slashbox site in the upper-left corner of most pages. It lives in the *htdocs/* subdirectory of each Slash site's home directory. (A site named "firewheel", installed as per the section "Before You Begin" in Chapter 2, would have the FAQ at */usr/ local/slash/site/firewheel/htdocs/faq.shtml.*)

Any frequently asked question is fair game for the FAQ. In hopes of stemming the tide of repeated questions clogging the administrative mailbox, update this file regularly. Any standard HTML editor will do, from *vi* to *emacs* to Netscape Communicator. Questions should progress from general to specific. The default FAQ is a good example, though it is devoted to the Slash program and not to any particular site.

The FAQ will take care of general questions, but new controversies will arise on occasion. The site may experience a mysterious outage, create a new Section, or change hardware and IP addresses. Consider adding a Topic for regular site issues. This will immediately mark related Stories as important and allow unconcerned users to filter out the sort of omphaloskepsis that often plagues such Stories.

The nice thing about dedicated site-related Stories is that they provide a clearer opportunity for users to interact with Authors and administrators using the familiar interface. There's a sense of immediacy and heightened community in these Stories. Popular sites might consider making this a monthly or even weekly feature. Very popular sites could even make a dedicated Story comment Section.

Of course, this presumes that Authors read and respond to their posted Stories. For larger sites, it may be prohibitive to read each and every comment, but Authors should consider at least skimming the responses. This is the single best way to gauge reader reaction—for every opinion someone bothered to post, a dozen more people may feel the same way. (This rule of thumb may fall apart with comments consisting of ASCII art cartoon characters.) Sites that aspire to "digital-age journalism" will see the largest benefit, especially if Authors comment on Stories written exclusively for the site.

There are other avenues of feedback, of course. The relative URL */authors.pl* lists all of the site Authors with their preferred contact information. This can include email and personal web site addresses. While Slash provides a flexible system for users to express their thoughts and opinions, many readers prefer the immediacy of email, especially for personal questions and site issues. Anything that helps establish Authors as real people, instead of mysterious hooded figures, will help users work within the site more smoothly. (This obviously does not apply for sites dedicated to mysterious hooded and bearded figures, such as Slashcode.)

Finding and Generating Content

While the discussion features help retain readers, threads have a half-life measured in days, if not hours. Compare this to Usenet, where users can debate a single thread for months. By its very nature, Slash encourages short bursts of ferocious activity, and is best suited for frequent Story turnover.* Picture Dr. Frankenstein in his laboratory, stitching together his monster. "Igor," he yells. "Go dig up something interesting!"

Original Content Versus Linked Stories

There are two main sources of Stories: original content and links to other sites. Fittingly, there are two main groups that suggest Stories: Authors and site users. The type of site governs which source and group will produce the most content. A news site (such as Slashdot) will likely post more links garnered from user submissions, while a personal weblog (such as Tangent.org) will post mostly unique content written by the Authors. These don't preclude other options, of course.

Chapter 4 discussed the mechanics of approving submissions, and the section "Setting the Tone" in this chapter suggested finding an appropriate niche for the site. With these in mind, how can administrators create or find new unique content?

The easiest way to generate new content is to make it a duty of Authors. Each week, each Author could write an opinion piece, book review, or fresh news story. Of course, this is much easier if Authors are paid for their work—volunteer contributors either need copious amounts of free time or very flexible deadlines.

---

* The engine is flexible enough to handle several different approaches. Of course, because Slash was built to run Slashdot, it assumes that default sites will behave like Slashdot.

Another approach is to request exclusive content from the reader base. Depending on the subject matter and formality, it may be wise to create some submission guidelines to ensure accuracy and applicability. Again, the possibility of financial remuneration tends to attract more reliable submissions, but even the promise of fame (such as it is) will often motivate potential writers.

Since Slash Version 2.2, Stories have had both an author and poster field. This allows finer-grained customization. It's easier to keep track of who is posting Stories while giving credit to the actual author of a Story. It's possible to create an Author who can create a Story but not post it. It's even possible to modify the Story display templates slightly to display the actual author instead of the poster. For sites such as Newsforge, where the writer of a piece matters more than the person who actually posted it, this is very handy.

Whether working with Authors or users, cultivate the habit of editorial review. This can be as informal as choosing a Topic and approximate due date and fixing any broken formatting before publishing or as complicated as accepting several drafts. At the very least, someone besides the writer should proofread the Story before it goes live.* Especially when working with an outside contributor, the acting editor can often suggest subject refinements (if it's been covered before on the site) and additional avenues of research.

Occasionally, a unique Story will generate controversy above and beyond good discussion. The site owner is ultimately responsible for anything posted. Regardless of whether this is fair or accurate, it's best to mark potentially sensitive Stories as the opinion of the author, not necessarily the Author or the site owners. Even standard Stories should have the author clearly marked, along with appropriate contact information. The author should also be encouraged to participate in the subsequent discussion.

The final issue is that of ownership. If authors are paid for their content, do they retain subsequent publishing and distribution rights? Who owns the copyright on the material? Hopefully this will never need to be tested, but an attorney-reviewed, written contract can stave off realms of future trouble. Even if authors go unpaid, it is advisable to present a standard agreement. At the very least, consider allowing authors to publish their own writings as they see fit after the Story is archived.

Knowing when to publish

Timing is critical to publishing. Slash allows Authors to post stories automatically (for more on automatic posting, see the section "Story Fields" in Chapter 4). This feature can occasionally lead to multiple Stories all appearing at once. To avoid

---

* Of course, the quickest way to find a mistake is to have someone else point it out to you immediately after it's been published.

this clumping, space out fresh content. When queueing a Story, check the future publication dates of other Stories, and adjust the schedule accordingly.

For most sites, this is not a problem—the bulk of the Stories come from user submissions, and people rarely submit more than a paragraph. Larger sites, such as Slashdot, can adopt informal habits. For example, Slashdot often posts book reviews on Tuesdays and Thursdays, around the middle of the day, and feature articles sometime before lunch. This is prime reading time, and the fresh content usually generates a lot of traffic. Movie reviews come on Sundays when the readership has dropped off somewhat.

Finally, don't be afraid to wait on a controversial story to see how things turn out. Unless you're involved in the cutthroat business of news reporting, where first-to-link brings big rewards, your site will attract more readers with the types of stories covered than by always being first on the scene. It may be better to be a little conservative and avoid red-faced mistakes than to rush to judgment and create ill will. The proper balance between speed and accuracy is up to you.

Promoting the Site

A Slash site may have insightful Stories. The Authors may be highly motivated and excellent writers. The design may be clean and attractive. Without visitors to submit and comment upon Stories, the power of the Slash engine will go unused. While standard Internet advertising techniques may apply,* Slash sites have several unique promotional features.

The easiest way to attract visitors is to rely on word of mouth. Happy, provoked, challenged, and interested readers will often pass along links to their friends and colleagues. This is relatively painless. It requires only that the site provide compelling content worth passing along often enough to retain new visitors who perpetuate the cycle. The measure of how long a user will stay within a particular web site is called *stickiness*.

The Slash engine provides a lot of help. Few, if any, other site management programs have comment systems with comparable power or sophistication. It's easy to post and read comments. It's easy to filter and sort comments. It's easy to receive feedback on comments in the form of moderation scores or replies. It's convenient for a user to share her thoughts with the rest of the world, and thousands do just that every day on hundreds of sites around the world.

Of course, only good content leading to good discussion will attract and maintain the kind of userbase most sites desire. The other guidelines in this chapter will

---

* Assuming anyone ever figures out the rules.

help. A site still struggling to find one new story per day will have to reconsider its target audience before relying on word of mouth.

RSS Feeds

Another good source of promotion is the daily headline mailing feature. If users are allowed to forward interesting Story summaries (with links), this can draw additional readers. If the headline summary does not contain advertising, consider adding a small notice granting permission for personal redistribution.

As mentioned in the section "Secrets of Headline Swapping: XML, RDF, and RSS" in Chapter 9, Slash automatically publishes Story headlines in RSS format. The latest news on one Slash site can appear automagically in a Slashbox on another site. Better yet, any application that speaks RSS can grab headlines every half hour, updating a portal site, mailing news to a cell phone via SMS, or even adding new links to a web browser or desktop window.

Sophisticated Internet news junkies and other Slash administrators can easily find the headline files, but regular users may not know that they can "subscribe" to their favorite sites, let alone where the RSS files live. Because this process is automated, it is a fantastically useful way to distribute Story links. Once it begins, the administrator never needs to modify the RSS aggregator.

The site as a whole has its own headline file, available at *http://siteurl/robots.rss*. Each individual Section also publishes a more specialized file, available at *http://siteurl/section.rss*.

This is a very convenient feature, but few endusers (or even Slash site administrators!) are aware of its existence. The issue is making users aware of the RSS feeds. Consider adding a prominent link marked "Syndication" to a page which explains the benefits of the service. Also provide links to RSS-aware software, such as Mozilla and the Nautilus desktop manager.

Also, register each new Slash site with the *Yet Another Slash Site* (YASS) registry on *http://slashcode.com/*. This service purports to be the largest and most comprehensive listing of Slash sites in the known universe. In addition, it also collects headlines via RSS, providing a very clever search function of current Stories across all sites. This is an excellent place to find potential new Slashboxes.

Several other RSS registries exist. One such site is xmlTree (*http://www.xmltree.com/*), which is not limited to Slash sites. It allows webmasters to submit links to their feeds. Registering your site there will reach a slightly different audience.

Cross-Site Promotion

More formally, standard web page links can attract several visitors. The original Slash license required site administrators to display a small graphic linking back to Slashdot.* A good graphic artist can create small, attractive link images. Users can embed these in their own web pages, providing additional site links. These links tend to be highly targeted, focusing on the sort of people who read the web sites.

Other similar or trusted sites may be interested in cross-promotion. Both sites might agree to promote the other in a prominent block, or to mention the site in appropriate Story introductions. (The Autonode feature, described in the section "Extra Story-Editing Features" in Chapter 4, has a similar function.) This feature can be a mixed blessing. If used inappropriately or too often, users may wonder why an equestrian site links to a site for modern-day anchorites.

Attracting Links

Judging by the occasional unsolicited commercial email, many people still consider search engine placement to be important. In the days of the excellent Google (*http://www.google.com/*), this seems less important. Instead of requiring users to submit site information manually, Google scours the Net, ranking pages based on relevance.† If the other techniques for attracting visitors work, and if the site has quality information, it will soon achieve a favorable Google ranking.

For highly specialized sites, this can often produce search results with site links ranked very highly. A Slash site dedicated to professional hockey, however, might have to compete with several other sites. In that case, a little work manually approaching the larger, categorized search engines (*http://www.yahoo.com/*, *http://dmoz.org/*, etc.) may attract new visitors. This is less likely to pay off than spending the time fine-turning Topics, however.

Finally, other weblogs can often be an excellent source of links. While RSS feeds and search results automatically provide links, a human editor writing commentary and analysis on a story found elsewhere provides a sort of validation or recommendation that can resonate with other people. Don't be afraid to submit good, on-topic Stories to related sites. Encourage users with their own weblogs to promote the site by linking to their Stories, when appropriate.

A site that knows its purpose, caters to its users, and receives a little administrative attention now and then will have no trouble attracting users. It just takes time.

---

* This is no longer required, though linking to Slashcode would be neighborly.

† In general, the more links to a page from highly relevant sites, the more relevant the site will be. Google explains its algorithm in more detail at *http://www.google.com/technology/*.

Managing Authors

As the arbiters of officially sanctioned material, Authors command tremendous trust. They must balance several simultaneous factors, whether they know it or not. Who is the target audience? Does it matter who posts a Story? How much personality should Authors expose in their Stories? Who wrote the Story? It's OK to have an opinion, and some sites demand it. Even those that make no claims to do journalism should strive to be fair and even-handed.

There are three major sources of good Authors. They may be the site owners and administrators, or employees of the site owner (in the case of an Intranet site). They may be respected members of the community which the site serves. They may also be trusted site users, promoted from within. In general, the less formal the relationship, the more trust Authors require.

From a practical standpoint, recruiting an Author with expertise in a Section is an easy way to divide responsibilities. In each Section, the Author could be the final authority. This does not necessarily preclude Authors from sharing the work between Sections.

Public sites that purport to have a serious purpose need to create a set of Author Guidelines. These can be as informal as three rules in a block somewhere or as formal as a signed and notarized document. (A simple page will suffice for most sites.) Having written (and understandable!) guidelines in place before trouble surfaces can head things off at the pass.

At the very least, site owners and administrators should answer the following questions:

Why are there Authors?
> Do they exist to clean out the queue? Does each Author maintain a site Section? Are they full-fledged partners, or do they merely assist the site administrator?

What responsibilities do Authors have?
> Do Authors log in when they have time? Daily, on a set schedule? Should an Author update his Section with a new Story three times weekly? Who monitors the access and moderation logs? Who handles banner ads and feature articles?

What should Authors do?
> Who should delete submissions from the queue? Who decides if a good but not-quite-on-topic Story should be published? Do Authors moderate to promote good posts or to weed out noise and filler? Do they research and write up potential new Stories or edit fresh content submitted by trusted users?

What can Authors do?

If Authors are allowed unlimited moderation points, how often should they use them? What are the rules for deleting a post? Can an Author approve Stories in another Author's Section? How much trust does the administrator bestow on an Author? Who can change variables, and who can promote (and demote) other Authors?

How should Authors handle submission comments?

Is there a standard format for distinguishing between the user's words and those of the Author? Should Authors add comments to most Stories, only to promote discussion, or only to clarify things? How much editing is allowed?

How are Story updates handled?

When should a new development have its own Story, and when should the Introduction to an old Story be updated? Is there a regular feature for corrections and updates, a la Slashdot's "Slashback" feature? How often should Stories be published on a given subject within a Topic?

How do Authors communicate with users?

Do Authors regularly read and respond to Story comments? Do they have a site-specific email address? Does the site crew make regular appearances in an IRC channel? Is there a devoted Section or Story for metacomments?

What is the point of the site?

Having chosen a tone and regularly evaluating the evolution of the site, where are things going? What changes will come in the future?

However formal or informal these guidelines are, they exist to encourage Authors to use their best judgment. Most guidelines can be made public in the spirit of journalistic integrity, honesty, and openness. (If the Authors receive financial compensation for their work, that should be kept private, of course.) If users know what to expect from the mysterious robed figures behind the site, they will watch vigilantly to keep the Authors and administrators on the straight and narrow.

Managing Users

Most of the innovations in Slash came about to make the user experience more pleasant—for example, user accounts, moderation, meta-moderation, and comment filters. If the central concept of Slash publishing is the Story, the most important item in the site as a whole is the individual user. Though posting Stories is the most visible administrative activity, managing users (and their expectations) will have the greatest effect on the future of the site.

Slash encourages user participation on a level rarely matched elsewhere. The simple act of registration bestows the power to customize Slashboxes, maintain a posting history, keep a public journal (since Version 2.2), and develop community standards for comments. The trick is to try to channel user participation so that it is constructive and interesting.

The Ubiquitous Anonymous User

Anonymity is the first bugaboo to consider. By default, Slash allows users without accounts to post comments, credited to the Anonymous User. This act is similar to providing paint and paintbrushes for random passers-by to create a wall mural. Users with valid accounts can also choose to post their comments anonymously. In either case, folks can provide valuable information or what some might call "utter rubbish" with little fear of retaliation.

Though creating an account is very simple, even three or four steps will immediately weed out drive-by users. If commenting on a Story as the Anonymous User is nodding at fellow pedestrians, registration is shaking hands and swapping business cards. It implies a potentially recurring relationship. As such, requiring posters to have valid accounts can encourage more responsible behavior. Of course, a bored adolescent with a fake email address can still gain an account, and even a mediocre Perl hacker can register dozens of accounts with a simple bot.

The decision to allow truly anonymous posting depends on many factors. Does the nature of the site value free speech above all else? Who is responsible for what is posted? Is there a need for anonymity, for personal or legal protection? Are the site owners susceptible to damages in cases of slander or intellectual property disputes?*

The Nearly Self-Governing Moderation System

The moderation system added another layer of accountability. Originally limited to a handful of trusted users, it attempted to separate the wheat from the chaff. For smaller sites, if the Authors can easily read a day's worth of comments, they can promote, demote, and even delete material without involving the users. A site receiving hundreds of comments daily will need to enlist the help of its users.

Any technological solution that includes human judgment introduces unpredictable behavior. What one user considers "insightful" might be "insipid tripe from Bovine University" to another. A genuinely held but abrasive opinion might be considered "flamebait," and a technically well-written but vapid piece of prose may sucker in

---

* Unfortunately, these questions will probably go unsettled for now. They're likely to be answered in courtrooms and legislatures, not necessarily in the server farms and cubicles that actually run the Net.

moderators to award high points. In theory, the available pool should be diverse enough that over time, fewer posts stick out.

Due to the built-in normalizing effect (see Chapter 6), a site can develop moderator groupthink. This is normal—most communities pass through the "us versus them" stage on the road to maturity. Skimming the top and bottom comments, by score, will give administrators an idea of how well the system performs.

On the whole, the system works fairly well by default. The two largest problems are that some users develop an emotional attachment to karma, and the system is a vague feedback mechanism.* People will occasionally click the wrong buttons. Some people will always treat their karma like a game score. A small number of posts will become evidence that the moderation system is horribly broken beyond repair. There will always be variables to tweak and little rights to wrong. In the end, though, if users care enough about the site to complain about losing a point on an obscure variable used in three places in the code, something's being done correctly.

The moderation system is highly tweakable and always evolving. You could spend weeks finding the right balance of comments, points, and tokens, not to mention fine-tuning meta-moderation ratios. It may be more worth your time to handle the inevitable conflicts on a case-by-case basis. Remember that the purpose of moderation is to help people organize information. The system can only make suggestions; it cannot reason on its own.

The Content Filter Cold War

As usual, part of any sizable userbase tends towards mischief rather than well-reasoned commentary. Administrative consistency and clarity, peer pressure, and the moderation system all encourage good behavior. Unfortunately, it's not always sufficient. Preventing such mischief is tricky. It requires a delicate balance of technological magic, psychology, and keeping things easy to use for the majority of the users.

For example, consider Slash's comment-filtering system (described in the section "The Comment Filters List" in Chapter 6). An administrator with a little regex kung-fu can quickly craft patterns to dissuade a rash of odd comments. Like bacteria developing immunity to antibiotics, though, a sufficiently motivated imp might only have to substitute letters for numbers (changing "first post!" into "f1rst p0st!", for example) to bypass the filter.

---

* Truth be told, Slash's moderation is the worst system out there, except for all of the others.

Sufficiently bored mischief-makers can easily come to see this as a game. Few people have the know-how or motivation to craft the one true regular expression to match all possibilities,* leaving administrators behind the power curve. In this case, it is far easier to destroy than to create.

Worse yet, the more filters, the greater the possibility a valid post may be rejected. Very few regular users wish to be casualties in the ongoing Cold War between administrator and graffiti artist. The 80% solution afforded by automatic filtering is best left to the most egregious abuses. Moderation (and perhaps deletion) should be able to handle the rest.

The Last-Resort Delete Button

Occasionally, it may be necessary to delete a Story or a comment. Because this is irreversable without dabbling in database backups, it should be a last resort. It may be rare, but a site of any reasonable size will confront this issue sooner or later.

Slashdot, for example, takes an unapologetic free-speech policy. All comments are available to anyone who wishes to read them. This includes rampant off-topic speculation and ramblings as well as potentially anonymous whistleblowers and people too lazy to create accounts. The only deleted comments in Slashdot history, as of this writing, violated U.S. federal law and put the site in legal danger.

This approach may not be appropriate for your site. There is no shame in enforcing a no-nonsense, "If you can't say something meaningful, don't bother to post" policy. Whatever you choose, be consistent. Think about your deletion policy beforehand. Publish it. Solicit comments. The fewer surprises your users and Authors have to face, the less friction there will be.

Deleting duplicate Stories is easy, if someone catches the booboo early enough. If users have already posted to both Stories, it's probably best to update the second to mark it as a duplicate. Simply deleting it will condemn potentially insightful comments to the void unnecessarily. Future versions of Slash may allow moving comments between Stories, but for now, admit to the mistake and resist the temptation to pull a Ministry of Truth–style retcon. Users will notice.

Anti-Abuse Features

One cost of free speech is putting up with people who have nothing to say but speak anyway. One powerful but unknown set of Slash features is designed to protect your site against the Internet equivalent of vandalism. Hopefully you will never have to use them, but they exist, and they can help when things get hairy.

---

* Of the few people who know how to do this, most know better.

Formkeys

Formkeys are designed to prevent users from submitting HTML forms multiple times, whether by accident or on purpose. This helps to defend the submission queue or the comment system from bots designed to flood the site. Whenever a user hits Reply to a comment or otherwise reaches a form, Slash generates a random and unique formkey associated with that form. It stores this key in the database and in a hidden HTML input field. If and when the user submits the comment, Slash checks the formkey sent with the comment against the key in the database. If they match, the post is allowed. Otherwise, the post is forbidden.

Formkeys cannot be reused. This prevents a user from hitting the Submit button several times in a row, or from accidentally reloading a submitted page. Formkeys are also not easily faked—a cracker would somehow have to guess a 10-character key composed of numbers and upper- and lowercase letters while it is active and unused. In practice, it seems to work pretty well.

Besides preventing multiple posts, the formkey system can enforce limits on posting activity. These limits include the number of comments that can be made in a 24-hour period, the frequency at which posts can be submitted, and the maximum number of unused formkeys available. Several configuration variables govern this behavior. (They are discussed in Table E-4. See also the *docs/formkeys.txt* file in the Slash distribution.)

Formkeys do have a few potential pitfalls. First, a determined mischief-maker can write a bot that can request a new form, pull out the valid formkey, and submit the form. There is no way to prevent this. Finding the right combination of the `speed_limit` and `max_allowed` variables will help. Also, the potential exists for formkey collisions between users. It's mathematically rare but possible.* Finally, verbose or quick human posters may run into the speed or maximum-post limits. Each site must confront its own version of the Malthusian dilemma: make things easy for valuable contributers (butter) or make things difficult for potential miscreants (guns).

IPIDs, NetIDs, and blacklists

The strongest and harshest penalty for abuse is banning. Because Slashdot receives an unbelievable number of scripted attacks, the Slashteam invented some tools to block people who refuse to play nicely with others. This is a controversial technique and is really the last resort. Hopefully you will never have to use these tools.

---

* A beta version of Slash had this problem. The random-number generator in each *mod_perl* child all used the same seed and produced the same "random" numbers. Each child now has its own seed.

All user requests are logged into the `accesslog` table in the database. This includes the user's IP address and a subnet ID.* These values are never stored directly. Instead, they are hashed with a one-way MD5 algorithm. Because the same original value will always produce the same hash, the hash is stored in the database instead of in raw IP addresses.

The `comments`, `submissions`, and `formkeys` tables all track IPIDs and NetIDs as well, even for anonymous users. This allows administrators to isolate certain patterns of undesirable behavior on a few hosts or networks.

By default, only the comment posting code within *comments.pl* uses this data. It calls the `getIsTroll` method within *Slash::DB::MySQL* and performs several checks to judge if a user or network has abused posting privileges too often. First, it checks to see if the number of downward moderations for the user's IPID within the last `istroll_ipid_hours` exceeds the value of `istroll_downmods_ip`. Next, it performs a similar check on the NetID, using `istroll_downmods_subnet`. If the user has an account, it performs a final check, using `istroll_downmods_uid` and `istroll_downmods_user`. If all of these tests pass (that is, if the user's IPID, NetID, or UID has not received too many downward moderations in the appropriate time period), the user is allowed to post her comment. These configuration variables can be set at will. You can disable this feature entirely by setting the `istroll_downmods_type` values to impossibly high numbers, or `istroll_type_hours` values to 0.

Stronger medicine involves banning users or networks from the site altogether. The *Slash::Apache::Banlist* module provides an Apache handler that will accept or reject incoming user requests based on their NetID or IPID. This is not enabled by default and requires editing the relevant Apache configuration file. Open the *sitename.conf* file and find the first `PerlAccessHandler` directive. Change the file to read:

```
PerlAccessHandlerSlash::Apache::Banlist
PerlAccessHandlerSlash::Apache::User
PerlCleanupHandler      Slash::Apache::Log
PerlCleanupHandler      Slash::Apache::Log::UserLog
```

This will cause *mod_perl* to turn away banned users before doing anything else. Don't forget to restart the web server if you make this change.

UIDs, IPIDs, and NetIDs must be banned manually by an Author. This is performed on the Edit User pages (see the section "Editing Authors" in Chapter 3. When viewing the information of any user, the page will list all IPIDs he has used.

---

* While the remote IP address is available through standard HTTP headers with various degrees of accuracy, the actual subnet portion is not. Slash assumes a subnet mask of 255.255.255.0. This is usually accurate enough in the rare cases when it is necessary.

These are links. If followed, they will bring up the Edit User page for that IPID. The three links at the top of the page lead to statistics, listing the top site abusers and the read-only and banned lists. Each list shows UIDs, IPIDs, and NetIDs where applicable. These are also links to the Edit User page.

Each IPID or NetID viewed on this page will also have a list of all comments associated with the ID. If too many of these comments break site rules, you can ban the ID. Simply check the Banned box and click on the Save admin button. Be sure to fill in the Reason box. This is not required, but it will be presented to banned users. Users and IDs can also be unbanned by unchecking this box.

Banning should be a temporary measure and should be as limited as possible while still being effective. If you need to ban a UID, ban only the UID. Banning an IP address is trickier. A user with a dynamic connection to the Internet can simply request a new IP address and return to make more mischief, leaving the ban to fall upon some other hapless soul. Worse yet, many users connect through proxy servers and firewalls that use one apparent IP address for dozens or hundreds of users.

Banning a NetID to squelch a particularly troublesome miscreant can be more effective, but it will likely affect many more innocent people. Your best hope is that someone will contact the appropriate network administrator who can kindly but firmly apply a user re-education tool. If this seems harsh, it is. Still, if it comes down to shutting off a few users temporarily to keep the site usable for most users, few people who've actually run a large web site will fault your decision. We hope that you'll never have to deal with this situation.

As is the case with most of Slash's automatic features, the best tool for shaping the site to taste is the three-pound, grayish-pink blob given to all Authors when they accept the job. Treat your users like rational, clever adults, and they will tend to behave that way.

9

Basic Site Customization

Slash was designed to be fully functional out of the box. Like a freshman dorm room, it could use a little personality. This chapter will help you redecorate your site. Thanks to the introduction of templates in Slash 2.0, you can change your site's layout, look and feel, and even behavior using only the web interface. This chapter focuses on wall decorations, while Chapter 10 delves into deeper tricks, including colors, page layout, and rewiring the outlets to put a TV in the lavatory.

Blocks and Slashboxes

Earlier versions of Slash scattered display elements throughout blocks and the Perl code itself. Blocks were more useful—unlike code, they could be edited through the backSlash interface. Most displayable elements have been moved into templates in the latest versions. However, *static blocks* are still useful for stable site elements, and *portald blocks* (updated by the *portald* task) still handle automatically updated content.

The Site Block Editor

Clicking on the *Blocks* link in the Admin menu brings up the Site Block Editor. From here, you can edit any block by choosing its name from either pop-up menu and clicking Edit Block. The Editor displays the same fields when editing both static and portald blocks, but some fields apply only to portald blocks (see Figure 9-1). Note that you must have a seclev over 100 and equal to or greater than the seclev of the block you wish to edit.

The Block field stores the actual block contents. This will be displayed as a Slashbox or used by the system. Generally, static blocks can be changed only from this

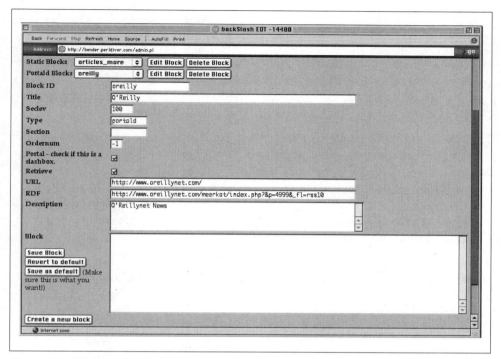

Figure 9-1. The Site Block Editor

form; the *portald* daemon will update the Block field on a regular basis. Any manual modifications will be replaced.

Each block has a unique block ID, used as an internal reference, and a Title, which appears in the user interface. As with Topic IDs and Topic names, block IDs should be concise, and titles descriptive. Since block IDs appear in URLs and in the database, they should contain only alphanumeric characters and not spaces.

The Seclev field limits which Authors can modify the block. An Author can modify only blocks with a seclev less than or equal to his. Slash will display all appropriate blocks in the Block Editor pop-up menu. The Type field sets whether the block is static or portald, and it governs the menu in which the title appears. The Section field can constrain the block to appear only within a specific Section. Left blank, the block will be allowed to appear in all Sections.

Ordernum governs the placement of a block on site pages where it appears. If positive, the block will be part of the default view of a site page. (This includes the main page and section homepages as seen by the Anonymous User or by users who haven't customized their Slashboxes.) As the name implies, Slash displays these default blocks in numerical order by their Ordernum. If set to −1 or 0, the block will not display by default. A user must manually add it so his custom view of the homepage, as described in the section "Slash User Preferences" in Chapter 1.

Most static blocks have an Ordernum of 0, indicating that they shouldn't be displayed anywhere. Instead, Slash uses them internally. Blocks of this type generally have the Portal checkbox unchecked. Unchecked, this will also prevent a portald block from appearing in the Slashbox list, without having to be deleted.

The Site Block Editor provides a convenient backup and restore mechanism. After making considerable customizations to a static block, an Author can save the block's current contents as the new default value by clicking the Save as Default button. Slash stores default contents in a separate column of the block's table in the database. If an Author makes an unintentionally catastrophic change to a block, the default can serve as a fallback position. Click the Revert to Default button to set the block's contents to the saved default.

The Description field appears to Authors only through the Block Editor. It provides an explanation about the purpose of a block. Slash requires no value here, but it is a good idea to include descriptive text for each block. The remaining Block Editor fields apply solely to portald blocks.

Secrets of Headline Swapping: XML, RDF, and RSS

While Slash itself updates some portald blocks (such as the Poll Slashbox), most Slashboxes contain content fetched from other sites on the Web. The *portald* daemon is the gateway to an underground network of promiscuous headline and link swapping. Any web site that publishes its headlines using the RSS format can populate a new Slashbox.

RDF Site Summary (RSS) is an *eXtensible Markup Language* (XML) implementation of the *Resource Description Framework* (RDF). RDF is a W3C-recommended schema for presenting metadata about web site content. Netscape created RSS to describe "channels" (site content descriptions) in a product named "My Netscape". The marriage of XML (easily parsed by computer programs, fairly human-readable) and RDF (rich semantics for describing content) makes RSS useful (if hard to describe without acronym dropping).

The beauty of RSS and *portald* is that an administrator needs to know very little about either to make things work.* To add a new Slashbox, simply tell Slash where to find the RSS file published by a particular site. The *portald* daemon will

---

* To learn all about RSS, start with the article "RSS and You" by Slash developer Chris Nandor, published on the Perl.com web site at *http://www.perl.com/pub/2000/01/rss.html*.

fetch the file, parse the XML, render it into appropriate HTML, and wrap the results in a Slashbox. (For a detailed explanation, see the section "The portald Task" in Chapter 11.)

O'Reilly's *Meerkat* open wire service publishes customized RSS-formatted summaries of news headlines. Meerkat (at *http://meerkat.oreillynet.com/*) provides several predefined profiles, including one with O'Reilly news. The URL for the RSS-encoded summary is *http://www.oreillynet.com/meerkat/index.php?&p=4999&_fl=rss10*. With this information, it's easy to create a Meerkat Slashbox.

First, click the Create a New Block button to bring up an empty Block Editor. Fill in the form with appropriate values:

Field name	Value
Block ID	oreilly
Title	O'Reilly and Associates News
Seclev	100
Type	portald
Section	Leave blank
Ordernum	−1
Portal	Checked

The Retrieve checkbox controls whether *portald* will actually retrieve the RSS file from the remote site. Leave it unchecked if the other site will be down for a while. If left unchecked permanently, the block contents will not change even if the publishing site updates the RSS file.

The RDF field must contain the URL of the RSS file for the remote site. The URL field should contain the URL of the homepage of the source site. If provided, the block title, shown in the title bar of the generated Slashbox, will be linked to the URL.

To find new sources of RSS content, start with other Slash sites. The *slashd* daemon publishes site headlines in four formats: RSS 0.9, RSS 1.0, WML (for wireless web devices such as cell phones and PDAs), and the simple "Backslash" format (including its Document Type Definition), at the following URLs:

Format	URL
RSS 0.9	*/slashsite.rdf*
RSS 1.0	*/slashsite.rss*
WML 1.1	*/slashsite.wml*
"Backslash"	*/slashsite.xml*
Backslash DTD	*/backslash.dtd*

Slash also publishes headlines for each site Section. Section names are used as the base filenames. A newly installed server will publish files, including */articles.rdf*, */features.xml*, and */slash.rss*. Other Slash sites, including those on the YASS list at *http://slashcode.com/sites.html* will publish headlines at these URLs unless the administrators have renamed the Sections or have disabled RSS file generation.

The xmlTree web site, at *http://www.xmltree.com/*, is a great source of RSS and XML content. It provides a searchable database of resources in a wide variety of XML formats. Users can filter by XML document type, browsing a hierarchical tree of content categories for source sites. Public Slash sites should consider adding their XML headline URLs to the xmlTree database.

Static Slashboxes

Blocks with static content can also be Slashboxes. The default Slash theme comes with several Slashboxes with tiny forms for major search engines (including Google, MetaCrawler, and Yahoo!). Creating a new static Slashbox is easy.

Start by capturing the HTML code for the search form on the target site. For example, consider the Internet Movie Database (*http://us.imdb.com/*). Choose the view source option in the web browser and locate the <FORM></FORM> tag pair enclosing the search form elements. The HTML will probably not work as is. Most site search forms use a relative URL in the ACTION attribute of the <FORM> tag. A *relative* URL omits the protocol and hostname, pointing to a resource on the same host as the containing page. Relative URLs use syntax similar to Unix file paths; if the URL begins with a slash, it is relative to the root of the site:

```
<IMG SRC="/images/cr.gif"> (points to http://thissite.com/images/cr.gif)
```

If the URL begins with a filename or directory name, it is relative to the directory of the containing page:

```
<IMG SRC="images/cr.gif"> (points to cr.gif in the images subdirectory of the current directory)
<IMG SRC="cr.gif"> (points to cr.gif in the current directory)
```

If the URL begins with two periods (..), it is relative to some parent directory of the current directory. Each pair of periods moves up one more level of the file hierarchy:

```
<IMG SRC="../cr.gif"> (points to cr.gif in the parent directory of the current directory)
<IMG SRC="../images/cr.gif"> (points to cr.gif in the images directory, which has the same
   parent directory as the current directory)
```

Change any ACTION parameter in the <FORM> tag to an absolute URL by supplying the protocol, hostname, and any necessary directory names in the path. Web browsers will guess at any missing components, and sometimes even get it right. The <FORM> tag for the IMDB search form resembles:

```
<form action="/Find" method=post>
```

The corresponding absolute URL becomes:*

```
<form action="http://us.imdb.com/Find" method="post">
```

If the form on the target site uses an image for the submit button (<INPUT TYPE="IMAGE"> versus <INPUT TYPE="SUBMIT">), copying the form verbatim will make the Slashbox load the image from the target site. It is easy to replace an image button with a regular submit button. The IMDB form uses such an image:

```
<input type=image height=21 width=31 border=0 value="Go" name="Go"
       src="http://i.imdb.com/f163.gif" align=absmiddle><br clear=left>
```

which can be replaced with:

```
<input type="submit" name="Go" value="Go">
```

Retain the NAME and VALUE attributes, which may be required by the program that processes the form. Only the form widget tags are strictly necessary. Anything else, including table elements (TR or TD), font and style information (FONT, DIV, or STYLE tags with CLASS attributes) can be removed. These generally provide layout and formatting information and, at best, will not work within a Slashbox.

The final HTML for an IMDB search Slashbox might be:

```
<form action="http://us.imdb.com/Find" method="post">
<select name=select>
<option selected>All</option>
<option>Titles</option>
<option>My Movies</option>
<option>People</option>
<option>Characters</option>
<option>Quotes</option>
<option>Bios</option>
<option>Plots</option>
</select> <input type=text name="for" size=14> <input
type="submit" value="Go" name="Go"><br>
<a href="http://us.imdb.com/search">More searches</a> | <a
href="http://us.imdb.com/Help/search-tips">Tips</a>
</form>
```

---

* Strictly speaking, valid HTML requires quotes around all tag attributes.

Create a new block with this HTML in the Block field and set the other fields as follows:

Field name	Value
Block ID	`imdb`
Title	`Internet Movie Database`
Seclev	`100`
Type	`portald`
Section	Leave blank
Ordernum	−1
Portal	Checked
Retrieve	Unchecked
URL	*http://us.imdb.com/*
RDF	Leave blank
Description:	Search form for IMDB

The resulting Slashbox will resemble Figure 9-2.

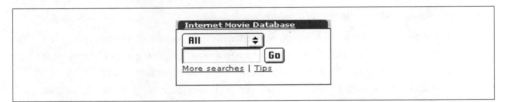

Figure 9-2. IMDB Search Form Slashbox

Default Static Blocks

The default theme comes with several predefined static blocks. Slash uses these blocks in normal operations, so any modifications will change site appearance or behavior. Without the proper precautions (such as editing the underlying Slash source code to remove references to the ill-fated block), deleting a static block will have a detrimental effect. Many of these blocks are initially blank. The most important are:

features

> This is the first Slashbox displayed by default on uncustomized homepages (Ordernum = 1). It can contain announcements or links to stories that have aged off the homepage but deserve continued exposure.

mysite

> The default contents of an unmodified User Space Slashbox. The default contents explain the Slashbox and how to modify it. See Figure 1-7 for more details.

colors

> Color blocks define a set of colors used in generated HTML pages. Colors are stored as a comma-delimited list of HTML hex triplet codes, such as #000000. The templates that control site layout and appearance use these values in COLOR and BGCOLOR attributes. If a block named *section*_colors exists (in which *section* is the name of a site Section, e.g., *articles*_colors), those colors will take precedence over the standard color block. See the section "Section Blocks: Colors and Boxes" in Chapter 10 for information on the Site Colors interface.

name_more

> The contents of a more block appear as the introductory text in the Older Stuff Slashbox. The Section field of the block will contain the name of the Section for which the contents will apply. If set to index, the block is valid for the site homepage.

index_qlinks

> The contents of a Quick Links block appear inside a Quick Links Slashbox. As with the more blocks, each Section can have a separate block. This is a good place to link to common sites within a Section. For example, see the Slash development links on Slashcode.

topics

> This block contains the HTML code for an array of Topic Icons suitable to display across the top of each site page. This is a good visual overview of the Topics in which stories were most recently posted. The *slashd* daemon generates this block automatically, so any manual changes will be overwritten. The default theme does not display the topics block. Enabling this requires editing templates, as described in the section "Section Templates" in Chapter 10.

Managing User Polls

Everyone loves to be consulted, to have an opinion that matters. Thus, it's no surprise that Slash users enjoy polls. It can be a fun and easy way to solicit opinions from the user community on an important or trivial question.

The User View of Polls

A user first sees a Slash poll on the site homepage. A special Poll Slashbox (see Figure 9-3) presents a question with multiple possible responses. To vote, the user selects a response and clicks the Vote button to see the results. The results page shows the current vote tally, along with user comments on the poll. From the Poll Slashbox, users can skip directly to the results page via the *Results* link, or can list all site polls with the *Polls* link.

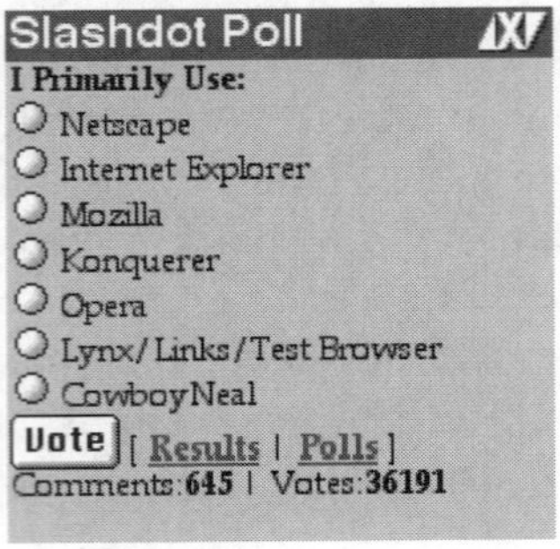

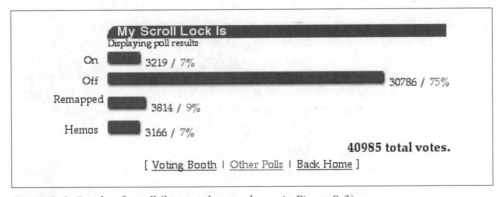

Figure 9-3. A typical Poll Slashbox

Slash plots poll results on a horizontal bar graph (see Figure 9-4). To the right of each option are two numbers: the number of votes for that response and the percentage of the total votes. The total number of votes for all options appears in the lower right, beneath the graph. The *Voting Booth* link takes you to a special Pollbooth page with the poll in the center of the page, the *Other Polls* link produces a page listing all of the site's archived polls, and the *Back Home* link leads to the site homepage.

Figure 9-4. Results of a poll (but not the one shown in Figure 9-3)

Vote Early, Vote Often

When a user, registered or anonymous, votes on a Slash poll, the software records the vote, the user's ID (if applicable), and the user's IP address. This helps, somewhat, to prevent repeat voting by the same user in the same poll. However, as the default Slash theme says, "This whole thing is wildly inaccurate. Rounding errors, ballot stuffers, dynamic IPs, firewalls. If you're using these numbers to do anything important, you're insane." Although such use of poll results doesn't really fit the DSM-IV criteria for clinical psychosis, determined users can easily skew the results.

A simple mechanism to stack any web poll, even those of major sporting sites, is an automated process, or *bot*. With the Perl LWP library, for example, it is trivial to register new users in bulk, to process the registration emails for the initial passwords, to log onto the site as each new user in turn, and to vote on the poll.*
Slash has mechanisms to detect and deter mass registrations from the same IP address, but this does not ensure the integrity of poll results. It may be more difficult to play Richard Daly with Slash 2.2, but do not discount it entirely.

Clicking the *Polls* link in the Poll Slashbox, the *Other Polls* link on a Poll Results page, or the *Past Polls* link in a navigation bar brings up a list of all polls currently running on the site. Each poll question is linked to the corresponding results page, and the poll start date follows the question. The list displays 20 polls at a time. Subsequent lists are available through the *More Polls* link.

Administering Polls

Authors have the ability to create new polls and edit existing polls (including the results—one more reason for skepticism). The Author's view of the polls list page includes an *Edit* link for each oll. The Admin menu also includes a *Poll* link, which leads to the Edit Poll page (see Figure 9-5).

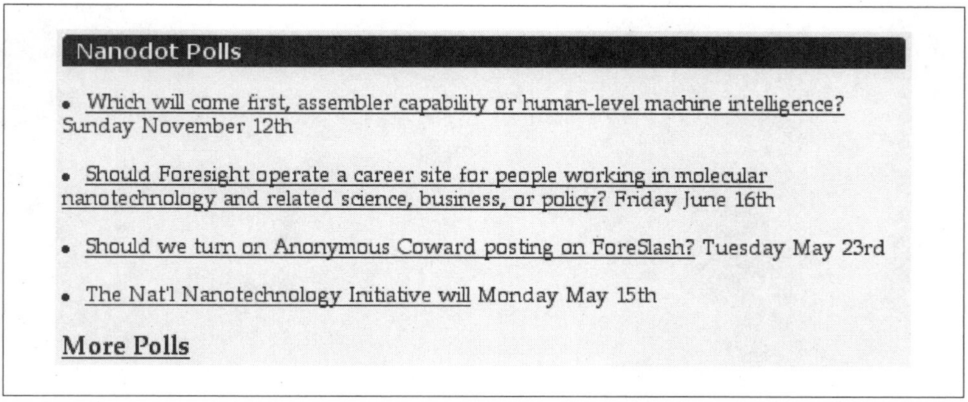

Nanodot Polls

- Which will come first, assembler capability or human-level machine intelligence? Sunday November 12th

- Should Foresight operate a career site for people working in molecular nanotechnology and related science, business, or policy? Friday June 16th

- Should we turn on Anonymous Coward posting on ForeSlash? Tuesday May 23rd

- The Nat'l Nanotechnology Initiative will Monday May 15th

More Polls

Figure 9-5. The Edit Poll page

Each poll will be assigned a unique ID automatically. The optional SID field allows the poll to be attached to a Story. When a user views a Story, the associated poll will appear in a Poll Slashbox. This allows Slash administrators to gauge user opinions on a Topic related to a current Story. Checking the Appears on homepage

---

* A superb introduction to writing such web clients (or rather, more socially useful ones) is Clinton Wong's *Web Client Programming with Perl*, available on the web as an O'Reilly Open Book at *http://www.oreilly.com/openbook/webclient/*.

box sets the value of the `currentqid` admin variable to the current poll's ID. The poll will then appear on the site homepage.

The Question and Answers text boxes are straightforward. Each poll can have up to eight answers.* The box after each Answer contains the current number of votes for that response. The box after the Question contains the current number of votes for all responses. Authors with sufficient privileges to edit polls can also edit result numbers. In the case of ballot stuffing, this can correct errors. Nothing prevents an Author from modifying the results himself, though, except guilt and shame. (Cheat carefully, because the total number of votes is not automatically adjusted to match the revised figures.)

The Slash web interface provides no mechanism for deleting polls. The only way to do so is to issue SQL commands directly to the database. (Appendix B describes the Slash Database Tables in more detail.)

---

* This is a limitation of the interface, not of the database. If you need more answers, feel free to modify the appropriate template to add more options.

10

Advanced Customization

Straight out of the box, Slash performs a lot like Slashdot and Slashcode. There's no reason your site has to do the same. Each new site will occupy its own ecological niche and has the potential to do something a little different. Perhaps it will cover different Topics. It may go as far as introducing a new interface, or even completely new behavior. Slash makes this possible.

This chapter explores the kinds of changes that Slash allows. It starts by discussing visual changes—site colors, blocks, and basic templates. Things get more complex by adding a banner ad package. Next, it walks through installing themes (new looks) and plugins (new actions) created by other users, before delving into an example plugin. From there, it explores changes to the Slash code itself. Finally, it describes the internationalization and localization features that allow Slash to serve the world community.

Changing the Look

Straight out of the tarball, Slash is readily modifiable by administrators without the ability or inclination to dig into thousands of lines of Perl code or arcane configuration files. Most of the appropriate options on the Admin menu have been covered earlier but are mentioned here for the sake of completeness. All serious site administrators will perform the following basic customizations.

Slash configuration variables control much of the site's internal behavior. These range from site directories to moderation controls and include toggles for almost every optional feature Slash supports. Plugins and themes may add their own (the section "Modifying Configuration Variables" in Chapter 3 describes how to edit and add variables). All default variables have verbose descriptions.

The (three) standard Topics are also ripe for customization. It's likely that any new site administrator will be able to come up with a dozen possible categories under which to group Stories. Besides that, the Topic icons themselves are an important part of the site's look and feel. The section "Managing Topics" in Chapter 7 discusses this in more detail.

Dividing a site into Sections not only allows an additional layer of Story grouping and a division of responsibilities between Authors, but provides further customization opportunities (the section "Managing Sections" in Chapter 7 explains the Section editing interface). Internally, Slash allows individual Sections to add and override features. While all Sections of a site share common users and database tables, they can appear so wildly divergent that no one would believe they belong to the same site.

Section Blocks: Colors and Boxes

The easiest thing to customize is a Section color scheme. This can be accomplished by creating a new color block. From the *Blocks* link in the Admin menu, click on the Create a new block button to reach the Site Block Editor (introduced in Figure 9-1). Color blocks are associated with Sections by a standard naming scheme. The Block ID field should be set to a value of *sectionname*_colors. To create a new color block for the Articles Section, use a block ID of `articles_colors`. Don't forget to set the Type field to `color`, or to choose an appropriate seclev and title. Ignore the other fields for now and click on the Save Block button.

Next, click on the *Colors* link in the Admin menu. This brings up the *Site Color Editor*, shown in Figure 10-1. Select the appropriate title from the pop-up menu and click on Edit Colors. The 10 textboxes each accept a hexadecimal color code string used to set a particular color. Slash passes these colors to templates, where they are used to color HTML elements.

For example, the default Slashcode theme uses its 10 colors as shown in Table 10-1. New templates and themes do not have to follow these standards. However, simply changing a Section's color block can have an immediate and dramatic effect on the look and feel of the site.

Table 10-1. How the default Slashcode theme uses its colors

Field	Use
Foreground Color 0	The font color used for Story titles
Foreground Color 1	The color of standard text and visited links
Foreground Color 2	The font color used when previewing a submitted comment
Foreground Color 3	The font color used to link to a comment, or to report moderator points

Table 10-1. How the default Slashcode theme uses its colors (continued)

Field	Use
Foreground Color 4	The background color used in some administrative menus
Background Color 0	The page background color
Background Color 1	A secondary background color, used underneath images such as the site slogan
Background Color 2	The background color of individual comment headings
Background Color 3	The color of normal links
Background Color 4	Not used

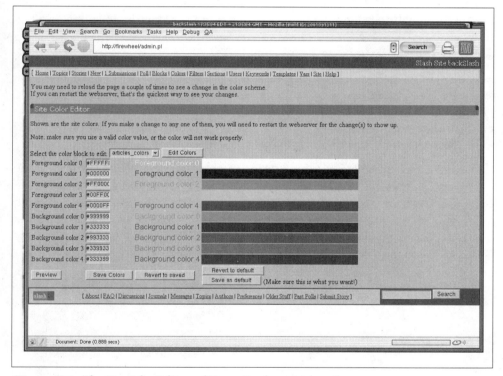

Figure 10-1. The Site Color Editor, editing a Funhouse color scheme

To add a blue tint to the Articles Section, modify the Background Color 0 and Background Color 3 boxes. Change the values to #DDDDFF and #0000FF, respectively. The Preview button displays the site homepage with the new colors without actually saving them in the database. Unfortunately, this works only when editing the default color block (for the Index Section).

Instead, click on the Save Colors button. Open a new browser window and visit a Story in the Articles Section. It should display with the new colors. Of course, none of the supplementary graphics have changed, so the corners of the title bars and the fine lines around the edges of comment header boxes will still use the old colors.* A decent graphic-editing program will be able to modify these graphics to use the new hexadecimal color codes. The GIMP (*http://www.gimp.org/*) is a very good choice.

As described in the section "The Site Block Editor" in Chapter 9, regular blocks can also be assigned to Sections. Additionally, any block with a block ID matching its Section will be displayed on all Stories within the Section. For example, a Review Section could have a block with submission guidelines. A News Section might have a block listing the most recent Stories. In general, these blocks are probably best left static, either updated by hand or automatically by a task.

Section Templates

Beyond simple color changes, Sections can have unique looks by using individual templates. The slashDisplay function, described in the section "Display Functions" in Appendix D, first looks for a template assigned to the current Section, loading the *default* template as a fallback. Though the same information will be provided to the new template, it can be displayed in a very different manner.

To create a new template for the Articles Section, use the *Templates* link in the Admin menu to bring up the Template Editor. As seen in Figure 10-2, the three pop-up menus provide great flexibility in selecting a precise template. As with many other Site Editors, be careful to click the appropriate button after making a selection. For example, choosing a different Section will not take effect until the Select section button is pressed.

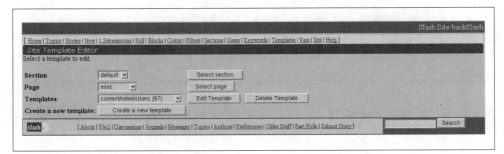

Figure 10-2. The Template editing menu, without a template selected

---

* The relevant graphics in the Slashcode theme include *cl.gif* (the left corner of a rounded bar), *cr.gif* (the right corner of a rounded bar), *gl.gif* (the left vertical bar of a comment or Story header box), and *gr.gif* (the corresponding right vertical bar).

Begin by choosing `article` for the Page field and click Select page. Next, choose the *display* option in the Template field and click the Edit Template button. This will bring up a page listing the template fields and values, including the all-important template description.

Because Slash does not yet have a mechanism to clone templates from the Admin menu, the most convenient way of changing the *default* template for the Articles Section is copy and paste. Open a new browser window and return to the Template Editor. Change the Page field to `article` and click the Create a new template button. This will bring up the editor with a blank template.

First, change the Template Section from default to Articles. Because nothing is yet assigned to the Articles Section, be sure to check the "new template section?" button. Copy the values from the other window for the Template page (the name of the applet that uses the template, i.e., `admin` or `users`), template name (the name of the page, as called by `slashDisplay`), title (a descriptive title), seclev (the seclev required to edit the template), and description (the purpose of the template and the variables it expects to receive). Also copy Template, the actual template code itself.

Editing the template code is straightforward (see Appendix C for details). For the sake of simplicity, add the dates of the previous and next Stories to their links. Find the lines that read:

```
[% n = BLOCK; PROCESS nextStory s=next; END %]
[% p = BLOCK; PROCESS nextStory s=prev; END %]
[% IF p %] <  [% p %][% END %]
[% IF n %] [% IF p %] | [% END %][% n %]  > [% END %]
<P> </TD><TD> </TD><TD VALIGN="TOP">
```

Modify them as follows and click the Save Template button:*

```
[% n = BLOCK; PROCESS nextStory s=next; END %]
[% p = BLOCK; PROCESS nextStory s=prev; END %]
[% IF p %] <  [% p; "($prev.section)" %][% END %]
[% IF n %] [% IF p %] | [% END %][% "($next.section)"; n %]  > [% END %]
<P> </TD><TD> </TD><TD VALIGN="TOP">
```

Any subsequent visits to a Story in the Articles Section will display the Section name alongside links to the previous and next Stories, if they exist. This is the tip of the iceberg as to the possible modifications.

---

* Depending on Slash configuration, templates may be cached in child processes. If this is the case, the web server will need to be stopped and restarted for the changes to take effect.

Customizing Template Behavior

There's much more to Slash templates than changing text output options. A common modification is adding banner ads to a site. Again, Slash's roots with Slashdot make this easy. Even site administrators responsible for internal sites can find some helpful ideas for further template editing.

Banner Ads

Many popular ad management packages have sprung up. There are several popular Apache modules for this purpose, including *mod_random* and *Adfu*. One, *mod_adbanners*, was written by Kurt Gray specifically for OSDN (neé Andover.net) sites, and works very well with Slash. It is available for download at *http://modadbanners.sourceforge.net/*. Installation of an Apache module is relatively simple. Follow the compilation directions in the section "Building Apache with mod_perl" in Chapter 2 and in the *INSTALL* file.*

After the module is installed and *httpd.conf* has been modified per the installation instructions, restart the web server to test the configuration. When everything works, you then must edit the configuration file for the site which will run banner ads. For firewheel, this file is */usr/local/slash/site/firewheel/firewheel.conf*. Copy the contents of the *docs/httpd.conf.example* file provided with the module into the configuration file, changing the file paths as appropriate for your system.

Next, copy the data and ad files to their proper destinations. The *.dat* files from */usr/local/adsystem/dat/* will go to the directory named in the AddBanner directive. The ads in */usr/local/adsystem/htdocs/banner/* should go into *htdocs/banner/* beneath the site directory. The Perl programs beneath */usr/local/adsystem/cgi-bin/* need to go into a directory somewhere beneath the site's *htdocs/* directory. You may need to enable a CGI handler for the directory in the configuration file. Finally, restart the web server.

Slash needs two more pieces of configuration to run banner ads. First, the *header* template must be modified to display the ad. With all of the included templates, this could be a daunting task. Luckily, the default Slash setup makes this task much easier. Instead of poking through the Template editing interface or grepping through server logs, simply visit the web page that should be modified, and bring up the HTML source. (In most web browsers, there will be an option for View Source, View Document Source, or something similar.) On the main homepage, this will produce a snippet resembling:

---

* *mod_adbanners* can also be built as an Apache DSO, if Apache has been configured for shared objects. This makes a site easier to administrate at the expense of possible compilation difficulties. See the Apache documentation, especially for the *apxs* utility.

```
<!DOCTYPE HTML PUBLIC "-//W3C//DTD HTML 3.2 Final//EN">
<html><head><title>firewheel: the homepage</title>

<!-- start template: ID 118, header;misc;default -->

</head>
<body BGCOLOR="#DDDDDD" TEXT="#222222" LINK="#660000" VLINK="#222222">

<table CELLPADDING="0" CELLSPACING="0" BORDER="0" WIDTH="99%" ALIGN="CENTER">
```

By default, Slash includes an HTML comment at the beginning of each template, providing identifying information. In this example, the specific header is *header;misc;default*, with a template ID of 118. Armed with this information, it's very easy to find the appropriate template in the Editor.

Use the *Templates* link in the Admin menu to reach the Template Editor. The starting values for Section and Page should be correct. Look in the Templates pop-up for the *header* template with the appropriate number. (The ID may vary from system to system.) This will bring up the text of the template. Luckily, the very first few lines are the ones to be changed:

```
[% IF constants.run_ads %]
<!-- ad code. You can use your own ad system - we use one that
sets an env variable in Apache that contains the ad itself and just put it
in this block -->
<!-- end ad code -->
[% END %]
```

This template snippet takes effect only if the run_ads configuration variable is set to true. By default, it isn't. This needs to be changed. Before that, however, the template must be modified. Since *mod_adbanners* is the ad system mentioned in the comment, it's safe to replace the comments with one simple template directive:

```
[% env.ad_banner_1 %]
```

Click the Save Template button. Next, follow the *Vars* link. Select the run_ads variable from the Select Variable Name menu and click Select Var. Change the Value from 0 to 1 and click Save.

Depending on template caching configuration, it may be necessary to restart the web server at this point. When this is complete, visit the site homepage *as a normal user* and marvel at the beautiful new banner bound to buy a boundless bevy of bandwidth.*

If the default position and look of the ad is slightly off-kilter, it's possible to tweak the template for a more balanced approach. Centering the ad can certainly help.

---

* Best of luck.

Return to the Template Editor, bring up the appropriate header block, and change the line that actually displays the ads to the following:

```
<div align="center">[% env.ad_banner_1 %]</div>
```

This will center the banner by wrapping it in HTML <div> tags. Other possibilities include turning it into a special ILAYER, wrapping it in a separate table, or performing all sorts of manipulations and edits. For more ideas on what templates can accomplish—and how—see Appendix C.

Themes and Plugins

Individual changes are fine, but occasionally someone will create such a work of art that it would be wrong not to share it with the world. Because Slash comes from that Free Software philosophy, it's adopted the same sort of "share and enjoy" outlook that has lead to the popularity of such organizations as CPAN (*http://www.cpan.org/*) and Themes.org (*http://www.themes.org*). The only thing that exceeds the thrill of creating something beautiful is finding out that other people are finding it just as useful. The first step towards mastery, though, is imitation.

Installing Plugins

Any complex program eventually grows to include some sort of plugin functionality.* Like the GIMP, Emacs, Perl, and Mozilla, Slash is also useful out of the box, but its true power is that it allows developers to build bigger and better things the original developers never imagined. This will probably become Slash's most important feature, as it moves beyond a simple yet powerful weblog program to become a full-powered application server.

Slash has long supported a feature called *plugins*. The plugin mechanism allows developers to bundle templates, applets, Perl modules, and database dumps together for distribution and installation on different machines. They can be as simple as a single program or as complicated as the standard Journal interface, adding amazing new functionality.

Slash Version 2.2 ships with 10 available plugins, not coincidentally in the *plugins/* directory (the section "Slash Plugin Directories" in Appendix A describes the directory structure in more detail.) These plugins are automatically installed in the Slash home directory and are made available to all sites when running the *install-slash-site* command. Finding new plugins is easy because Slashcode maintains a central repository at *http://slashcode.com/repository.pl*.

---

* Or the developers go crazy, trying to cram in yet another feature.

Installing new plugins is also simple. If Slash hasn't yet been installed, simply unpack the plugin tarball within the *plugins/* directory. This should create a new subdirectory containing all of the plugin files. From there, the normal Slash installation process will take over, automatically making the plugin available.

If Slash has already been installed, as is most likely the case, unpack the plugin within the *plugins/* directory under the Slash site directory. Using the example paths in the section "Before You Begin" in Chapter 2, given a plugin named *Print-1.1.tar.gz*, the appropriate commands to issue, as the root user, would be:

```
# cp Print-1.1.tar.gz /usr/local/slash/plugins/
# cd /usr/local/slash/plugins/
# tar xvfz Print-1.1.tar.gz
# ls Print/
```

This should unpack and list all of the files of the Print plugin. Installing a new site with *install-slashsite* will now prompt the installation of the Print plugin.

Adding the plugin to an existing site is also easy with the *install-plugin* tool, also found in the *bin/* directory. It has one required argument, the –u flag. As with all of the Slash command-line tools, this option gives the name of the virtual user associated with the particular site's database. For example, since the firewheel site uses a virtual user of `slash`, the command becomes: *bin/install-plugins -u slash*.

Other options include –l, which merely lists the available plugins, and –L, which automatically answers the question of creating symbolic links or actually copying plugin files. If followed by `y`, the tool creates symbolic links to the general plugin files within the site's *plugins/* directory. If followed by `n`, it copies the files. If this option is not provided, the tool will prompt for an answer.

Next, the tool displays a list of templates, strongly resembling that shown by the *install-slashsite* tool (described in the section "Installing the Slash Site" in Chapter 2). Installation proceeds in the same fashion. Plugins may display further instructions at the end of this process. Be sure to read this, because it may be necessary to edit a few existing templates or blocks.

Installing Themes

Themes and plugins are technically very similar—more like fraternal twins than cousins. The main difference is conceptual. Themes are intended to change the appearance of a site, while plugins change its behavior. Of course, plugins can often add templates, and themes can provide applets and tasks as well. Their internals are so similar; they use the same format for their installation lists.

The theme installation tool, *install-theme*, behaves in the same manner as *install-plugin*. It takes the same arguments, which enable the same features. The only difference is that it looks in the sitewide *themes/* directory for its installation targets. As such, a standard theme installation should be nearly self-explanatory.

```
# bin/install-theme -u slash -Ly

Please select which themes you would like?
1.      rhinelander "a virtual apple orchard"
2.      slashcode "Slashcode.com theme"
Hit 'a' to select all, otherwise select comma separated numbers or 'q' to quit
1
```

Creating a theme is little more (or less) than creating or editing templates as necessary, creating a *THEME* file, and distributing as necessary. Slash really only cares that a theme has a *THEME* file and is installed in the serverwide *themes/* directory. Otherwise, there's no important difference between the two.

Inside the Slashprint Plugin

A moderately experienced Perl programmer should be able to write a plugin, given sufficient information (say, Appendix D). Nothing beats a good example, though. The Print plugin is relatively simple and showcases just a few of the many features waiting to be created.

Plugin overview

The plugin itself does only one thing: displays a Story with minimal markup, suitable for printing. It accomplishes this task with one applet, three templates, and one small edit to an existing template. When unpacked, the plugin creates a directory resembling:

```
# ls -1R
.:
total 27
-rw-r--r--    1 slash    slash         236 Oct  1 21:15 Changes
-rw-r--r--    1 slash    slash       18049 Oct  1 21:16 GPL
-rw-rw-r--    1 slash    slash         701 Oct  1 21:05 INSTALL
-rw-rw-r--    1 slash    slash          58 Oct  1 21:05 MANIFEST
-rw-rw-r--    1 slash    slash         202 Oct  1 21:31 PLUGIN
-rwxr-xr-x    1 slash    slash        2441 Oct  1 21:09 print.pl*
drwxrwxr-x    2 slash    slash        1024 Oct  1 21:11 templates/

./templates:
total 4
-rw-rw-r--    1 slash    slash        1058 Oct  1 21:11 dispStory;print;misc
-rw-rw-r--    1 slash    slash         540 Oct  1 21:11 footer;print;misc
-rw-rw-r--    1 slash    slash         250 Oct  1 21:11 header;print;misc
```

The important files are *PLUGIN*, which tells *install-plugin* which files go where; *print.pl*, which contains the Perl code to accomplish the mission; and everything in *templates/*, which controls how Stories are displayed. The rest of the files are instructions and information for other developers.

The Print applet

Looking inside *print.pl* in Example 10-1, we see that it does only one thing. If passed a valid Story ID, it uses the special *print* templates to display the Story. Otherwise, it redirects the user to the site homepage. (This is based on code by Norbert "Momo_102" Kuemin and is available under the GNU General Public License, like Slash itself.)

Example 10-1. Contents of print.pl

```perl
#!/usr/bin/perl -w

use strict;
use Slash;
use Slash::Display;
use Slash::Utility;
use vars qw( $VERSION );
$VERSION = '1.11';

my $constants = getCurrentStatic();
my $user = getCurrentUser;
my $form = getCurrentForm();
my $slashdb = getCurrentDB();

my $sid = $form->{sid};
unless ($sid) {
        redirect($constants->{rootdir});
        return;
}

my $sect_title = $user->{currentSection}{title};

my $story       = $slashdb->getStory($sid);
my $topic       = $slashdb->getTopic($story->{tid});
my $author      = $slashdb->getAuthor($story->{uid},
        [qw( nickname fakeemail homepage )]);

$story->{storytime} = timeCalc($story->{time});

(my $adm, $user->{is_admin}) = ($user->{is_admin}, 0);

header($sect->{title});
$user->{is_admin} = $adm;

slashDisplay('dispStory', {
        user                    => $user,
        story                   => $story,
        topic                   => $topic,
        author                  => $author,
```

Example 10-1. Contents of print.pl (continued)

```
        section                 => $sect_title,
        displayLinks             => !$form->{nohtml},
}, { Nocomm => 1 });

slashDisplay('footer', {
        time                     => $slashdb->getTime(),
        story                    => $story,
        displayLinks             => !$form->{nohtml},
        autoPrint                => $form->{auto},
}, { Nocomm => 1 });
```

The first several lines use some standard Perl and Slash libraries to enable access
to certain functions used later. These functions are covered in more detail in
Appendix D:

```
my $constants = getCurrentStatic();
my $user = getCurrentUser;
my $form = getCurrentForm();
my $slashdb = getCurrentDB();
```

The following chunk of code initializes some handy data structures. $constants is
a Perl hash with the current names and values of the Slash configuration variables,
$user is information about the current user, $form is a Perl hash with the CGI
parameters passed through a form or a URI, and $slashdb is a Slash database
object, capable of performing all sorts of retrieval and storage operations.

```
my $sid = $form->{sid};
unless ($sid) {
        redirect($constants->{rootdir});
        return;
}
```

To print a Story, the plugin needs a valid Story ID. It looks in $form, but must
unfortunately redirect to the site homepage without an identifier. This is not very
robust, but if the print links are generated automatically, it will fail only if someone is playing around or if something is terribly broken. The rootdir configuration
variable points to the URI of the site homepage.

```
my $sect_title = $user->{currentSection}{title};

my $story        = $slashdb->getStory($sid);
my $topic        = $slashdb->getTopic($story->{tid});
my $author       = $slashdb->getAuthor($story->{uid},
        [qw( nickname fakeemail homepage )]);

$story->{storytime} = timeCalc($story->{time});
```

These lines grab important information that will be used in the templates. Note
that the getAuthor function can optionally grab only certain fields. This is slightly

more efficient than retrieving the complete structure at once. For a single record retrieval, it doesn't matter, but it is a good technique to know. `timeCalc` uses the user's preferred time display type to format the Story's time. The new value can be stored in a `$story` structure without affecting the Story in the database.

```
(my $adm, $user->{is_admin}) = ($user->{is_admin}, 0);

header($sect->{title});
$user->{is_admin} = $adm;
```

With the setup out of the way, it's time to print the HTML header. First, there's an ugly/clever hack to suppress the Admin menu. Looking at the `header`, currently in *Slash::Utility::Admin*, it prints the Admin menu if the `is_admin` flag is set for the user. That would mess up the clean, functional design, so the flag is temporarily set to a false value, then restored after the function call. (Calling `slashDisplay` directly is a better solution in this case, but sometimes that is not possible. For the purpose of demonstration, this is a good trick to know.) After the function call, the admin flag can be restored in `$user`.

```
slashDisplay('dispStory', {
        user                    => $user,
        story                   => $story,
        topic                   => $topic,
        author                  => $author,
        section                 => $sect_title,
        displayLinks            => !$form->{nohtml},
});
```

Finally, the most important part of the applet is a single call to `slashDisplay`. This function finds the appropriate template, named *dispStory*, and respects the `$options`, feeding it the arguments passed as the second parameter. It handles the act of sending the results to the user agent, so the return value is safely ignorable. Note the value of `displayLinks` will be the *boolean opposite* of any provided `nohtml` CGI parameter. If the parameter is not set or is set to 0, `displayLinks` will be true. If the parameter is set, the variable will be false. This value is important in two templates.

```
slashDisplay('footer', {
        time                    => $slashdb->getTime(),
        story                   => $story,
        displayLinks            => !$form->{nohtml},
        autoPrint               => $form->{auto},
});
```

As expected, this locates and displays the *footer* template in the Print Section. It uses an additional CGI parameter of `auto`.

The Print plugin templates

All that's left is some display magic, scattered about three templates. These must render a Story in printable format, using the previous information. Additionally, they should respect the nohtml and auto parameters to remove as much unprintable formatting as possible and to print automatically if possible, respectively. These templates must somehow be associated with the *print.pl* applet, so displayStory can find them easily. This is accomplished by assigning them to the print page in the default Section.

As shown in Example 10-2, the *header* template is very simple. It is processed by header immediately after the *html-header* template, closing some tags and adding in the name of the site and its slogan.

Example 10-2. The header template

```
</HEAD>
<BODY>
<H1>[% constants.sitename %]</H1>
<H2>[% constants.slogan %]</H2>
```

The *dispStory* template, shown in Example 10-3, does much more. It begins by checking the displayLinks flag. If set to true, it sets the title and topic variables to valid HTML links to the Story and its Topics. Otherwise, it uses plain text. Performing this check here makes the display logic cleaner.

Example 10-3. The dispStory template

```
[% IF displayLinks;
        title = "<a href=
\"$constants.rootdir/$story.section/\">$section.title</a>: $story.title";
        topic = "<a href=
\"$constants.rootdir/search.pl?topic=$topic.tid\">$topic.alttext</A>";
ELSE;
        title = story.title;
        topic = topic.alttext;
END %]

<h2 align="left">[% story.title %]</h2>
<table border="0" valign="left">
<tr><th align="left">Date:</th><td>[% story.storytime %]</td></tr>
<tr><th align="left">Author:</th><td>[% author.nickname %]</td></tr>
<tr><th align="left">Topic:</th><td>[% topic %]</td></tr>

[% IF constants.use_dept %]
        <tr><td colspan="2">from the <em>[% story.dept %]</em> dept.</td></tr>
[% END %]
```

Example 10-3. The dispStory template (continued)

```
</table>
<p>[% story.introtext %]</p>
<p>[% story.bodytext %]</p>
```

The next chunk simply creates an HTML table and interpolates the Story information into the right table cells. The only interesting thing to note is the line that checks to see if the use_dept configuration variable is set. The printed Story should match the Story as displayed on a web browser.

The last few lines end the table and display the text of the Story. The plugin is currently limited in that it does not strip links out of either introtext or bodytext. There is no convenient, built-in mechanism for doing so. Patches are welcome.

The *footer* template in Example 10-4 takes care of the last bits of data, adding some convenient text to the page. The first block again checks the displayLinks variable, assigning either a clickable link or a plain text URI and Story title to url. This is then displayed beneath a horizontal line, with a modified version of the standard copyright notice and the time of printing.

Example 10-4. The footer template

```
[% IF displayLinks;
        url = "<a href=
\"$constants.rootdir/article.pl?sid=$story.sid\">$story.title</a>";
ELSE;
        url = "$story.title (http:$constants.rootdir/article.pl?sid=$story.sid)";
END %]

<hr />
<P >All trademarks and copyrights on this page are owned by their respective
companies.</P>
<P>
printed from [% url %] on [% time %]
</P>

[% IF autoPrint %]
<script language="JavaScript1.2">
<!--
        if (window.print) { window.print(); }
//-->
</script>
[% END %]

</BODY>
</HTML>
```

The final block uses the autoPrint parameter. If true, the template sends a tiny JavaScript snippet to the web browser. This attempts to verify that the current browser window can pop up a print dialog. If so, it does so. The default behavior of the template is not to include this feature. It can be handy, however.

The resulting page will look something like Figure 10-3. Hopefully the Story is more interesting, though.

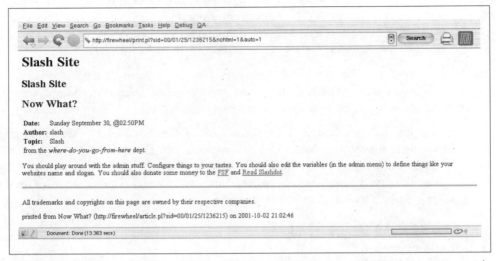

Figure 10-3. The printable version of a default Story on a freshly installed site

Modifying the Code Itself

Occasionally, even the most die-hard Perl hackers themselves want to roll up their sleeves and get to work. Perhaps an administrator will find a feature that's just not quite right, or come up with an excellent idea to make Slash much better for her users. Someone else may think of something that can't be done in a plugin.

Whatever the case, it's possible to change the underlying Slash modules themselves. Some parts are scary and some are simple. For a moderately experienced Perl programmer, a little intuition and a little knowledge of Slash architecture and behavior will open the doors to all sorts of possibilities. (Of course, administrators who don't know much Perl aren't entirely out of luck. Posting a request on Slashcode can attract the attention of a capable coder.)

Be aware that modifying the core code may leave you stranded when it comes time to update to a newer version of Slash. Anything that can be done as a plugin should be. If it's truly necessary to change the code itself, check with the Slash development team to see if there are plans to do such a thing already. If they can guide you in creating a patch that will be accepted in the next revision, your life will be much easier.

An Example: Applying Content Filters Based on User Karma

The best way to illustrate modifying Slash is with an example. Shortly after Slash 2.2 went into beta testing, the new content filters (see the section "The Comment Filters List" in Chapter 6) tripped up several experienced users. Unfortunately, the content filters applied to all users equally. The tools used to catch some undesirable content put a burden on valued contributors.

One possible solution is to relax the filtering as users accumulate karma. That is, users who earn the trust of the community can be expected to conduct themselves appropriately. The easiest approach is to hijack the content filtering code, applying it only to users with karma below a certain level. A more proper fix is to add an optional karma level to each content filter, applying it only to users with karma below that level.

Finding what to change

Having identified the problem, the next step is to figure out what needs to change. This is the most difficult part in any modification, especially for people who lack an intimate understanding of the code. Intuition and a little detective work will help, but choosing the right starting point is the real trick. The obvious starting point is the place in the code that actually applies content filters to user comments. Unfortunately, this isn't immediately obvious. Perhaps clues will appear while chasing down other leads.

Obviously, any extra fields added to content filters will require a change to the filter-editing page. This is part of the Admin menu controlled by the *admin.pl* applet. This file runs the whole menu, with several available options. Looking at the `main` function, it reads the `op` parameter from the user agent to decide which action to perform. Clicking the *Edit Filters* link with a web browser brings up the appropriate page. Viewing the source reveals two potential `op` values, "listfilters" and "editfilter". The second one is correct, in this case.

admin.pl executes a function called `editFilter`. This is a gold mine of information. It calls other functions on the database object, specifically `createContentFilter`, `setContentFilter`, `getContentFilter`, and `deleteContentFilter`. Additionally, it uses a template named *editFilter*. The next step to understanding these filters is to investigate the database functions. How are they stored, and how should a new field be added?

The easiest way to find Slash functions is with the standard Unix *grep* utility. Granted, the database access will be somewhere in the *Slash::DB* hierarchy, but the specific location could be in any of several files. To find a subroutine declaration, use a command similar to *grep -r 'sub createContentFilter' *.* This reveals the next stop: *Slash::DB::MySQL.*

Looking at the `createContentFilter` function reveals that it is a thin wrapper around `sqlInsert`, putting the appropriate fields into the `content_filters` database table. Looking at the database schema for the table will reveal the last piece of the puzzle.

Within MySQL, the appropriate command is simply *describe content_filters;*. This will display a nicely formatted summary of the table design:

```
+----------------+---------------------+------+-----+---------+----------------+
| Field          | Type                | Null | Key | Default | Extra          |
+----------------+---------------------+------+-----+---------+----------------+
| filter_id      | tinyint(3) unsigned |      | PRI | NULL    | auto_increment |
| form           | varchar(20)         |      | MUL |         |                |
| regex          | varchar(100)        |      | MUL |         |                |
| modifier       | varchar(5)          |      |     |         |                |
| field          | varchar(20)         |      | MUL |         |                |
| ratio          | float(6,4)          |      |     | 0.0000  |                |
| minimum_match  | mediumint(6)        |      |     | 0       |                |
| minimum_length | mediumint(9)        |      |     | 0       |                |
| err_message    | varchar(150)        | YES  |     |         |                |
+----------------+---------------------+------+-----+---------+----------------+
9 rows in set (0.01 sec)
```

There's clearly room for an extra field, but what should it be? The name `karma` seems clear enough. How should it be declared? It ought to match the karma field in the user tables. Issuing the *show tables;* command reveals several user tables. Looking through the likely suspects for a karma field eventually leads to `users_info`, which uses a tinyint of nine places, defaulting to a value of 0.

The plan is now in place. Editing the `comment_filters` table to add this field is mostly straightforward. Of course, the better solution requires a little more work. Instead of updating the code on just one machine, why not create a patch against the Slash distribution for other administrators?

There are several different approaches, but all of them require some way of keeping unmodified files around to provide a sort of baseline. Copying the whole Slash directory (as unpacked from the tarball) is easy. Copying each file to a temporary backup (say, *MANIFEST* to *~MANIFEST*) is simple. For developers familiar with CVS,* making patches against the Slash repository is also easy (*cvs diff -u filename > filename.patch*). Whatever the solution, having a non-modified version of the source available makes it possible to recover from horrible, smoldering ruin.

---

* Karl Fogel's excellent *Open Source Development with CVS* can be perused online at *http://www.red-bean.com/cvsbook/* and is well worth reading.

Instead of issuing SQL commands to modify the database directly, the patch-oriented approach prefers to change the database dump shipped with Slash. These all live under *sql/* directories. Grepping again for `content_filters` reveals that SQL files exist for MySQL, Oracle, and PostgreSQL. The MySQL directory also contains a file named *datadump.sql* that inserts the default filters.

Editing the *slashschema_create.sql* files is very straightforward. Simply find the Section that creates the `content_filters` table and add a field to it. For MySQL, the addition is:

```
karma mediumint DEFAULT '0' NOT NULL,
```

Why `mediumint` and not `tinyint(9)`, which was the described output of the `karma` field? Because the `users_info` definition was in the same file, it was easier to copy the karma field declaration than to create an entirely new one. This also makes it easier to edit the files for Oracle and PostgreSQL, which have slightly different syntax.* Having added one line to all three files, it's now safe to edit the database dump.

The dumped file lives in *themes/slashcode/sql/mysql/datadump.sql*. It contains around 20 default filters in raw SQL statements. They resemble:

```
INSERT INTO content_filters (regex, form, modifier, field, ratio, minimum_match,
minimum_length, err_message) VALUES ('^(?:\\s+)','comments','gi','postersubj',
0.0000,7,0,'Lots of space in the subject ... lots of space in the head.');
```

Since the schema set a default value for the new field, it's not strictly necessary to modify anything here, but there's no sense in doing a halfway job. Each field needs to have the karma field name added to the first list and the default value of 0 added to the second. A good text editor can perform this manipulation with a macro in no time. Otherwise, it shouldn't take too long to modify each line individually, producing:

```
INSERT INTO content_filters (regex, form, modifier, field, ratio, minimum_match,
minimum_length, err_message, karma) VALUES ('^(?:\\s+)','comments','gi',
'postersubj', 0.0000,7,0,'Lots of space in the subject ... lots of space in the
head.', 0);
```

Just like editing the schema, missing or misplaced commas can really wreak havok during installation.

Having added the new field, it's time to step back. The code that actually applies filters is still banging around somewhere within the big bundle of Slash modules.

---

* Make sure the previous line ends with a comma, or the database will give strange errors when trying to create the new table.

Intuition says it probably uses one of the database methods to load the filters, though. Grepping for getContentFilter reveals a likely suspect:

```
Slash/Utility/Access.pm: my $filters = $slashdb->getContentFilters($formname,
$field);
```

Indeed, this line is part of the filterOk function, itself called from various places in *comments.pl* and *submit.pl*. This must be the place. Reading through the code, it reads all of the content filters into an array reference. Looping through the filters, it applies each to the appropriate field. The important bits of the function are:

```
my $slashdb = getCurrentDB();
my $user = getCurrentUser();
my $filters = $slashdb->getContentFilters($formname, $field);

for (@$filters) {
        my($number_match, $regex);
        my $raw_regex          = $_->[2];
        my $modifier           = 'g' if $_->[3] =~ /g/;
        my $case               = 'i' if $_->[3] =~ /i/;
        my $field              = $_->[4];
        my $ratio              = $_->[5];
        my $minimum_match      = $_->[6];
        my $minimum_length     = $_->[7];
        my $err_message        = $_->[8];
        my $isTrollish         = 0;

        # apply filter to comment
}
```

It appears that each filter is itself an array reference, containing several fields from the content_filters table. Nothing can change here until the database access code is modified. This is the fun part.

Changing the content filter subroutines

Everything that accesses the content_filters table needs to be updated. Again, *grep* comes to the rescue. The simple command *grep -r 'content_filters' * | grep '.pm'* reveals that only *Slash::DB::MySQL* touches the table. This is a big assumption to make, but it turns out to be safe, in this case.

Consistency is nice, and all of the filter subroutines in the database package follow the form *verbContentFilter(s)*. Simply searching for "ContentFilters" brings up each of five subroutines in turn.

As it happens, getContentFilters needs no editing. It selects all fields from the table with the otherwise dubious SQL construct SELECT * FROM content_filters. As the karma field was added at the end, nothing should break, though if your database administrator catches you writing this kind of select, you may break.

Moving on, setContentFilter updates a filter in the database with values pulled from a variable named $form. This represents another decision point. The hash key to hold the karma must correspond to the HTML field name used in the template. For the sake of consistency, karma will work as well as anything else. The change is easy: add a comma to the previously last hash item and one more entry. The modified update call becomes:

```
$self->sqlUpdate("content_filters", {
        regex         => $form->{regex},
        form          => $formname,
        modifier      => $form->{modifier},
        field         => $form->{field},
        ratio         => $form->{ratio},
        minimum_match    => $form->{minimum_match},
        minimum_length   => $form->{minimum_length},
        err_message      => $form->{err_message},

        # this line was added
        karma         => $form->{karma},

        }, "filter_id=$form->{filter_id}"
);
```

createContentFilter is very similar. Instead of an update, it performs an insert. The karma field has a default value of 0, so it's not really necessary to modify this method. In the interest of clarity, there's no reason not to add a single line. Predictably, adding one comma and a line turn the guts of this function into:

```
$self->sqlInsert("content_filters", {
        regex         => '',
        form          => $formname,
        modifier      => '',
        field         => '',
        ratio         => 0,
        err_message      => '',
        minimum_match    => 0,
        minimum_length   => 0,

        # this line was added
        karma         => 0,
});
```

deleteContentFilter doesn't care about the fields, issuing a simple SQL delete. getContentFilter isn't used in the code anywhere, and it doesn't appear to care about field names either. Both functions go unmodified.

Adding a karma check

Returning to *Slash::Utility::Access*, there's now enough information to add a karma check. Consulting the schema again, if the database returns the fields in order, the karma value will be in position 9 of the array. Here come the most difficult decisions of all. Should karma filtering apply all the time? Should it have a configuration variable to disable it? When should the code check? Backward compatibility is worth considering. If administrators upgrade, will the code still perform as they expect?

As things turn out, the default value of 0 was a good choice. If the ninth field of the filter does not evaluate to true in Perl terms, there's no reason to check the user karma. If it does evaluate to true, the code should check to see if the user's karma exceeds the karma limit, skipping the filter check as necessary. It could be nice to have a configuration variable that disables this new behavior entirely, however.

The $user variable is a reference to a hash full of all sorts of useful data. One of these is the karma field, conveniently accessible.* Finally, it makes sense to do this check as early as possible. If a filter will be skipped, there's no point in assigning to several variables and applying regular expressions. Skipping the filter is safe because the method returns only a failure, exiting the loop early, if a filter fails. The result, added to the top of the loop, is:

```
for (@$filters) {

        # skip this filter if there's a karma limit and the user is over it
        if ($_->[9]) {
                next if $user->{karma} > $_->[9];
        }
```

Modifying the content filters menu

The only things left to change are the parts of the Admin menu that allow content filters to be edited. These are the *admin.pl* file and the *editFilter* template, which are highly complimentary. Editing HTML is relatively easy, so the first stop is the template.

Templates live in two places. For distribution purposes, they exist in plain-text files in *templates/* directories. Because *editFilter* is part of the Admin plugin, its full path is *plugins/Admin/templates/editFilter;admin;default*. The sidebar "How Slash Calls Templates" in Appendix C explains the peculiar naming convention. Otherwise, the standard Template Editing feature of the Admin menu updates the live template in the database.

---

* Again, *grep* would come to the rescue for anyone who didn't immediately guess this. After digging around in the code for a while, things like this start to make sense.

Adding a form widget to modify the karma value is very simple; it's just a matter of copying the HTML used to modify another value. The `ratio` box looks to be a good choice.* Replacing all instances of "ratio" with "karma" and writing a short explanation produces the following HTML:

```
<TR>
        <TD WIDTH="40">
                <B>Karma Level</B>
                <BR>If non-zero, the karma level above which this filter will not
                be applied to a user's comments.<BR><BR>
        </TD>
        <TD>  </TD>
        <TD VALIGN="top">
                <BR>[% filter.karma %]
        </TD>
        <TD VALIGN="top">
                <INPUT TYPE="text" LENGTH="8" NAME="karma"
                        VALUE="[% filter.karma %]">
                </INPUT>
        </TD>
</TR>
```

With these changes, the filter-editing page will now show the existing karma value and will send a form field back to the server with a new value. All that's left is to capture the new value and handle it appropriately.

Returning to `editFilter` in *admin.pl*, it appears that `$form` should already be set with the updated values. Good—the content filter inserting and updating functions should work automatically. The only thing left to do is to modify the display feature to send the new field to the template.

The code builds a list of desired fields and passes it to `getContentFilter`. This returns a reference to a hash, with the field names as keys. The only thing required is to add the karma field to the array, and everything should work as expected. The new code is:

```
my @values = qw(regex form modifier field ratio minimum_match
        minimum_length err_message karma);
```

With that, the hard work is over, and the tedious work of debugging can begin. The most common mistake is forgetting a comma when adding an item to a list. Authors are allowed a spot of *deus ex machina*, however, so everything works automatically the first time.

---

* Copy and Paste is still a time-honored software development shortcut.

When you've finished testing your new masterpiece, strongly consider submitting it to be included in the main Slash distribution. Not only will it earn you certain fame and fortune (or at least gratitude), but it will make your life easier when it comes time to upgrade. Consult the *docs/slashstyle.pod* file distributed with Slash for suggestions on proposing, creating, and submitting code changes.

Internationalization

Though Slashdot was originally the brainchild of Midwest American geeks, the site has reached a worldwide audience. Extending the successful idea, several native language sites sprang up using the Slash code. Of these, Barrapunto (*http://www.barrapunto.com/*) may be the best known. It's the Spanish-language equivalent of Slashdot. Other international sites cater to Italian (*http://slash-italian.kenobi.it/*), Hebrew (*http://www.orik.co.il/*), and Japanese (*http://slashdot.ne.jp/*) audiences. Potential administrators with non-English speaking audiences can adjust their site to serve up nearly any language represented by computers.*

Beginning with Slash 2.0, most of the text aimed at endusers has moved to templates. This makes it possible for administrators to translate things without having to edit comments buried in Perl code. From the Admin menu, it's possible to change the templates, blocks, and all other messages stored in the database.

Of course, the underlying software must also support internationalization. By default, MySQL operates on the ISO-8859-1 or Latin character set. The choice of character set governs the string sorting order. (For example, a character set without accent marks over vowels will treat "è" much differently than "e".) This directly affects GROUP BY and ORDER BY clauses.

Depending on compile-time options, MySQL can switch character sets as necessary. Official binaries from MySQL.com have compiled-in support for complex character sets, including multi-byte sets. The server must be started with the additional clause —*default-character-set* to specify anything besides ISO-8859-1. Changing this value on a server with existing databases may cause some of the indexes to be wrong. It's also possible to use a character set not compiled into the binaries. Check the MySQL manual for more information. Of course, complex characters may not be allowed in table and column names until MySQL Version 4.0, but Slash does not provide these by default.†

---

* This may or may not include EBCDIC. It does include Unicode.

† MySQL versions newer than 3.23.14 have these options. At the time of this writing, the latest version is 3.23.43. The relevant part of the manual is currently at *http://www.mysql.com/doc/C/b/ Character_sets.html*. If that does not work, a search for "character sets" should reveal the latest information.

Perl itself has embraced Unicode in recent releases. The current stable release, 5.6.1, includes several important fixes to make things work. Internal character-handling techniques work on characters, which may or may not be bytes. In particular, Unicode characters are often several bytes long. It is highly recommended to stay abreast of the most recent stable release.

For the most part, built-in Perl functions transparently switch to operating on characters instead of bytes, when necessary. It's still possible to make some unportable assumptions. Things such as regular expressions might specify a range of "word characters" that apply only to the U.S. English character set, leaving out valid accented characters.

The underlying data stores and structures will need to remain in English, for practical reasons—renaming a database table could introduce a messy set of dependencies requiring someone to go through reams of Slash modules and templates to sort things out. The same goes for errors and warnings aimed at developers and administrators. Authors may not need to read much English to perform their duties, but woe to anyone trying to decipher messages in the site error log.

The final verdict is mixed. Yes, it's possible to set up and maintain a Slash site catering to an often-overlooked set of Net users. Like setting up the early versions of Slash, the path is rocky. Anyone with language skills looking for an opportunity to contribute back, developer or not, will likely be welcome to help make Slash as useful for the rest of the world as it is for native English speakers.

11

Advanced Administration

Administrators and Authors can run a successful Slash site quite well with the information presented in previous chapters. A bit of initial customization and preventative maintenance will keep the site running for ages. There's a class of people, though, who like to take things apart to see what makes them tick.* The relative ease of Perl programming and certain design decisions by the Slashteam make this especially appropriate.

This chapter explores Slash architecture from a nuts-and-bolts perspective. Readers with a little Perl, SQL, and Unix under their belts will get a feel for the architecture of the program as it works. It's a little noisy behind the curtain, and sometimes the floor is greasy. Step carefully.

To perform advanced administration, you must understand the Slash architecture, API, and even several common database tables. The good news is that you don't have to be an expert to do interesting things. That's the Perl way. This chapter should be read in conjunction with Appendix A, Appendix B, and Appendix D. (They may be short on suspense, but they're tall on detail.)

Tasks

All of a site's tasks live in the *tasks/* subdirectory. They must be valid Perl files (or symbolic links to valid Perl files). Their names must end in ".pl" and should contain only alphanumeric characters or the hyphen.

---

* Some of them go on to write software and even books about software. That doesn't mean they'll ever put their little brothers' alarm clocks back together. (Sorry!)

Internally, tasks must provide two pieces of information: a time specification used to schedule the task and a Perl subroutine to be called at the appropriate time. *slashd* makes two Perl variables, in the main package, available to all tasks. These are $me, containing the name of the task, and %task, a hash of all available tasks, keyed by their names. A very simple example task might only print a status message. In its entirety, it could be:

```perl
#!/usr/bin/perl -w

use strict;

# variables made available from slashd
use vars qw( %task $me );

$task{$me}{timespec} = '10 * * * *';
$task{$me}{code} = sub { print "Running $me!\n" };

1;
```

At its heart, the task simply adds its own information to the task hash. Nothing prevents it from manipulating other tasks, except good neighborly manners. As *slashd* runs under the *strict* pragma, with warnings enabled, so should all tasks. This means predeclaring the two necessary variables. Additionally, all tasks must return a true value at the end. This alerts *slashd* to the success or failure of an installation attempt.

The time specification, a simple string with five fields, will look familiar to anyone who's used *cron*. In order, the fields represent the minute, hour, day of month, month, and day of week. Each field takes numbers (0–59 for minute, 0–23 for hour, and so forth) or an asterisk, signifying any. In the previous example, the task will run at 10 minutes past the hour, every hour. A task with a timespec of * 0 * * * will run once every day, at midnight. A few default Slash tasks need to occur every few minutes. The timespec for *freshenup.pl* is 1-59/3 * * * *, which means that it will be run every three minutes, starting at the first minute past the hour.*

The task subroutine can be almost arbitrarily complex. It has access to the standard *Slash*, *Slash::Display*, and *Slash::Utility* packages. Additionally, it can use other Perl modules and declare subroutines as needed. As *slashd* executes all tasks in the main package, namespace collisions between tasks are possible. Defensive Perl programming on the part of task writers will minimize the risk. Be aware of this.

---

* The crontab(5) manpage on any well-installed Unix system provides more detailed documentation.

All tasks are invoked through their subroutine references. *slashd* passes four variables to provide context to all tasks. In order, they are:

$virtual_user

> The name of the *DBIx::Password* user associated with the appropriate database for the site.

$constants

> A hash reference filled with configuration variables. Most of these are available in the vars database table. Note that changes to this hash are not reflected in the database.

$slashdb

> The current database object. This allows method calls to access and manipulate database tables directly.

$user

> A hash reference containing information about the currently authenticated user. As tasks operate outside of the web server context, this will be the Anonymous User.

Tasks have access to the site database as well as to the normal filesystem. The *slashd* launch script (usually */etc/rc.d/init.d/slash*, but potentially */etc/init.d/slash*) takes care to launch the task as the appropriate user; however, this account can still wreak havok if compromised. A poorly written or malicious task could destroy the database, post secret system information as a Story, or even open up a back door for further compromise. Of course, this also means tasks can perform powerful operations, such as database integrity checking, log merging, and submission queue manipulation.

The launcher takes three potential arguments: *start*, *stop*, and *restart*. It will stop, start, or restart a new instance of *slashd* as the appropriate system user for each installed site. The tasks should normally operate on their own without intervention. They will need to be restarted when modifying or adding tasks, whether they are new or have a plugin or theme. Also, poorly written tasks may contribute to a slow memory leak. If *slashd* grows and uses too much memory, simply restart it, then fix the leak.

Extra Task Options

Besides the timespec and code fields, tasks can provide extra information to the scheduler. For example, if a task adds a standalone hash key with a nonzero value, *slashd* will refuse to schedule it. This is useful for creating tasks that should only ever be run manually.

Tasks are also allowed to take extra options to change their behavior. These extra options will be made available through the `$constants->{task_options}` hash. This is currently available only when they are run manually, however. *slashd* has no provision for passing options to tasks. A task that can optionally update user settings could expect a uid option, with code something like:

```
my $uid = $constants->{task_options} || $constants->anonymous_coward_uid;
```

Be aware that *slashd* will not run tasks that would have run in the past. That is, if the administrator shuts down the task one minute before *portald* is set to run, the scheduler will not run the task until its next iteration. If the task ends abruptly, or if someone stops it for maintenance, routine tasks will not run. Slashboxes will keep their old content, moderator points will not regenerate, and users will become keenly aware of all of the little niceties that go on behind the scenes.

For sites running multiple web servers, it is usually sufficient to run *slashd* on only one server, presumably on the one exporting directories via NFS. (Slashdot does this.) For tasks that truly need to run on multiple machines, it may be necessary to use a more sophisticated mechanism to report tasks:

```
use Sys::Hostname;

my $host = hostname();
my %allowed = map { $_ => 1 } (split/\,/, $constants->{$me . '_allow'});

if ($allowed{$host}) {
        $task{$me}{timespec} = '30 * * * *';
        $task{$me}{code} \&do_something;
}
```

For further efficiency, consider running tasks against a backup database, if you have one. Depending on the replication type and refresh rate, it may be appropriate to trade some data freshness (information created by the task) for the privilege of leaving your main database unfettered by regular, potentially expensive tasks. Slashdot uses this to good effect. Not all tasks can be migrated, but less important things such as generating access logs can relieve load on a busy server.

The Slash Daemon and Tasks

As implied way back in the section "The Slash Publishing Cycle" in Chapter 1, Slash relies on several external processes to do things outside the standard web publishing cycle. Some tasks need to happen at predetermined times (e.g., rotating logs and mailing out daily headline lists). Other jobs, such as doling out moderator points, take up time or memory that a *mod_perl* process cannot spare.

slashd

The venerable *slashd* daemon is the parent and guardian of all tasks. For each unique site, it schedules and launches all tasks found in the site's *tasks/* directory. Slash installs *slashd* to launch as a system daemon at boot time, so it should always be running when any Slash site is accessible. Each Slash site has its own *slashd* process. The only difference between these instances is that each will use the virtual user appropriate to its assigned site.

As it runs, *slashd* writes copious information to the *slashd.log* file beneath the associated site's *logs/* directory. (The *slashd* running for ghostwheel will write its log to */usr/local/slash/site/ghostwheel/logs/slashd.log*). If a site appears to be "stuck," check this log to make sure that the daemon is running as expected. The `slashd_verbosity` configuration variable controls the amount of logging. *slashd* checks this variable regularly, so an administrator can temporarily raise the debugging level and monitor the log if problems arise. The available values are 0, 1, and 2.

At level 0, *slashd* will log errors and warnings, *slashd* startup and shutdown messages, and the number and names of tasks that were successfully and unsuccessfully scheduled. Level 1 adds task ending times, the length of time tasks take to complete, and extra warnings if a task tried to schedule itself for some point in the past. At level 2, *slashd* records the name and the time at which the first task is scheduled. Also, when a task has completed, it logs the number of seconds until a task runs again.

Fatal errors include a tragic failure to find any valid tasks and the presence of severely malformed tasks. These are both rare and tend to explode only when the daemon starts. Warnings are also rare. They include invalid task files (in which the task returns bad data or does not compile), bad time specifications in task files, and a warning if *slashd* is not running under the GMT time zone. For the most part, it's easy to forget this daemon is actually there.

Trusting a long-running process to run arbitrary Perl programs automatically is a bit of a security risk. *slashd* does check for the most egregious of security holes. It will log an error and die if a task directory or an individual task program has the world-writable permission bit set. It is still a wise idea to check any tasks from third parties for suspicious code. Tasks run as the user specified them to the *install-slashsite* command. On a properly secured box, this may prevent root exploits, but it is sufficient to wreak havok on the web site and in the database. Standard good system administration practices apply.

The dailyStuff Task

As its name implies, the *dailyStuff* task runs daily, taking care of common maintenance and update tasks. First, it calculates some basic statistics and emails them to
the addresses listed in the `stats_reports` configuration variable. This report
includes the total number of hits for the previous day, the number of unique hits
(based on host addresses), the total number of hits to the site to date, the number
of hits to the homepage, and a summary of all articles viewed more than 100 times
that day.

Next, the task creates a daily mailing. All Stories posted in the previous day are
converted to plain text. They're fed through the *dailynews* and *dailyheadlines* templates. This produces two separate messages, one consisting of just the headlines
and the other including headlines, introductions, and extended copy.
dailyStuff sends each out only to users who have subscribed to either mailing. As
an artifact from earlier versions, it logs this activity to a file in each site log directory named *messaged.log*.

Next, *dailyStuff* performs some routine maintanance. It looks through the active
discussions for everything older than `discussion_archive` days. These archived
discussions are considered closed. No more comments will be allowed. For ongoing discussions, threads headed by comments past their expiration date (the `dis-
cussionrecycle` variable) will also be deleted.

Finally, it's time to delete some old data. The poll voting logs are purged. The
moderator and meta-moderator logs older than `archive_delay` are cleared. All
formkeys older than `formkey_timeframe` are deleted, and the access logs older than
two days are dumped. This prevents stale information from clogging up the
database. It does take a bit of database power, though, so it should run during a
lull in site activity. By default, Slash schedules *dailyStuff* for 6:07 A.M. GMT. That's
bedtime, at least in Holland, Michigan.

The moderatord Task

As its name implies, *moderatord* has the unenviable job of allocating, distributing,
and recycling moderator points. The sidebar "Mommy, Where Do Moderation
Points Come From?" in Chapter 6 discusses the moderation algorithms in greater
detail. This daemon writes its messages to *moderatord.log* in each site's log directory. Of course, if the `allow_moderation` variable is false, the task has nothing to
do, and takes long holiday weekends.

To perform its work, *moderatord* first compares two configuration variables,
`totalComments` and `lastComments`. These variables are automatically generated by

the system and should not be manipulated directly. It subtracts `lastComments` from `totalComments` to determine the number of comments that have been added since the task last ran. Without new comments, there is nothing to do, and the task ends. Otherwise, `lastComments` is updated with the current value of `totalComments`.

moderatord then attempts to recycle expired moderation points, based on the current value of the `stir` variable.* Next, it creates tokens, based on the number of new comments, and distributes them randomly. Each user, selected from a pool of potential moderators, will receive one token. After this lottery, the task looks for all users with the number of tokens set in the `maxtokens` variable. It automatically exchanges these tokens for moderator points. These users will be notified of their good fortune they next time they request a page.

The task's second job is to reconcile meta-moderations. To be eligible for reconciliation, a moderation must be judged by a certain number of meta-moderators. Two configuration variables are involved: `m2_consensus` dictates how many meta-moderators must agree on the fate of a moderation, and `m2_batchsize` controls how many meta-moderations are processed in one iteration of the task. Without a batchsize, *moderatord* will reconcile all new meta-moderations each time it runs.

For each meta-moderation, the task reviews the meta-moderator votes. The most popular option, either "fair" or "unfair", rules the day. In case of a tie, the moderation is ruled as fair. Otherwise, *moderatord* divides the meta-moderators into two groups: those who agreed with the ultimate result and those who disagreed. For example, if eight users rule a moderation fair and two mark it unfair, the eight would be put in a pile labeled "consenters" and the two in a pile labeled "dissenters".

To uncover suspicious meta-moderation, *moderatord* uses two configuration variables. `m2_minority_trigger` specifies an allowed percentage of disagreement. If the number of dissenters divided by the total number of meta-moderators is less than this ratio, Slash penalizes the dissenters the number of karma points stored in `m2_dissension_penalty`.† If a meta-moderator disagrees often enough, he will find himself unable to meta-moderate. Luckily, the default values of the configuration variables make it very unlikely that an innocent black sheep will be penalized for an honest disagreement. The penalized moderations are also updated, with their flag set to the value 8, for easy administrative access. (The SQL command *SELECT*

---

* For larger sites, this may be counterproductive. On Slashdot, the `stirPool` method in *Slash::DB::Static::MySQL* never recycles points. A significant portion of the thousands of points bestowed weekly go unused. Eventually, Slashdot would be overrun with excess points—far more than the number of moderatable comments. Experimentation is the only way to know how well this will work on your site.

† Though the default value of this variable is –1, its *absolute value* is subtracted from the user's karma.

mmid, uid FROM metamodlog WHERE flag = '8'; will find all questionable meta-moderations and the user ID of the meta-moderators.)

Having punished malicious users as necessary, *moderatord* next rewards diligent meta-moderators. If the ratio of consensus to dissent exceeds the value of m2_consensus_trigger, the system randomly bestows m2_reward_pool points. A user can receive only one karma point per reward period, though. Also, users cannot exceed maxkarma points. It next updates the database, marking the meta-moderations as processed.

If the messaging plugin is installed, the task prepares a message summarizing the results of the reconciliation, including the comment details and the consensus judgment of the meta-moderators.

moderatord uses a special template to format its logs, found in *data;misc;default*. The getData function in the *Slash* package loads the *data* template. This is an unwieldy beast, containing several smaller Sections that don't yet merit their own templates. The *moderatord* task records vital information on the number of comments, the number of recycled tokens, the pool of eligible moderators, and the freshly promoted moderators. This file can rapidly grow quite large, so be sure to rotate it regularly.

The portald Task

The *portald* task has the all-important job of fetching fresh content from other web sites. Even if a user has read or skipped all of the current Stories, she may find an eye-catching link to somewhere else. This task simply fetches all portald blocks from the database, requests the contents of the associated URLs, and updates the blocks in the database with the results.

When *portald* first runs, it writes a message to its log file, *portald.log*, in the site-specific log directory. Next, it checks for any site-specific retrieval tasks. If the site's *sbin/* directory contains a file named *portald-site*, the task will execute it. This file can be used to update anything besides a block, such as the *motd* (message of the day) template. In practice, it may be easier to create a new task, but you have the option.

Next, *portald* fetches information about all blocks with with the retrieve field set to 1. It retrieves remoted RSS files by way of the *XML::RSS* module. This can fail if the remote site is unreachable or if the RSS file is invalid. The task logs an error in this case. Otherwise, the block replaces the current contents of the block, *in memory* with the decoded RSS information. Note that the task will make some attempts to handle broken XML gracefully. Several feeds fail to encode the "&" character correctly, for example.

Not all blocks have to be associated with RSS feeds. *portald* updates a few special blocks. For example, it chooses a random block to be the next "rand" block. It counts the latest poll votes and updates the Pollbooth block. It runs the *uptime* and *ps aux* commands to gather server and site statistics for the special uptime Slashbox.

Finally, *portald* commits all of the changed blocks to the database. It calls `newSemi-RandomBlock` in the *portald-site* file, if it both exist. The task then logs a final message and exits.

A single configuration variable modifies *portald* behavior. `http_proxy` allows a firewalled site to communicate with the outside world through another. By default, *portald* runs once an hour, at 37 minutes past the hour. Popular sites may wish to increase this value slightly, though it's considered impolite to request an RSS file more than once every 20 minutes. If 1,000 bots requested your files every 30 seconds, actual human readers would have trouble getting through. Be kind.

The task writes its process ID to the *portald.pid* file in the site log directory. This means that only one process can update the site at a time. (It should not be an issue, but it can happen.) If it fails to run, portald blocks will not be updated regularly. If this happens, check to see if a stale *pid* file is blocking access. The log file will contain an error in this case.

Slash Utilities

Though (or because) it's a web site management program, Slash comes with several command-line utilities to make your life easier. It's possible to run a successful site without ever using any of these programs, but they're fiercely useful. Of the programs in the Slash binaries directory (*/usr/local/slash/bin/*), the most important is *install-slashsite*, which was described way back in the section "Installing the Slash Site" in Chapter 2. The other utilities are invoked in a similar fashion.

template-tool

The *template-tool* utility provides access to templates stored in the database. If you are proficient with a Unix text editor, this is the most conveninent way to work with templates.* As with all Slash utilities, the tool is invoked from the command line. The single most important option is the -u flag. It takes one argument: the virtual user of the site. The default value is `slash`; if that is the name of your virtual user, you may skip this flag. The other all-important option is -h, which briefly

---

* Jon Udell (*http://udell.roninhouse.com/*) and his newsgroup have discussed ways to improve the lackluster editing controls available in modern web browsers. To date, there is no robust, cross-platform solution.

describes the other available flags. The program will exit if this option is present, regardless of the presence of any other flags.

Editing templates is much easier with *template-tool.* To modify `index;index;` `default`, first extract it from the database to the filesystem. Edit it with your preferred text editor. Finally, update the database with the file. The following example assumes a virtual user of `chelle`:

```
[slash@waterwheel /home/slash]$ /usr/local/slash/bin/template-tool
-u chelle -d index
dumping template to ./index;index;default
dumping template to ./index;index;light

[slash@waterwheel /home/slash]$ vi index\;index\;default

[slash@waterwheel /home/slash]$ /usr/local/slash/bin/template-tool
-u chelle -s index\;index\;default
```

Several things are notable in this example. First, beware of the template naming convention. Some Unix shells (including GNU *bash,* the default on many Linux distributions) use a semicolon to separate commands on a single line. These characters must be escaped, or the shell will interpret them as such, instead of passing them to *template-tool.* Also note the –d and –s flags. The former dumps named templates to files, and the latter saves files to the database. These files are in the same format as files in theme and plugin *templates/* directories. Finally, the –d flag does not take an option. If provided, the template name must be the last value on the command line. If you forget this, you will get odd results.

If you know the name of the template you wish to edit, this is a great solution. Otherwise, the –l flag will list all installed templates. This is handy, but can produce several dozen screens of data. For the purpose of this discussion, only one is shown here:

```
[slash@waterwheel /home/slash]$ /usr/local/slash/bin/template-tool -u chelle -l
--------------------------------------------------------
Tpid: 122 Name: index
Page: index Section: default

Description:
This is the main block of html and code that gets evaled to create the main
index page.

* is_moderator = boolean for whether current user has moderator access
* stories = string containing all the stories
* boxes = string containing all the slashboxes
--------------------------------------------------------
```

The first section shows the template's vital statistics. This example uses *index;index;default,* which has a unique ID of 122 in the database. (This will vary between installations.) It includes the description and lists the variables passed to the template. This is usually sufficient information to find the appropriate template to edit.

Armed with this information, it's easier to correct a flaw in the admittedly contrived first example: specifying only a name of "index" dumped two *index* templates. There are several options. Using the -i flag tells *template-tool* to interpret the name as the template ID. The -S and -P options specify the template page and Section, respectively. The following commands are all functionally equivalent for this installation:

```
[slash@waterwheel /home/slash]$ /usr/local/slash/bin/template-tool
-u chelle -d -i 122

[slash@waterwheel /home/slash]$ /usr/local/slash/bin/template-tool
-u chelle -S default -d index

[slash@waterwheel /home/slash]$ /usr/local/slash/bin/template-tool
-u chelle -S default -P index -d index
```

The Section and page flags can both act as wildcards. If no template ID or template name were provided, *template-tool* would work on all templates matching those criteria. A little imprecision when dumping templates is acceptable, but can be very dangerous when updating or deleting templates. It is far better to provide too much information than too little. If you can manage it, using the template ID is the most accurate method.

template-tool can also be used to create new templates with the -B (for Boilerplate) option. It takes one argument, the name of the file to create. This name has no bearing on the name of the template; it is used only for temporary storage and editing. If there is a template name (as opposed to the filename) provided, the tool will use it when writing the new template. Otherwise, the new template will have a name of *generic*. This option also respects the -P and -S flags, if they are present. The default values are misc and default, respectively. The following example creates a file named *newtemplate*, describing a template named *index* in the Cats Section:

```
[slash@waterwheel /home/slash]$ /usr/local/slash/bin/template-tool
-u chelle -B newtemplate -S cats index
```

The resulting file (*newtemplate*) will need to be edited. Its contents will resemble:

```
__section__
cats
__description__
You should describe stuff here.
__title__
Useless title to template
__page__
misc
```

```
__lang__
en_US
__name__
index
__template__
This is where you would put all of your HTML and such to be displayed. See
Template(3) for more information about syntax.
__seclev__
10000
```

runtask

The *runtask* program is used to run tasks manually, without having to wait for their next scheduled execution time. This is handy for testing and for tasks that normally execute only once a day. It can be used to run any task in a site's *tasks/* directory. As with all other Slash utilities, the –u flag provides the virtual username associated with the site. The only other required argument is the name of the task to run.

The following example runs the *new_motd.pl* task for the virtual user chelle. Note that the ".pl" extension is not necessary in the task name. It can be included or excluded.

[slash@waterwheel /home/slash]$ **/usr/local/slash/bin/runtask -u chelle new_motd**

The –o flag allows you to pass a string of options to the task. These take the form of "key=value" and are separated by commas. The *counthits.pl* task parses data from the accesslog table and updates Story counts accordingly. It supports three options: since (parse hits only since this date), replace (replace the Story's hit total, do not add to it), and sid (update only one Story). To update the hits since 8 September 2001 on the Story identified by 01/09/06/1236215, the command would be:

[slash@waterwheel /home/slash]$ **/usr/local/slash/bin/runtask -u chelle**
-o since=20010908,sid=01/09/06/1236215 counthits

Note that the name of the task must be the final argument on the line. Also beware that, in the case of duplicate keys passed with the –o flag, the value of the latter pair will overwrite that of the former.

As a final caveat, *runtask* attempts to switch to the system user associated with a site. On the waterwheel machine, attempting to run a task for stampworld (system user jojo) as the system user associated with chelledot (slash) produces an error:

[slash@waterwheel /home/slash]$ **/usr/local/slash/bin/runtask -u tara run_portald**

```
can't set uid/gid to 507/509 (503/503 230 100 81 10 500)
at /usr/local/slash/bin/runtask line 188, <GEN0> line 1.
```

Either run this program as the root user (who has the ability to switch user and group IDs) or as the system user associated with the site (which obviates the need to switch IDs):

```
[jojo@waterwheel /home/slash]$ /usr/local/slash/bin/runtask -u tara run_portald

Sat Nov 10 19:10:33 2001 runtask run_portald.pl begin
Sat Nov 10 19:10:37 2001 runtask run_portald.pl end:   (ran in 3.08s)
```

Slash Architecture

With Slash up and running, you will probably want to make things look a little more homey. The key to advanced customization is understanding how Slash fits together. This appendix walks through the basic design and explains how things run. It is intended to help you understand how the individual components work, so you will be prepared to make your own changes.

The Apache Request Cycle

Slash is tied heavily to the Apache request cycle. Further, it is broken into multiple components, each supported by its own libraries. This modularization makes it possible to modify one kind of behavior without having to know how the underlying support structure works. The only pieces of Slash that do not fit this model are the housekeeping daemons, covered in the section "The Slash Daemon and Tasks" in Chapter 11.

Apache begins life by reading its configuration file, performing any initializations its modules require (see Figure A-1). Slash uses this stage to initialize several of its own components. For instance, the guest user is created during this stage. Slash also creates all of the menus for a site and stores all of the constant site configuration data (e.g., site name, document root, administrator name, etc.) in a hash. Consequently, any changes to this information require a complete restart of the web server to take effect. Global requirements are stored in */usr/local/slash/httpd/slash.conf,* and each site has its own configuration file in the root of its site directory. This information can be retrieved with the getCurrentStatic function.

Slash uses the *Apache::ModuleConfig* Perl module to store this data. It provides each Slash and Apache module with its own space for storing module-specific data. Because this information is stored on a per-site basis, it is possible to host

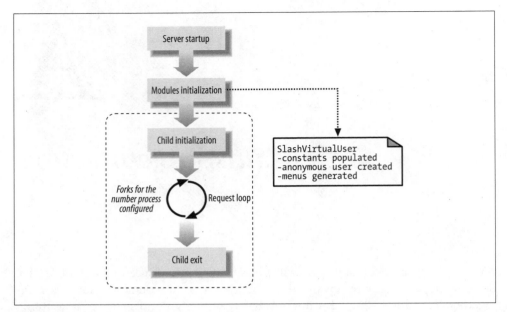

Figure A-1. Apache startup

multiple Slash sites for different groups on a single server, without fear of one group modifying information for another group. This allows Slash to be used in an ASP environment.

After the initialization stage, the server begins to handle requests. Apache breaks each request into two stages (see Figure A-2). The first stage is URI translation, in which the server decides which resource to send to the client. On large Slash sites, the index page can be cached to disk on a regular basis, and guest users can be redirected there. Users with authentication credentials are sent to the next stage, to see if they really can be authenticated.

Requests for user information via the "~" URI are also handled at this layer. This makes it easy for users to look each other up through a common convention. (For example, see *http://slashdot.org/~krow/*.) Both of these options can be enabled by uncommenting the appropriate `PerlTransHandler` directives in the site configuration file.

Requests then pass through the authentication layer. Users are logged in, if possible, and several objects (user and form data, as well as cookies) are created and stored for use in site applets and libraries. If you write any of your own handlers, be aware that these objects are invalid until this stage.

All registered users have a unique user ID, which is the primary mechanism used to identify users. The user object is populated with values from the database (see Appendix D). This object will be used throughout the request, and some values

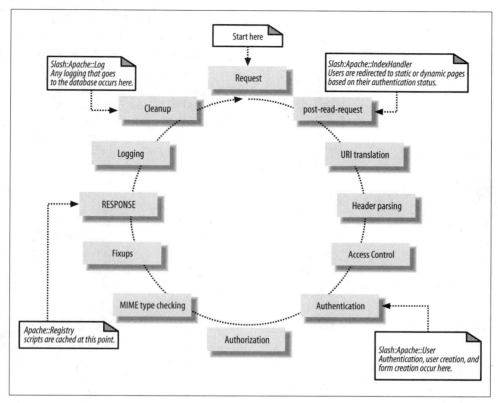

Figure A-2. the Apache request cycle

may be modified temporarily. For example, if a user changes her comment view, the view type will change in the user object, but will not be saved to the database. Two additional flags may be set. If the user has not been authenticated as a registered user, the anonymous flag will be true. If the user is authenticated and has a security level over 100, an administrator flag will be set to true (the section "Editing Authors" in Chapter 3 describes the different possible seclevs).

Similarly, a form object is created from any CGI parameters found in either the query string or as the body of a POST request. This object is also available to subsequent stages of the request. Certain pieces of information are also used in the user object, namely cookie information (an *Apache::Cookie* object).

In the next stage, Apache calls the applets through *Apache::Registry*. These programs are compiled only the first time they are accessed. All future requests call the compiled versions, for a nice speed boost. While all applets are unique, they have several commonalities. For example, all applets determine the pages they will display based on an op key. These keys are referred to as *opcodes*.

Finally, Slash collects data from the user request and stores it in the database with a custom log module. Though Apache has a logging stage, Slash uses the cleanup stage so that the work occurs after the user has disconnected from the web server. The collected information is used to calculate statistics, update user records, and calculate changes to user karma. The requested page is also recorded without its file extension. Any extra information passed to the `Slash::Utility::writelog` function is also stored, along with the parameters used in the request. The child process then returns to the available pool, awaiting a new request. If you need to record additional information on your site, look at the *Slash::Apache::Log* module.

How Information Is Stored

Slash is very much tied to the database and was designed around the idea that all data will come from the database. Despite this, it tries to avoid being tied to any one database and fetching as little data as necessary. All information in Slash finds its way to the database at one point or another. Generated pages also come from the database but not always through a direct path.

Inheritance and Database Independence

All Slash libraries that access the database follow a standard method of achieving database independence. Consider *Slash::DB*, the core library used to gain information about the internal workings of the system. A client application gains access to the *Slash::DB* object's methods by calling it:

```
my $user = getCurrentVirtualUser();
my $slashdb = Slash::DB->new($user);
```

A *DBIx::Password* virtual username provides the *Slash::DB* object with two vital pieces of information. First, the library provides a handler to the correct database. Second, it can tell the module what type of database is being used. (Only MySQL and PostgreSQL are supported. As of this writing, Oracle support is not yet finished.) This is all the information that a well-written library needs. At no point should any application that uses a database from Slash need to understand anything specific to the database. If you decide to extend Slash, keep to this rule, or you will find that porting will become an even larger, hairier gorilla.

To provide their objects with the ability to reuse database handles, cache prepared statements, and recover from failure robustly, all database objects inherit from *Slash::DB::Utility*. This parent class also provides default new, get, set, create, and exists methods. If you use this library, you will find it much easier to create your own database objects.

Cache Is King

Web site systems typically go through the same evolutionary stages. They begin by using flat files (sometimes exclusively). Display is hardcoded and is troublesome to modify. They eventually migrate to a database, making things much easier to edit. Soon, the administrators discover that even the fastest, best-designed database cannot keep up with the page view rate of a large web site. Though Slash uses the database heavily, it gets around this limitation by caching as much data as possible in the Apache process. It also writes as many pages as possible to flat files, so that the database does not have to be called as often. Because of the cache, RAM is the single most important physical factor in running Slash.

Before you customize your site in any detail, you need to understand how the cache works. Slash's aggressive caching enables sites to scale to large volumes of served pages. Anything that may not change frequently is cached. This trades memory for speed, with convincing results. At the time of this writing, the cached index page needed to execute only 3 SELECTs on the database, while the non-cached page cost 37. Keep in mind, however, that caching can work against you. If you change a template or add a new Topic and notice that the old information is still present, you're probably getting stale information.

The default installation assumes the resulting site will be medium to very large. The Slashcode web site has additional information about tuning to use less resources. Slash has been run on a low-end server with only 64 MB of RAM, though it required several modifications to the Apache configuration files. In a similar situation, change `cache_enabled` to a false value and set the maximum number of allowed Apache processes to a very low number (5, for example). This can also be helpful when designing a site. It will be slower serving pages, but faster than having to restart the web server to see significant changes. Disabling the cache on a production site is inadvisable unless your server has very low memory and a very low page view rate.

Caching begins in the startup stage of the Apache request cycle. Certain variables are stored before the initial fork occurs, leaving them in shared memory. These variables include the site configuration variables, template names, and data for the Anonymous User. Because of this, any new templates or changed variables will not be visible until the server is restarted. Edited templates will be fine.

Other components are cached only for a shorter period of time. They are divided into two camps. The first contains methods such as `Slash::DB::getDescriptions`, which returns information used for most drop-down menus in the system. This data is cached separately in each child process. If the `MaxRequest` directive is set to handle 10,000 requests (as is recommended), any cached menu will last for a maximum of 10,000 requests. The second camp of cached data is timed. This group includes Stories, blocks, and templates. Stories honor the `stories_cache` variable, blocks and templates the `block_expire` setting.

How Information Is Displayed

All of the HTML rendered in user agents comes from templates. Templates themselves are the core of the display system, determining the look and feel of the site. Template logic all lives in the *Slash::Display* module and the `slashDisplay` function, which are described in the section "Display Functions" in Appendix D. Templates are called either directly from applets or from widgets. Widgets are a holdover from earlier versions of Slash (found in the *Slash* module, where elephants go to die). In modern versions, widgets are used only for drawing boxes with the *fancybox* template. For example, to draw a sidebar box on a page, use the `Slash::templatebox` function, passing the name of the template to use. Similar calls exist for creating Poll Booth and portald Slashboxes.

To improve performance, templates are compiled and cached. The cache keeps only a set number of compiled templates in memory. This can be controlled by the `template_cache_size` configuration variable. One final note: the template language attribute is currently unused. It is intended to support internationalization, which is not yet complete.

Slash Directory Structures

The first glimpse of Slash's odd bundle of files and directories may evoke memories of using Unix for the first time. Navigating the interconnections to find one specific file is difficult without some sort of roadmap. Take heart. For the most part, there's an underlying organization behind the apparent chaos. Understanding how everything fits together is very important to advanced customization.

The Slash Home Directory

The Slash home directory (*/usr/local/slash*, by default) holds several files and directories. A typical directory listing could be:

```
[slash@firewheel /usr/local/slash]$ ls -lp
total 9
drwxr-xr-x    2 slash    slash    1024 Aug 22 16:22 bin/
drwxr-xr-x    2 slash    slash    1024 Aug 22 16:43 httpd/
drwxr-xr-x   11 slash    slash    1024 Aug 22 16:23 plugins/
drwxr-xr-x    2 slash    slash    1024 Aug 22 16:45 sbin/
drwxr-xr-x    3 slash    slash    1024 Aug 22 16:27 site/
-rw-r--r--    1 slash    slash      22 Aug 22 16:27 slash.sites
```

```
-rw-r--r--    1 slash    slash          6 Aug 22 16:44 slashd.slash.pid
drwxr-xr-x    5 slash    slash       1024 Aug 22 16:22 sql/
drwxr-xr-x    3 slash    slash       1024 Aug 22 16:23 themes/
```

This directory holds data and utilities for all of the Slash sites installed on the server. For example, files in the *bin/* directory are standard administrative tools. They can be used on any installed site, given a proper *DBIx::Password* virtual user. (This will be covered later.)

Perhaps the most important file in this directory is *slash.sites*. This is a very simple configuration file, used to install new sites and schedule tasks. Each separate site has an entry. On a server hosting three sites, this file might read:

```
slash:slash:firewheel
roger:zelazny:ghostwheel
annie:dillard:prayerwheel
```

The firewheel site uses a virtual user named `slash` and a system user of the same name. ghostwheel uses the `roger` virtual user and the `zelazny` system user. The prayerwheel site follows the same pattern.

The Slash/Apache configuration files live in *httpd/*. The *slash.conf* file contains Apache directives used to enable the installed sites. It tells *mod_perl* to compile and include all of the Perl modules necessary to run Slash. The *slash.conf.def* file holds the default values and is used to generate a new configuration file, if necessary. These files live under the Slash home directory for the sake of convenience—they are easier to find and modify this way.

The *plugins/* directory holds all installed plugins. Each plugin should create its own named subdirectory. For example, the Journal plugin lives in *plugins/Journal/*, relative to the Slash home directory. Plugins are described more fully in the section "Themes and Plugins" in Chapter 10.

The *sbin/* directory contains the Slash daemon and tasks (*moderatord, portald,* and *slashd*). The Slash daemon (*slashd*) runs these automatically, as detailed in the section "The Slash Daemon and Tasks" in Chapter 11. They can also be run as necessary through supplementary programs in *bin/*.

The *site/* directory holds individual site directories. The firewheel machine hosts a public site available as firewheel and a testing site called localhost. The *site/* directory contains a subdirectory for each. The site-specific directories are described in the next section.

```
[slash@firewheel /usr/local/slash/site]# ls -lp
total 2
drwxr-xr-x    8 slash    slash       1024 Aug 22 16:27 firewheel/
drwxr-xr-x    8 slash    slash       1024 Aug 22 16:29 localhost/
```

The *sql/* directory holds the SQL commands used to install a new site. These are arranged further by database type. For example, if *install-slashsite* creates a new site running on MySQL, it will execute all of the SQL files in the *sql/mysql/* directory. These files install the basic tables and indexes and fill in the basic default values.

The *themes/* directory holds all installed themes. As with plugins, a theme in this directory is made available to installed sites, but it is not installed unless explicitly selected with either the *install-slashsite* or *install-theme* utility. On a fresh installation of Slash 2.2, this does not matter because it includes only the slashcode theme. This is, of course, installed in *themes/slashcode/*. Themes are described in the section "Themes and Plugins" in Chapter 10.

Slash Site Directories

Each individual site running on a Slash server has its own directory, holding site-specific logs, configuration files, and installed web programs and files. The firewheel site's directory is:

```
[slash@firewheel /usr/local/slash/site/firewheel]$ ls -lp
total 8
drwxr-xr-x    2 slash    slash         1024 Aug 22 16:27 backups/
drwxr-xr-x    3 slash    slash         1024 Aug 22 16:27 htdocs/
-rw-r--r--    1 slash    slash         1607 Aug 22 16:27 firewheel.conf
drwxr-xr-x    2 slash    slash         1024 Aug 27 12:25 logs/
drwxr-xr-x    2 slash    slash         1024 Aug 27 12:24 misc/
drwxr-xr-x    2 slash    slash         1024 Aug 22 16:27 sbin/
drwxr-xr-x    2 slash    slash         1024 Aug 22 16:27 tasks/
```

The only file in this directory is the all-important site configuration file. Like the directory itself, it derives its name from the name of the site it supports. In this case, the firewheel site lives in the *firewheel* directory and is configured by the *firewheel.conf* file. Like *slash.conf*, this file also contains Apache directives. It sets up a virtual host for the site, binding to a port and IP address and specifying the site's root directory. The *install-slashsite* program creates this file automatically and edits *slash.conf* file to include it.

It is possible to perform site-specific configuration within this file. For example, the default behavior is not to compile site templates when the server starts. This compilation step saves time in the long run but costs extra memory and slows startup. To enable this feature, set the `SlashCompileTemplates` directive to "On". A less drastic optimization is to uncomment the `PerlTransHandler` directive, allowing Apache to redirect anonymous users to the static page generated by a scheduled task. Any other Apache or *mod_perl* directive that makes sense within a Virtual-Host block can be added to this file.

The *backups/* directory is created automatically but is currently unused. In the future, Slash may add a task that automatically stores site backups here. In the meantime, it is a good place for weekly log backups, if they're important to you.

The *htdocs/* directory holds all applets, images, and HTML files intended to be publicly accessible to Slash web users. This directory also contains an *images/* subdirectory, which contains a directory named *topics/*. As described in the section "Installing the Slash Site" in Chapter 2, many of the default files may be symbolic links to plugins and theme files installed serverwide. For example, the *admin.pl* applet on firewheel is linked to */usr/local/slash/plugins/Admin/admin.pl*. Similarly, *comments.pl* points to */usr/local/slash/themes/slashcode/htdocs/comments.pl*.

These directories can contain standard HTML files, executable files separate from Slash, and images. Apache will serve any other file as its configuration dictates. This allows site administrators to add web pages to a Slash site which are not necessarily managed by Slash. In practice, this may be little used.*

The *logs/* directory hosts site-specific log files. This includes daemon logs and *pid* files, such as *slashd.log* and *slashd.pid*. By default, this directory does not contain the site's Apache logs. Instead, they may be found in */usr/local/apache/logs/*.† The names of these logs take the format *sitename_access_log* and *sitename_error_log*. In a multiple–web server configuration, each server will keep its own logs.

The *misc/* directory contains miscellaneous data files. These normally supplement various plugins and themes. The files are usually symbolic links to the appropriate sitewide plugin or theme directory.

The *sbin/* directory holds administrative programs and daemons. There are currently no files installed here by default.

The *tasks/* directory contains task files. These are small programs run automatically by the *slashd* daemon to perform housekeeping at regular intervals. Many plugins and themes add their own tasks, so files here are usually symbolic links to the actual tasks stored in the appropriate sitewide directory.

Slash Theme Directories

Themes are installed on a serverwide basis. Each theme has an eponymous subdirectory within */usr/local/slash/themes/*. This directory contains a *THEME* file, which lists the theme components by type. The theme installer uses this file to determine

---

* Be aware that any files with the *.pl*, *.shtml*, or *.inc* extensions will be handled by handlers defined in *sitename.conf*. Consult this file for more details.

† This may be configured by editing the `ErrorLog` and `CustomLog` directives in the site configuration file.

how and where to install the theme. The directory of the default slashcode theme resembles:

```
[slash@firewheel /usr/local/slash/site/themes/slashcode]# ls -lp
total 19
-rw-r--r--    1 slash     slash         7606 Aug 22 16:22 THEME
drwxr-xr-x    2 slash     slash         1024 Aug 22 16:22 backup/
drwxr-xr-x    3 slash     slash         1024 Aug 22 16:23 htdocs/
drwxr-xr-x    2 slash     slash         1024 Aug 22 16:22 logs/
drwxr-xr-x    2 slash     slash         1024 Aug 22 16:23 misc/
drwxr-xr-x    5 slash     slash         1024 Aug 22 16:23 sql/
drwxr-xr-x    2 slash     slash         1024 Aug 22 16:23 tasks/
drwxr-xr-x    2 slash     slash         5120 Aug 22 16:23 templates/
```

The *backup/* directory is currently unused.

The *htdocs/* directory contains applets and HTML files, as well as an *images/* subdirectory. All files that produce output for users directly live in this directory. Themes can add any kind of file Apache can serve, as well as subdirectories. For example, the slashcode theme includes several new Topic icons in the *images/topics/* subdirectory.

The *logs/* directory can hold logs and other supplementary files for tasks associated with a theme. It is unused by default.

The *misc/* directory holds miscellaneous data files for the theme. The slashcode theme contains the *spamarmor* file, featuring several Perl regular expressions used to spam-proof user email addresses.

The *sql/* directory holds SQL files used to create or modify the database during theme installation. By convention, each supported database type should have its own subdirectory. This allows the installer to choose the appropriate SQL commands for the site.*

The *tasks/* directory contains tasks associated with the theme. This will be scheduled and executed by *slashd* automatically.

The *templates/* directory is the most important theme subdirectory. It holds the template files that produce output. These are not used directly from the filesystem, however. Straight from the tarball, all template files have extra, nonprintable data. The theme installer breaks these files apart and inserts the results into the templates table in the database. These files follow a very strict naming scheme, discussed in the sidebar "How Slash Calls Templates" in Appendix C.

---

* Though Slash has offered *some* support for PostgreSQL and Oracle, only MySQL is officially supported. Any SQL files that create or modify tables will probably need some porting to other databases. This is a good place to get involved with the Slashcode project.

While this is an excellent place to find a specific template, modifying the files in this directory will have no effect on an installed theme. This directory highlights an interesting Slash design decision. While it would be easier to install templates from a SQL file, it is more convenient for users and coders to read and modify templates as files (especially with the *template-tool*). As discussed in the section "Finding what to change" in Chapter 10, finding the right thing to change is easier with a directory full of files than with a database full of text.

Slash Plugin Directories

Themes and plugins are very similar. Each installed plugin has its own named subdirectory beneath */usr/local/slash/plugins/*. All files needed to install and to run the plugin live in this directory. The most important file is the *PLUGIN* file, used by *install-slashsite* to install the plugin. As you should expect by now, plugin files will be symbolically linked or copied to site-specific directories during this process. A typical (if contrived) plugin directory will resemble:

```
[slash@firewheel /usr/local/slash/plugins/SamplePlugin]# ls -lp
total 5
-rw-r--r--    1 slash    slash        231 Aug 22 16:22 PLUGIN
-rwxr-xr-x    1 slash    slash       6543 Aug 22 16:22 SamplePlugin.pm
-rwxr-xr-x    1 slash    slash       1429 Aug 22 16:23 sampleplugin.pl
drwxr-xr-x    2 slash    slash       1024 Aug 22 16:23 sql/
drwxr-xr-x    2 slash    slash       1024 Aug 22 16:23 tasks/
drwxr-xr-x    2 slash    slash       1024 Aug 22 16:23 templates/
```

A plugin may include multiple applet files (*sampleplugin.pl*) and associated Perl modules (*SamplePlugin.pm*). These must follow normal Perl and *mod_perl* rules. Modules can be nestled in subdirectories if their package names so require.

Most modules include a *templates/* directory, containing templates specific to the plugin. Plugins can also include tasks in a *tasks/* directory. For example, a plugin might collect hourly statistics or retrieve files from external sites. Many plugins also include SQL files, within the *sql/* directory, to modify the database. Most of the default plugins have generic enough SQL to work on most databases without modification.

The only hard and fast plugin rule is that each must contain a *PLUGIN* file. Just like *THEME*, this associates files with types, so that *install-slashsite* can install files correctly. Any other organization, including directory consistency, only helps administrators. Don't miss the chance to make your life easier, though. The section "Inside the Slashprint Plugin" in Chapter 10 dissects a plugin, strictly for example purposes.

THEME and PLUGIN Directives

The *THEME* and *PLUGIN* installation files are very similar. They both share the same syntax and differ only in the order in which they are called. Themes are installed first so they can list which plugins they expect to exist. This allows themes to override templates provided by plugins. A theme or plugin is required to have the appropriate file in its root directory. The current directives for *THEME* and *PLUGIN* files are:

image
> An image to be placed into the site's image directory

topic
> An image to be placed into the site's Topic image directory

htdoc
> A file to be placed into the site's document root directory

task
> A file to be placed into the site's task directory

template
> a template to be installed into the site's database

mysql_prep
> SQL commands to be run to prepare the site's database (to create a new table or add fields to an existing table)

mysql_dump
> SQL commands to insert new data into the site's database

More directives are likely to be added over time. Right now, there are no means by which to require a certain version of any given theme or plugin, so the theme or plugin that is found is used.

Slash Libraries

Slash 1.x consisted of one big library that had to be added to Perl's include path manually. This was a suboptimal situation, with everything stuck in one huge file. Worse, there was no namespace protection. Slash 2.x split everything from *Slash.pm* into several separate libraries. (*Slash* still exists, but is reserved for legacy applications.) The Slash:: namespace is reserved for Slash modules on the CPAN. Note, however, that Slash does not follow a strict object-oriented design, as do many Perl modules. It uses OOP where the need is clear and other techniques where OOP is unnecessary.

Slash::Utility contains most of the common routines used to fetch data. It hosts getCurrentUser, getCurrentForm, and other functions commonly used when writing plugins. The library itself exports functions from several child modules. This is all hidden by *Slash::Utility* but should be kept in mind if you need to read the source code.

Slash::DB holds the Slash database logic. This governs everything that generates and works with SQL. This class has two important subclasses. *Slash::DB::Utility* holds all of the common, database-neutral methods. Database-specific functions live in modules named after the appropriate database, such as *Slash::DB::MySQL* for MySQL. (The PostgreSQL module actually inherits from the MySQL module, overriding a few functions as necessary. This makes it much easier to port Slash functions to a new database.)

The *Slash::Install* library holds all of the logic used by the different install scripts. This includes parsing the *PLUGIN* and *THEME* files. No methods are exported to web applets by default. It does include methods for modifying the site_info table.

While the previously mentioned libraries make up the bulk of the Slash API, most non-trivial plugins contain their own libraries—*Slash::Journal* for journals, *Slash::Messages* for the messaging system, and *Slash::Search* for the search routines, for example.

Some of these libraries have good documentation in POD format. Others offer little more than the source code. Reading the source is the last, but best, resort. The code itself is guaranteed to be the most up-to-date documentation. If you're feeling especially magnanimous, writing documentation is a great way to contribute to the project while teaching yourself the gory details.

B

Common Slash Database Tables

Slash is designed so that users (and administrators) should never really need to know anything about the underlying database, in normal operation. For programmers, the database is abstracted behind a standard programming interface. Furthermore, most of the display and calculation functions hide the existence of the database.

Keep in mind that when (not if) these tables change, any assumptions you have about the database will probably break your code. If the API is not flexible enough for your needs, consult the Slash development list to see if anyone else has found a solution. Even if nothing comes up, you stand a better chance of having a patch integrated into the main distribution. Your career as a Slash site administrator will be long and happy if you do not have to merge several custom patches with each upgrade. That said, there are several reasons why you might need to explore the database schema:

You want to write a plugin
> Most plugins will need to use only the API provided by *Slash::DB*, but certain data structures (such as $user) correspond very closely to table fields.

You want to use an unsupported database vendor
> You may also wish to use a database not directly supported by Slash, especially in an organization that is standardized on one platform. Porting Slash to a new database may be your only recourse. As of Version 2.2, Slash has run on three database platforms: MySQL, PostgreSQL, and Oracle. The Slashteam actively supports only MySQL. The others are maintained by outside groups and tend to lag behind slightly.

You want to extend the schema

> Here be Dragons. Modifying the schema is a good way to make upgrades extremely difficult. The current schema will look "wrong" by normalizing rules but has been optimized to assume that database time is much more expensive than processing time.

> Generally, people want to add additional fields for users or Stories. Slash allows for this with the "param" tables. They associate unique key/pair values with the primary keys on the users and stories tables. Sending additional key/value pairs to methods such as setUser() or setStory() will create additional parameters. They can be accessed as normal. This obviates most of the need for extra columns in the tables.

You need a key for a method

> The generic get and set methods from *Slash::DB* work directly on the tables, based on column names. Being familiar with the type of information stored will help you retrieve the information you need.

It really cannot be stressed enough that modifying the schema is the best way to get yourself into trouble with Slash. New versions of Slash will expect the default schema and will not upgrade modified versions well. The Slashteam makes no promises to freeze the schema between releases—it frequently changes even between minor versions. Scripts are provided to handle conversions during upgrades, however.

Foreign Keys

Slash was designed with MySQL in mind. MySQL lacks the traditional foreign-key relationship paradigm supported in most other relational databases. The Slash schema identifies these relationships but does not enforce them. If you delete any row containing the primary key of another table, you must take special care to remove all references. A common mistake is to remove a Topic without updating all Stories, polls, and discussions that refer to it.

The major keys are:

uid

> A unique integer used to identify users.

sid

> A unique identifier for Stories, based on the date of posting.

tid/topic

A unique identifier for Topics. In earlier versions, this was a string based on the Topic name. It is now an integer.

section

The string name of the Section to which a given object belongs.

qid

A unique identifier for a poll.

discussion

The unique identifier for a discussion. Discussions own comments.

If you are using MySQL, several SQL commands will come in handy. *DESC* `table` displays the column names and types that make up a table, *SHOW INDEX FROM* `table` shows the indexes active on a table, *SHOW TABLES* lists all of the tables within the current database, and *SHOW CREATE TABLE* `table` gives the SQL commands used to create the table.

When issuing SQL directly into the database, keep in mind that you are bypassing all of the safeties and business logic that Slash has in place to keep your site running smoothly. Sometimes, this is the only way to restore a site to working condition. Before working on a table, you may wish to create a backup. The SQL command *CREATE TABLE mytemp INSERT * from* `table` will do this. Use *DELETE* `table` and then *INSERT INTO* `table` *SELECT * FROM mytemp*.

Common Table Schemas

The following sections describe the basic groupings of tables. They do not include entity relationship diagrams or example create statements. These can be found in the *docs/* and *sql/* subdirectories, respectively. Because of the schema changes between versions, going into specific detail would render most of this information worthless. Consult the files provided with your specific version of Slash (including *docs/slashtables.pod*) for the latest information on the tables' current relationships, entities, and attributes.

Access Log

`access_log` will be the largest table on busy sites. It keeps track of all hits to HTML, SHTML, and Perl files. Because of its size, only two days' worth of content is ever kept. The purpose of this table is to create the nightly statistics and calculate the time when a user last used the system. It can also be used to create more detailed reports on site usage.* It contains the fields:

host_addr
> The address of the user who made the request

op
> The name of the page requested, without its file extension

uid
> The user ID of the user making the request

ts
> The date and time of the request

section
> The name of the Section to which the requested page belonged

query_string
> The arguments of the user request

dat
> A miscellaneous field used for additional information logged via `writeLog`

Authors Cache

For performance reasons, the `authors_cache` table contains information about all current and past site Authors. The `refresh_authors_cache` task rebuilds this table nightly. Consequently, if you set the `author` flag on a user, she will not be in the system until the next day. If this is a problem, consider running the task by hand. Nothing in this table is original data. It is all built from other tables.

Blocks

The block tables are a throwback to Slash versions before 2.0. Unless you are adding RSS files, it is best to avoid these tables. They may go through drastic changes in the future. These tables have only a few important attributes:

bid
> The name of a block.

block
> The contents of a block.

---

* To log additional information to this table, modify the `handler` function in *Slash::Apache::Log*.

seclev
>   The security level required to edit a block from the admin interface.

type
>   Whether a block is a portald or a text block. This is almost always portald.

url
>   The URL of the RSS file to be requested.

ordernum
>   The default position of a block on a page.

Code Params

The `code_param` table holds most of the "codes" for the site. These are key/value pairs used in drop-down and pop-up menus. This table makes it easier to change the labels of menu items, to make things clearer, or to translate them into other languages. There is currently no web interface to modify these values, so they must be changed with SQL commands.

Discussions, Comments, and Moderation

The comment tables have changed drastically in successive versions of the code. As Slashdot has grown, the comment system had to be redesigned to handle ever-increasing traffic loads. Each entity within the comment tables represents a single comment. The notable fields are:

uid
>   The user ID of the user who posted the comment

lastmod
>   The user ID of the last user to moderate the comment

reason
>   The last moderation label applied to the comment

pid
>   The comment ID of the parent comment, used to build the threaded view

points
>   The current score of the comment

Moderation information is kept with a comment to allow Slash to undo moderations when the moderator posts to a Story. The moderation tables belong to the discussion system. As comments are attached to discussions (not just Stories), there is also a `sid` attribute in the comment table. (It keeps this name for historical reasons.)

Content Filters

The content_filters table holds data for all of the content filters in the system, as described in the section "Comment Filters" in Chapter 6. Keep in mind that filters are created and then defined. If you are not careful, you can end up cluttering this table with filters that were never defined.

formkeys

The formkeys table contains unique keys created whenever a user accesses a form. These control how quickly and how often a user can make a submission and can help prevent bots from filling up the submission bin, posting junk comments, and other denial of service attacks.

Site Information

The site_info table holds information about the installation of the site. This information is viewable through the *Info* link in the Admin menu. It cannot be modified through the web interface and is changed only when additional plugins or themes are installed.

Menus

The menus table contains all of the information needed to create menus for any page. For example, the *admin* entries are used to build the Admin menu. It is read when Apache first starts up (as described in Appendix A). There is no way to add or delete entries from the web interface at this point. The important attributes of this table are:

seclev
> The minimum seclev a user needs to view this menu.

menuorder
> The order in which a menu entry will appear in the list. If multiple items have the same value, they will appear in the order in which they were added to the table.

label
> The name of the menu that appears in the menu bar.

Polls

Polls take up three tables. pollquestions lists the current questions and their total vote counts. pollanswers contains the poll answers. For now, questions are limited to eight answers apiece. This is only a limitation of the interface. The final table, pollvoters, keeps track of the daily votes. This is designed to prevent users from voting multiple times in a day and is wiped clean every night. All three tables use the qid key from the pollquestions table to represent a single poll.

Related Links

The related_links table represents the related links displayed with a Story from */articles.pl.* The structure is quite simple. A keyword is associated with a link and a name title. Only admins with a seclev of 10,000 can edit this table through the *Keywords* link of the Admin menu.

Sections and Topics

The sections and topics tables hold information for each Section and Topic in the system. Each entity represents a unique Topic or Section. The sections table also keeps the current article count and the current poll question for the Section. Deleting rows from these tables will orphan Stories. This will produce Stories with no Topics to be displayed or Stories that cannot be found (if they were published within the Section only). This is an excellent way to destabilize your site.

The section_topics table keeps track of Topics assigned to Sections. It has two attributes. The first is section, the primary key of the sections table. The second is tid, the primary key from topics.

Sessions

The session table keeps track of Author and administrator sessions. This allows you to see what your peers are doing, which is especially handy in preventing duplicate Story updates. In the 1.x versions of Slash, this table was also used to authenticate Authors. Expect to see this table changed or removed in favor of a system that can track all users.

Stories

The Story tables hold data on all accepted Stories. The stories table also holds pointers to other tables with related information (such as comment headers and Topic IDs). An important additional table is story_param. If the setStory() function is called with a key that is not part of the standard Stories schema, it will add the data to the story_param table. This can be used to attach additional information to a Story (for example, a screenshot.) Slash validates values by looking in the section_extras table. There is no web interface to this table yet. Notable attributes are:

aid

> The UID of the author who created the Story

title

> The title of the Story

introtext

> The introductory text of the Story

bodytext

> The optional extended text of the Story

relatedtext

> The contents of the `Related Text` box attached to the Story

writestatus

> A flag indicating whether to display the Story

Submissions

The `submissions` table holds all potential Stories that have ever been submitted to the site. Slash never deletes information from this table. When a submission is deleted in the Submissions menu, it is removed only from the display list. Depending on diskspace and site traffic, it's worth archiving and/or deleting old Stories every now and then. (On Slashdot, this happens annually.) While old submissions may not seem relevant today, recalling previous Stories can be handy.

The delete field in the schema has three values. If the value is 0, the submission has not been touched. A value of 1 means that it was deleted without being posted, and a 2 means that it was posted. A future version of Slash will add a web interface to view deleted submissions.

Templates

Each row of the `templates` table represents a template. The keys are `name`, `section`, and `page`. An additional attribute is `language`, though it is currently unused. With the *template-tool*, there should be no need to touch this table. See the section "template-tool" in Chapter 11 for more details.

Users

User information is currently spread out over six tables. This is intended to reduce the amount of data in a single table. (Other databases can easily reduce this to two or three tables.) Like the Story tables, there is a `users_param` table. Calling the `setUser()` function with a new value will store the extra data in the `users_param` table with the user. The `author` flag is set this way. Following is a not-entirely-exhaustive list of the important user fields:

uid
>   A unique integer used to identify the user. This is automatically generated by the database.

nickname
>   The user's preferred "handle".

realemail
>   The user's real email address, used only for system mailings.

fakeemail
>   The email address displayed for the user. This exists to foil address harvesters employed by spammers.

homepage
>   A URL to the user's homepage.

password
>   The user's password, stored in an MD5 hash format.

signature
>   A hopefully witty slogan attached to the user's comments.

seclev
>   The user's security level.

matchname
>   A normalized form of the user's `nickname`, with letters forced to lowercase and spaces removed. This is used to prevent near-duplicate usernames.

realname
>   The user's real name.

bio
>   A short biography of the user.

totalmods
>   The total number of moderation points ever given to the user.

tokens
>   The current number of tokens the user has, used by the moderation system to grant moderation points.

lastgranted

The last date at which the user received moderation points.

karma

A very rough estimation of the user's participation in the site.

maillist

A boolean value to determine if the user wants to receive daily headline mailings.

totalcomments

The total number of comments ever posted by the user.

lastmm

The last comment meta-moderated by the user.

posttype

The user's preferred posting mode.

maxcommentsize

The maximum size of a comment to be displayed without being truncated. The full comment will be available by following a *Read the rest of this comment* link.

hardthresh

A boolean value that determins whether the user wants to see the availability of comments below his current threshold.

extopic

A list of Topics the user never wants to see displayed.

exaid

A list of Authors the user never wants to see displayed.

exsection

A list of Sections the user never wants to see displayed.

exboxes

A list of boxes the user wants to see on the site homepage.

willing

A boolean flag indicating if the user is willing to moderate.

dfid

The unique identifier of the date format the user prefers.

tzcode

> The time zone code corresponding to the user's preferred time zone.

noicons

> A boolean flag indicating whether the user wants to see icons.

light

> A boolean flag indicating whether the user wants to see the simple version of the site.

C

The Slash Template Language

Since Version 2.0, Slash has used Andy Wardley's excellent Template Toolkit (*http://www.template-toolkit.org/*) to separate content from presentation. This allows Authors and administrators to change the look and feel of the site without having to modify large amounts of Perl code. Of course, this does require learning a little bit about the Template Toolkit language, as well as a few Slash-specific additions.

Template Basics

Templates are text files with embedded rules for including and formatting variable data. These rules are called *directives*. The simplest directives merely tell the template processor to insert the contents of a named variable in the current location. (If it helps, think of them as serious "Mad-Libs".) A sample template might be:

```
Hello, [% name %].  How are you today?
```

If "Pater" were provided as the name variable, the output would be:

```
Hello, Pater.  How are you today?
```

Directives always occur within special tags so that the template processor and the readers can distinguish between regular text and instructions. The default Slash templates always use tags of the style [% DIRECTIVE %]. Each tag can contain multiple directives, separated by a semicolon. For clarity's sake, most of the examples in this appendix will use the more verbose style.

Variables (and templates) aren't limited to plain text. They can contain anything from HTML to XML to PostScript. In a Slash context, variables generally hold either plain text from the database or HTML used in menus.

Furthermore, variables can be modified within templates. New variables can be created. The following example creates two new variables (automagically spring-ing into existence, armed for battle), assigning values:

```
[% counter = 0 %]
[% fullname = "$firstname $lastname" %]
```

In the second directive, the variables `firstname` and `lastname` already exist. The leading sigil is used to distinguish between variable names and literal text. Other-wise, the template could not tell whether `fullname` should contain "firstname lastname"[*] or "Eva Dell-Harlow".[†]

Complex Template Variables

Variables can be arbitrarily complex. The Toolkit will go to great lengths to inter-pret a directive. For example, the following template will display a Slash user's nickname:

```
User: [% user.nickname %]
```

`user` may refer to a Perl hash table with a key named `nickname` or to a Perl object with a method named `nickname`. Within the template, they are functionally equiva-lent. The hard work goes on behind the scenes.

Lists and arrays[‡] are handled differently from hashes. Given an array named `user` containing two items, "KKelly" and "3659", the directives to access the first and second[§] elements are:

```
Nickname: [% user.0 %]
UID: [% user.1 %]
```

Standard Slash Template Variables

Slash automatically provides several variables to its templates. In template terms, these are `env` (HTTP environmental variables), `constants` (site configuration vari-ables), `user` (user information and preferences), and `form` (the contents of submit-ted HTML forms).

---

[*] Provided, of course, that variables named `firstname` and `lastname` exist, and have the appropriate values.

[†] Yes, it should be "Yves Adele Harlow." What kind of a Slash book would this be without one homophonic misspelling?

[‡] For the purpose of introduction, this chapter treats the two terms as interchangeable.

[§] The first *element* of a list is at the 0th *position*. If it helps, things work the same way in Perl and C. It's zeroes all the way down!

Template Control Structures

As if variable interpolation weren't enough, Slash templates can also use *control structures*. These should be immediately familiar to anyone who has programmed in a procedural language. Control structures are template declarations that modify the flow of control. Instead of processing each line, one at a time, in order, templates can loop over a data set, repeat an operation a certain number of times, and even choose to process or to ignore things based on given conditions.

As with all template directives besides simple variable access, control structures begin with an uppercased token and may be followed with an expression. For example, the *userInfo* template (in *themes/slashcode/templates/userInfo;users;default*, relative to the Slash home directory) lists all Stories submitted by a current user with a loop similar to:

```
[% FOREACH story = stories %]
<A HREF="[% constants.rootdir %]/article.pl?sid=[% story.sid %]">
[% story.title %]</A><br>
[% END %]
```

The variable `stories` is an array containing one or more structures with `sid` and `title` fields. This code loops through the array, assigning `story` to each item in turn, creating a new HTML link to the Story each time. The FOREACH field marks the beginning of the loop and the END field marks the end. Anything inside—whether other control structures, plain text, or text mixed with directives—will be evaluated on each loop iteration. For example, it's easy to number list items automatically:

```
[% i = 0 %]
Rank:               Name
---------------------
[FOREACH user = users %]
#[% i++ %]          [% user %]
[% END %]
```

Given users "Buffy", "Dave", "Leon", and "Gayle", this will produce:

```
Rank:               Name
---------------------
#1                  Buffy
#2                  Dave
#3                  Leon
#4                  Gayle
```

Templates can also perform operations if certain conditions are true. The simplest test is the IF directive. The *userInfo* template uses similar code to add a link to the Moderator Guidelines if the user has moderator points:*

```
[% IF mod_flag %]
<P>You're a moderator!  Please read the
<A HREF="[% constants.rootdir %]/moderation.shtml">Moderator
Guidelines</A> before you do any moderation.
[% END %]
```

As with FOREACH, the condition begins with IF and ends at END. The template will interpolate and display the text inside the condition if and only if the contents of mod_flag are true. If there is no variable of that name, or if it contains an empty string or the value of 0, nothing will be displayed.

The ELSE directive provides an alternate path. It is possible to provide a different message to users without moderator points:

```
[% IF mod_flag %]
        <P>You're a moderator!  Please read the
        <A HREF="[% constants.rootdir %]/moderation.shtml">Moderator
        Guidelines</A> before you do any moderation.
[% ELSE %]
        You're not a moderator.  Please brush up on the
        <A HREF="[% constants.rootdir %]/moderation.shtml">Moderator
        Guidelines</A> for next time!
[% END %]
```

If mod_flag is true, things work as in the previous example. Otherwise, the second message will be shown. To make things even easier, the ELSIF directive allows several different options:

```
[% USE Slash %]
[% IF mod_flag %]
        <P>You're a moderator!  Please read the
        <A HREF="[% constants.rootdir %]/moderation.shtml">Moderator
        Guidelines</A> before you do any moderation.
[% ELSIF Slash.isAnon(user.id) %]
        You're not logged in.  You'll never get moderator points this way.
[% ELSE %]
        You're not a moderator.  Please brush up on the
        <A HREF="[% constants.rootdir %]/moderation.shtml">Moderator
        Guidelines</A> for next time!
[% END %]
```

This code adds another test in the middle. Users with moderation points will see the second message. Logged-in users without points will see the third message. Users for whom the isAnon call is true are not logged in and will see the second message. Checking to see if user.id is 1 would work on default installations, but

---

* Throughout this appendix, some long lines have been formatted to fit comfortably on the page.

this is not true of every site. Until the section "Calling Slash functions from templates" later in this appendix, just trust that the function call works and does what it says.

Standard mathematical and boolean comparators work in IF statements as would be expected. These include && (or and), || (or or), and ! ("not"), as well as == ("equals"), < ("is less than"), and > ("is greater than"). Grouping several comparisons is easier than nesting IF directives.

For example, one might say:

```
[% IF user.id > 1 && mod_flag %]
        You have [% user.points %] moderation points.
[% END %]
```

instead of:

```
[% IF user.id > 1 %]
        [% IF mod_flag %]
                You have [% user.points %] moderation points.
        [% END %]
[% END %]
```

Complex expressions will be much more readable with a judicious use of parentheses. Thankfully, the default Slash templates tend to be very straightforward.

One nice bit of syntactic sugar allows the UNLESS directive to perform a default action if the given condition is false. (Put another way, it says, "Do these things unless this is true.") Instead of writing:

```
[% IF ! useredit.registered %]
        This account is expired.  Please re-register.
[% END %]
```

one can write:

```
[% UNLESS useredit.registered %]
        This account is expired.  Please re-register.
[% END %]
```

This can make complex conditionals much more readable.

Looking for one of several possible alternatives can result in several lines of ELSIF clauses. The SWITCH and CASE directives perform the same operation more succinctly. The variable in the SWITCH is evaluated. Each subsequent CASE directive presents a possible value. If these match, everything until the next CASE or END directive will be evaluated:

```
[% SWITCH mailname %]
        [% CASE 'malda' %]
                Rob "CmdrTaco" Malda
        [% CASE 'hemos' %]
```

```
                    Hemos the Hamster
        [% CASE 'pater' %]
                    CowboyNeal, hero for the ages
        [% CASE 'nate' %]
                    Nate "Oostendorp" Oostendorp
    [% END %]
```

In other words, "Check the value of the `mailname` variable. If it is *malda*, produce the output Rob `"CmdrTaco" Malda`. If it is *hemos*...".

The `WHILE` directive allows another type of loop, a combination of `IF` and `FOREACH`. This can process a large number of records without having to generate or store them until absolutely necessary.

```
    [% WHILE num < 10 %]
            [% comment = comments.next; num = num + 1 %]
            Comment #[% num %] of 10: [% comment.title %], on [% comment.date %]
    [% END %]
```

The `LAST` and `NEXT` directives allow finer-grained control over loops. `LAST` stops the loop altogether, in effect saying, "This is the last pass through the loop, whether it's done or not." `NEXT` simply stops the current iteration, telling the loop to continue with the next element.

```
    [% FOREACH user = users %]
            [% IF user == 'Godzilla' %]
                    Noooo, Godzilla!  *** GAME OVER ***
                    [% LAST %]
            [% ELSIF user == 'Rodan' %]
                    Rodan has unlimited moderator points.  We're saved!
                    [% NEXT %]
            [% ELSE %]
                    [% user %] has entered the arena.  Flame on!
            [% END %]
    [% END %]
```

Template Blocks and Files

Just like software, templates can be combined into more complex entities. Another set of directives allows files and other templates, in part or as a whole, to be inserted or processed into the current template. This works with the previous directives, so a properly written template can include a certain menu for Authors and a regular menu (or no menu) for normal users.

Blocks

The `BLOCK` directive defines a block. This is a piece of a template that can be processed as necessary, like a sort of miniature template. Most blocks have names, such as `listcomment`:

```
[% BLOCK listcomment %]
        Comment #[% comment.num %] on [% comment.date %]
        [% comment.title %] by [% comment.username %]
[% END %]
```

The Template Toolkit also permits anonymous blocks. Instead of having a name, these blocks are captured to a variable. Several default Slash templates use this to great effect, such as *themes/slashcode/templates/display;article;default:*

```
[% p = BLOCK; PROCESS nextStory s=prev; END %]
[% IF p %] <  [% p %][% END %]
```

This creates an anonymous block, stored in the p variable. In addition, it processes the nextStory, setting the appropriate variable. Whatever nextStory produces will be the content of the block. If there's anything in p, it will be displayed. (This portion of the template produces links to the previous and next Stories, displayed right above the comment preference widgets on every Story page.)

Blocks (and templates in general) resemble subroutines in a very real sense. They can take arguments (just like templates) and are not limited to returning one value. The RETURN directive interrupts the current processing and returns control to the caller. This can be another template or block, or the program that invoked the template. The nextStory block in *themes/slashcode/templates/display;article;default* uses this to avoid creating a link to the same Story or to a Story that does not exist:

```
[% BLOCK nextStory;
    IF !s;
        RETURN;
    ELSIF s.title == story.title;
        RETURN;
    ELSE;
        ls.link = s.title;
        ls.sid = s.sid;
        ls.section = s.section;
        Slash.linkStory(ls);
    END;
END %]
```

Including and processing

The INCLUDE directive processes another template or block and includes the output at the current location. The template processor prefers blocks defined in the same template file to blocks defined in parent files but will look in the filesystem as a last resort. Any variables defined in the current template will be visible to the included template or block. The following template will produce:

```
A poem by Aaron:

Roses are red,
Violets are blue.
Hello, Aleatha, how do you do?

[% name = 'Aleatha' %]
A poem for [% name %]:

[% INCLUDE greeting %]
[% BLOCK greeting %]
        Roses are red,
        Violets are blue.
        Hello, [% name %], how do you do?
[% END %]
```

The same applies to templates loaded from a file.

Temporary variables can be defined only for the components, as well. Changing the INCLUDE directive in the previous example to [% INCLUDE greeting name="Zanzibar" %] produces a slightly different poem:

```
A poem by Aaron:

Roses are red,
Violets are blue.
Hello, Zanzibar, how do you do?
```

Unfortunately, this doesn't fix the meter of the poem.

Standard Template Toolkit behavior looks first for named blocks, then for files in the INCLUDE_PATH directories. In Slash context, this is the wrong behavior. Templates live in the database so Authors can modify them as necessary. They are also found under the site-specific directories, but these can quickly be out of date.

The Slash developers solved this problem by subclassing the *Template::Provider* package. As far as template writers are concerned, requesting a template by name Just Works, whether the user is in "admin", "default", or "light" mode, for example. TT2 is nothing if not flexible.

The PROCESS directive performs very similar behavior. It does not, however, offer any protection to variables. Instead, variables modified in a processed block will still be modified in the parent. Due to the internals, this is slightly faster than INCLUDE. Beware of behavior such as the following, though:

```
[% raw = 'Pb' %]
[% cooked = PROCESS transmogrify %]
Changed [% raw %] into [% cooked %]!

[% BLOCK transmogrify %]
        [% raw = 'Au' %]
        [% raw %]
[% END %]
```

While such an equation would be nice in the real world, it's a tautology, not the Philosopher's Stone.

Advanced Templates for Slash

As mentioned earlier, Slash adds some special magic to the Template Toolkit to perform its necessary magic. While the following manipulations all retain the essential flavor of TT2, Slash adds some handy idioms and tools.

Filters

Filters process the output of a block. They can perform any type of manipulation imaginable. In Slash templates, filters generally remove bad HTML and modify formatting as necessary. A standard FILTER directive converts significant HTML characters into their appropriate entities:

```
[% FILTER html %]
        These three bad boys are Trouble in raw HTML:  <, >, &.
[% END %]
```

This produces the following output, which ought to display properly in any web browser:

```
These three bad boys are Trouble in raw HTML: &lt;, &gt;, &amp;.
```

As usual, the Slash templates often take advantage of template shortcuts, running a variable through a filter and returning the result in one statement. These two lines are functionally equivalent:

```
Here is some HTML: [% FILTER html; potential_code; END %]
Here is some HTML: [% potential_code |. html %]
```

Slash Filters

Because it must deal with data from many different clients and from users with a wide range of skills and attitudes (from careless to malicious), Slash provides several of its own filters. These do everything from screening out unwanted HTML codes (no pop-up windows or embedded banner ads!) to creating valid URLs. For the morbidly curious, the real functions may be found in *Slash::Utility::Data*, but are exported by *Slash::Utility*. The following filters are available in all Slash templates:

strip_nohtml

Removes everything that looks like an HTML tag (anything between < and > brackets). It also removes the brackets and converts the ampersand into its entity (turning "&" into &).

strip_literal

Converts the three special HTML characters into their entities, so the text will be displayed in a web browser just as it appears in the string. Normally, if a user types a simple line of code such as x < y, a browser will try to interpret "< y" as the start of an HTML tag. This filter will produce x < y, which will display what the user intended.

strip_extrans

Converts the three tricky characters into their entities and preserves whitespace by encoding it into HTML entities. Blank lines are converted into <BR> tags, tabs are converted into spaces, and spaces become   entities.

strip_code

Performs the same operation as *strip_extrans* and wraps the results in <TT> tags. Most web browsers render such text with a monospace font.

strip_attribute

Converts the three troublesome characters into entities as well as double quotes, which become ". This is appropriate for values which will appear in attributes of an HTML tag, where a stray literal double-quote character would break things.

strip_plaintext

Removes bad HTML and adds whitespace to wrap potentially long lines. This does not affect text within HTML tags, only literal text. It does not convert the three special characters into their entities, but it uses the same heuristics to ensure that whitespace will be preserved when the text is rendered by a web browser.

strip_html

Removes bad HTML and adds whitespace to wrap potentially wrong lines. It does not convert any characters into entities, nor does it modify whitespace.

strip_anchor

Removes carriage returns and new lines but does no conversions. This is handy for anchor tags that stretch over several lines. If the link title is not nestled tightly against the tags, some clients will add extra spaces. The following example will produce a single line of HTML, not three:

```
[% FILTER strip_anchor %]<A HREF="foo">
        hi
</A>[% END %]
```

fixurl

Prepares a URL to be included within an HTML link tag. It removes spurious quotes (both double and single) and angle brackets and converts all special characters into HTML entities.

fudgeurl

Attempts to remove common link hijacking tricks by stripping out JavaScript and other nasty hacks.

fixparam

Encodes data intended to be parameters in a URL. It escapes significant data.

Several filters strip out "bad HTML." This is performed by the `stripBadHtml` subroutine in *Slash::Utility::Data*. It encodes the < and > characters and removes all unapproved HTML tags. Site administrators can allow and disallow tags as desired by modifying the `approvedtags` configuration variable. By default, Slash allows only HTML links and tags that format text. It runs all URLs through the *fudgeurl* filter, trying to prevent link exploits.

Functions and Templates

On their own, templates provide a tremendous amount of functionality. Being able to dereference complex data structures (whether hashes, objects, or method calls) makes most tasks very simple. The filtering mechanism, especially as extended by Slash, provides very common data-laundering operations. Even with all of these features, a few other standard manipulations are missing from the Toolkit.

Standard template functions

Perl itself provides several string manipulation operations. These come in very handy. Through still more magic, the Template Toolkit makes them available. Instead of being general-purpose functions, these appear in templates as methods

on variables. Given a variable named `domainname`, a template can force its contents
to lowercase with the `lc` function:

```
The converted domain name is [% domainname.lc %].
```

The following functions are commonly used throughout the Slash templates. They
work only on scalars and are meaningless when applied to anything but variables:

`uc`

 Uppercases the entire string

`lc`

 Lowercases the entire string

`ucfirst`

 Uppercases the first letter of the string

`lcfirst`

 Lowercases the first letter of the string

`substr`

 Extracts and optionally replaces a portion of the string

For example, to display only the first 10 characters of a name, use:

```
[% name.substr(0, 10) %]
```

The `rand` function applies to lists. It selects a random element from the list. For
example, the *index* template produces a whimsical message by choosing random
elements from three lists:

```
This page was generated by a [% group.rand %] of [% modifier.rand %]
[% type.rand %] for [% user.nickname %] ([% user.uid %]).
```

Calling Slash functions from templates

Fortunately, it's possible to call Slash functions from within templates, passing in
arguments and receiving back appropriate data. Users familiar with Perl packages
will have no trouble with the syntax. First, tell the template to refer to the Slash
package:

```
[% USE Slash %]
```

This directive tells the code where to find functions that will be called later. From
there, calling a function is as simple as accessing a variable. The *footer* template
lists all administrative users and their tasks with the following code:

```
[% IF user.is_admin %]
        [% Slash.currentAdminUsers() %]
[% ELSE %]
            <FONT SIZE="2" FACE="[% constants.mainfontface %]">
```

```
<I>[% INCLUDE motd %]</I></FONT>
[% END %]
```

Most functions will live in the *Slash* package. The syntax is consistent for calling functions in other packages. Passing arguments is also very easy. The *dispTheComments* template calls dispComment with one argument:

```
[% FOR C = comments %]
        [% Slash.dispComment(C) %]
[% END %]
```

The *discreate* template demonstrates passing multiple arguments as a list. Note the mixture of variables and hardcoded constants:

```
[% Slash.selectTopic('topic', topic, '', 1) %]
```

Finally, the *printCommentsMain* template passes several arguments as a Perl hash:

```
[% Slash.linkComment({
        sid => sid,
        pid => pid,
        color   => user.fg.3,
        subject => 'Top',
}) %]
```

For a comprehensive list of Slash functions, see Appendix D, or the documentation for *Slash*, readable with the command *perldoc Slash*.

Miscellaneous Arcana

The Template Toolkit is full of other convenient features, but most Slash templates use only the few functions described here. There's no reason to limit yourself, though, if you can make your site more powerful or easier to maintain. If you go on to write your own templates, there are a few extra things you should know.

Whitespace

By default, Slash templates preserve whitespace between directives. That is, two output-producing blocks, separated by a blank line or a space, will have the same whitespace character between their output. For example:

```
Katie has written [% num %] comment
        [% IF num > 1; 's'; END %]

.
```

given num of 2 will produce:

```
Katie has written 2 comment
s

.
```

How Slash Calls Templates

Internally, all template access goes through the `slashDisplay` function in *Slash::Display*. This function loads a template from the database by name, provides it with variables, processes it, and sends the results to the waiting web browser. Further, it loads the right template for user preferences.

Templates can be assigned to a Section and a page. (The defaults are `default` and `misc`, respectively.) The Section may or may not correspond to a literal Section on the site. By default, most templates live in the default Section. Other options are `admin`, for Authors and administrators, and `light`, a stripped-down version for low-bandwidth use. The page setting corresponds to the current Slash applet. For example, a user accessing user preferences via `users.pl` would have a page of `users`.

Besides being stored in the database, these values are preserved in template filenames in the distribution. For example, a template named *yourPending-Subs* in the default Section, assigned to the `submit` page, has a filename of *yourPendingSubs;submit;default.*

In general, most `slashDisplay` calls strongly resemble the `INCLUDE` directive. The `users.pl` applet displays the user information page with a simple call:

```
slashDisplay('userInfo', {
        title           => $title,
        nick            => $nick,
        useredit        => $requested_user,
        points          => $points,
        lastgranted     => $lastgranted,
        commentstruct   => $commentstruct || [],
        commentcount    => $commentcount,
        nickmatch_flag  => $nickmatch_flag,
        mod_flag        => $mod_flag,
        karma_flag      => $karma_flag,
        admin_block     => $admin_block,
        admin_flag      => $admin_flag,
        stories         => $stories,
        storycount      => $storycount,
});
```

Much of the site's look and feel can be changed by modifying the templates themselves. Unfortunately, changing the information passed to the templates requires editing the underlying Perl code.

One solution is to cram all directives and text together into an unreadable mess. A better approach is to enable whitespace chomping within a directive. The + and -

characters disable and enable this effect, respectively. Rewriting the example produces the intended effect:

```
Katie has written [% num %] comment
       [%- IF num > 1; 's'; END -%]
```

```
Katie has written 2 comments.
```

Idioms and More Information

The Slash templates frequently take advantage of several Template Toolkit idioms. Yet another example is the use of the *trinary conditional operator*. While SWITCH and CASE directives provide a compact way of writing several conditionals, the trinary comparator is a very terse way of writing a single conditional. It takes the form expression ? option if true : option if false. The earlier pluralization code can be simplified to:

```
Katie has written [% num %] comment[% num > 1 ? 's' ; '' %].
```

The Template Toolkit itself is much more powerful than this brief introduction indicates. It has many small features and interesting details that don't come up in the default Slash templates. For more information, read the excellent documentation at *http://www.template-toolkit.org/docs/*, or start with Dave Cross's tutorial at *http://www.perl.com/pub/a/2001/01/tt2.html.*

D

The Slash API

To add features to Slash in a plugin or a theme, it's helpful to know which functions exist. Most of the hard work of getting and setting information in the database and passing information to templates is already done. While some of the internals are still being rearranged, the core functions are very stable. Most plugins use only a handful of functions.

Browsing the Slash Documentation

Most of the Slash modules have inline documentation in POD format. Most of the documentation in *docs/* beneath the Slash source directory is also in this format. As discussed in the section "Getting help on Perl" in Chapter 2, this is the standard means of documenting Perl code. The *perldoc* utility can be used to find and display documentation for any installed Slash module. For example, to see which functions are available from the *Slash* module, use the command *perldoc Slash*. This will produce something like:

```
Slash(3)        User Contributed Perl Documentation        Slash(3)
NAME
        Slash - the BEAST

SYNOPSIS
                use Slash;  # figure the rest out ;-)

DESCRIPTION
        Slash is the code that runs Slashdot.

FUNCTIONS

        printComments(SID [, PID, CID])
```

```
Prints all that comment stuff.

...
```

All modules follow the same format. The tricky part is knowing which module contains the appropriate function. Only experience and knowledge of the Slash architecture will help (see Appendix A). Another good tool to use is *grep*, as described in the section "Finding what to change" in Chapter 10. It's worth keeping the unpacked Slash sources around for this reason. Once you have found the appropriate module, pass either its package name or its full filepath to *perldoc*. For *Slash::Utility::Anchor*, there are two possibilities:

```
# perldoc Slash::Utility::Anchor (read the documentation where it is installed)
# perldoc /usr/local/src/slash/Slash/Utility/Anchor/Anchor.pm (read the
  documentation from the unpacked source)
```

The *perldoc* command uses your preferred paging program, usually *less* or *more* on Linux systems. This is important for at least one convenient feature: it is possible to search for text. Hit the forward-slash key (/), then type the function name. For example, when displaying *Slash::Anchor*, type the command */header* and press Enter. Different pagers handle this differently, but this should highlight all occurrences of the string "header" in the file. In *less*, the n key moves to the next match, and N moves to the previous match. This is very helpful to find a particular function in a long document.

For undocumented functions, or for functions that don't make much sense, the -m parameter to *perldoc* will display the code of the module, instead of the embedded documentation. The same search features apply.

Finally, if you go to the trouble of figuring out a previously documented function, please consider writing up a short description and submitting it to the Slash project. See *perldoc perldoc* or any documented module for examples of POD. Writing documentation is easier than reading code, and it is (slightly) less thankless. You will earn good karma for it, though.

Initialization Functions

The following functions set up the Slash environment for applets, plugins, and tasks. Any non-trivial program will use most of these functions.

createEnvironment — sets up Slash to run scripts outside of the web environment

Synopsis

```
createEnvironment();
createEnvironment($virtual_user);
```

createEnvironment initializes several Slash components that would normally be set when running under Apache. This includes creating a database connection and setting the current user to the Anonymous User. It takes an optional single parameter, $virtual_user, which is the string name of the *DBIx::Password* virtual user associated with the database that will be used. Lacking this parameter, it will look through @ARGV for key/value pairs of the form "key=value". If it finds a key named virtual_user, it will use the associated value. It returns nothing and will perform no action if running under *mod_perl*. This function is exported from *Slash::Utility*.

Example

```
use Slash::Utility;
my $virtual_user = $ARGV[0];
createEnvironment($virtual_user);
```

---

getCurrentDB — returns the current *Slash::DB* object, which can be used for database operations

Synopsis

```
my $slashdb = getCurrentDB();
```

getCurrentDB retrieves the current database object (see the section "Database Functions" later in this appendix). It is exported from the *Slash::Utility* package, on behalf of *Slash::Utility::Environment*.

Example

```
use Slash::Utility;
my $slashdb = getCurrentDB();
```

---

getCurrentStatic — retrieves the current configuration variables by name or into a hash reference

Synopsis

```
my $constants = getCurrentStatic();
my $value = getCurrentStatic($name);
```

With no parameters, getCurrentStatic retrieves a hash reference of the current configuration variables in the vars table. Though they can be modified, the table will not be updated to reflect changes to hash values or keys. If a $name parameter is provided, this function will return the associated value from the table, if it exists. Otherwise, it will return the undefined value. This is exported from *Slash::Utility*.

Example

```
use Slash::Utility;
my $constants = getCurrentStatic();

my $rootdir = getCurrentStatic('rootdir');
```

---

getCurrentUser — retrieves information about the current user by key or as a hash reference

Synopsis

```
my $user = getCurrentUser();
my $value = getCurrentUser($name);
```

With no parameters, getCurrentUser returns a hash reference of the current user's information. If the optional $name parameter is provided, it returns the associated value within the user information, if present, and the undefined value if not. This is exported from *Slash::Utility*. If the program is not running under *mod_perl*, and if createEnvironment has not been called, the hash reference may be empty.

Example

```
use Slash::Utility;
my $user = getCurrentUser();

my $nickname = getCurrentUser('nickname');
```

---

getCurrentForm — retrieves form values from the current CGI request

Synopsis

```
my $form = getCurrentForm();
my $value = getCurrentForm($name);
```

With no parameters, getCurrentForm retrieves a hash reference of the current form information passed via user request. If the optional $name parameter is supplied, it returns only the associated value, if it exists, and the undefined value otherwise. This is generally useful only when running in the web server. However, if createEnvironment is called and no virtual user is provided, form values will be populated from @ARGV. This feature is rarely used. *Slash::Utility* exports this function.

Example
```
use Slash::Utility;
my $form = getCurrentForm();

my $op = getCurrentForm('op');
```

Database Functions

All of the following functions operate on the underlying database. They require a valid database object, as returned from getCurrentDB.

---

sqlSelect — returns one or more fields in a single row from a SQL statement

Synopsis
```
my $field = $slashdb->sqlSelect($select);
my $field = $slashdb->sqlSelect($select, $from);
my $field = $slashdb->sqlSelect($select, $from, $where);
my $field = $slashdb->sqlSelect($select, $from, $where, $other);
```

sqlSelect builds and executes a SQL statement from its parameters. It returns a field or fields from the first returned row. In scalar context, it returns the first field. In list context, it returns the entire row. In case of error, it logs the failed SQL statement and returns a false value.

The $select parameter is required. It must be a string containing a field (or a comma-separated list of fields) to select. The $from parameter is optional. If provided, it must be a string containing a table (or a comma-separated list of tables) from which to select. The $where parameter is also optional and will be used to construct a WHERE clause. The $other parameter is also optional and will be added, verbatim, to the end of the SQL statement. It can be used to add a GROUP BY or ORDER BY clause.

Example
```
my $num_users = $slashdb->sqlSelect('COUNT(*)', 'users');
my ($nick, $level) = $slashdb->sqlSelect('nickname, seclev', 'users',
"uid=$uid");
```

---

sqlSelectArrayRef — returns one row as an array reference from an executed SQL statement

Synopsis
```
my $arrref = $slashdb->sqlSelectArrayRef($select);
my $arrref = $slashdb->sqlSelectArrayRef($select, $from);
my $arrref = $slashdb->sqlSelectArrayRef($select, $from, $where);
my $arrref = $slashdb->sqlSelectArrayRef($select, $from, $where, $other);
```

sqlSelectArrayRef constructs and executes a SQL statement from its parameters. It takes the same parameters as sqlSelect and handles failures in the same way. If it succeeds, it returns a reference to an array of the fields of the first row selected from the database.

Example

```
my $userref = $slashdb->sqlSelectArrayRef('nickname, realemail', 'users',
"uid=$uid");
print "Username: $userref->[0], address: $userref->[1]\n";
```

---

sqlSelectHashref — returns a reference to a hash for a single row of results from a SQL statement

Synopsis

```
my $hashref = $slashdb->sqlSelectHashref($select);
my $hashref = $slashdb->sqlSelectHashref($select, $from);
my $hashref = $slashdb->sqlSelectHashref($select, $from, $where);
my $hashref = $slashdb->sqlSelectHashref($select, $from, $where, $other);
```

sqlSelectHashref constructs and executes a SQL statement from its parameters. If the execution succeeds, it returns a reference to a hash for the first row of results. The hash keys are the field names, and the values are the field values. This function takes the same parameters as sqlSelect and handles errors in the same way.

Example

```
my $user = $selfdb->sqlSelectHashref('*', 'users', "uid=$uid");
print "Username: $user->{nickname}, homepage: $user->{homepage}\n";
```

---

sqlSelectHash — returns a hash for a single row of results from a SQL statement

Synopsis

```
my %hash = $slashdb->sqlSelectHash($select);
my %hash = $slashdb->sqlSelectHash($select, $from);
my %hash = $slashdb->sqlSelectHash($select, $from, $where);
my %hash = $slashdb->sqlSelectHash($select, $from, $where, $other);
```

sqlSelectHash works exactly the same as sqlSelectHashRef, except that it creates a hash from the reference before returning the results. Note that it still returns only the first row of the result set.

Example

```
my %user = $selfdb->sqlSelectHash('*', 'users', "uid=$uid");
print "Username: $user{nickname}, homepage: $user{homepage}\n";
```

sqlSelectMany — prepares and executes a SQL statement, returning a *DBI* statement handle

Synopsis

```
my $sth = $slashdb->sqlSelectMany($select);
my $sth = $slashdb->sqlSelectMany($select, $from);
my $sth = $slashdb->sqlSelectMany($select, $from, $where);
my $sth = $slashdb->sqlSelectMany($select, $from, $where, $other);
```

sqlSelectMany provides access to the underlying DBI interface. It constructs a SQL statement from its parameters, returning a statement handle which can be used to retrieve the results. It takes the same parameters and handles errors in the same way as sqlSelect.

Example

```
my $sth = $slashdb->sqlSelectMany('nickname, realemail', 'users',
'seclev > 100');
while (my $row = $sth->fetchrow_hashref) {
    print "Author: $row->{nickname}, email: $row->{realemail}\n";
}
```

---

sqlSelectColArrayref — returns a reference to an array of the first column from each row of the results returned from a SQL statement

Synopsis

```
my $arr = $slashdb->sqlSelectColArrayref($select);
my $arr = $slashdb->sqlSelectColArrayref($select, $from);
my $arr = $slashdb->sqlSelectColArrayref($select, $from, $where);
my $arr = $slashdb->sqlSelectColArrayref($select, $from, $where, $other);
```

sqlSelectColArrayref constructs and executes a SQL statement, returning a reference to an array holding only the first column of each row of the results. It takes the same parameters as sqlSelect and handles errors in the same way. In practice, this is little used. Note that requesting multiple fields in the $select parameter will have little effect.

Example

```
my $col_ref = $slashdb->sqlSelectColArrayref('nickname', 'users', "uid < 100");
foreach my $usernick (@$col_ref) {
    print "User: $usernick\n";
}
```

sqlSelectAll — returns a reference to an array of arrays, one for each row retrieved from a SQL statement

Synopsis
```
my $arr_ref = $slashdb->sqlSelectAll($select);
my $arr_ref = $slashdb->sqlSelectAll($select, $from);
my $arr_ref = $slashdb->sqlSelectAll($select, $from, $where);
my $arr_ref = $slashdb->sqlSelectAll($select, $from, $where, $other);
```

sqlSelectAll builds and executes a SQL statement, returning a reference to an array, itself containing an array for each row of the result set. This trades memory use for speed. Instead of holding a database connection open to retrieve each row as necessary, it retrieves all of the results at once. This takes the same arguments and handles errors the same as sqlSelect.

Example
```
my $results = $slashdb->sqlSelectAll('nickname, realemail, karma', 'users',
'uid < 100');
foreach my $user (@$results) {
    print "Nick: $user->[0], email: $user->[1], karma: $user->[2]\n";
}
```

---

sqlSelectAllHashrefArray — returns a reference to an array of hashes, one for each row retrieved from a SQL statement

Synopsis
```
my $arr_ref = $slashdb->sqlSelectAllHashrefArray($select);
my $arr_ref = $slashdb->sqlSelectAllHashrefArray($select, $from);
my $arr_ref = $slashdb->sqlSelectAllHashrefArray($select, $from, $where);
my $arr_ref = $slashdb->sqlSelectAllHashrefArray($select, $from, $where, $other);
```

sqlSelectAllHashrefArray constructs and executes a SQL statement, retrieving all rows, storing each of them as a hash reference in an array. This takes the same arguments as sqlSelect and handles errors in the same manner. It trades memory for speed, returning its results as soon as possible, thereby closing the statement handle quickly.

Example
```
my $arr_ref = $slashdb->sqlSelectAllHashrefArray('nickname, realemail', 'users',
'uid < 1000');
foreach my $user (@$arr_ref) {
    print "Nickname: $user->{nickname}, email: $user->{realemail}\n";
}
```

sqlUpdate — updates rows in the database

Synopsis

```
my $rows = $slashdb->sqlUpdate($table, $data, $where);
```

sqlUpdate constructs and executes a SQL statement to update existing rows in a database table. It returns the number of updated rows. Most existing functions ignore the value, but it can be used to check the success or failure of the operation. The $table parameter is a string containing the name of the table or a comma-separated list of tables to update. $data must be a reference to a hash associating column names with the field values. The values will automatically be passed through sqlQuote unless the key starts with a single dash. The $where parameter is required and is used to add a WHERE clause to the statement. (The function automatically prepends WHERE to the value of $where.)

Example

```
# sig must be quoted, fakeemail probably should be
my %values = (
    karma             => -10,
    -sig              => 'Love,<br />Edwin "Snarky Boy" Redford',
    -fakeemail        => 'snark@tired-rant.com',
);
my $rows = $slashdb->sqlUpdate('users', \%values, "uid=$uid");
print "Updated okay!\n" if $rows;
```

---

sqlSelectAllHashref — returns a reference to a hash of hashes of rows returned from a SQL statement

Synopsis

```
my $hashref = $slashdb->sqlSelectAllHashref($id);
my $hashref = $slashdb->sqlSelectAllHashref($id, $select);
my $hashref = $slashdb->sqlSelectAllHashref($id, $select, $from);
my $hashref = $slashdb->sqlSelectAllHashref($id, $select, $from, $where);
my $hashref = $slashdb->sqlSelectAllHashref($id, $select, $from, $where, $other);
```

sqlSelectAllHashref builds and executes a SQL statement, returning a reference to a hash containing each row of the results as a separate hash. The leading $id parameter is the name of a field used as a key for each row hash in the parent hash reference. Otherwise, it uses the same parameters and handles errors in the same fashion as sqlSelect. This function trades memory for speed, returning all results and closing the statement handle as soon as possible. Note that the only order that can be imposed on the results can be done with the parent hash keys.

Example

```
my $hash_ref = $slashdb->sqlSelectAllHashref('uid', 'nickname, uid, realemail',
'users', "karma > $karma");
foreach my $uid (keys %$hash_ref) {
    print "User: $uid, nickname: $uid->{nickname}, email: $uid->{realemail}\n";
}
```

---

sqlInsert — inserts data into a table or tables in the database

Synopsis

```
my $rows = $slashdb->sqlInsert($table, $data);
my $rows = $slashdb->sqlInsert($table, $data, $delayed);
```

sqlInsert creates and executes a SQL statement intended to insert new data into a table or tables. The first two parameters are the same as those for sqlUpdate. The $delayed argument is optional. If it is provided and evaluates to true, the function will perform a delayed insert. This allows the current process to continue immediately. Additionally, the update operation will not preempt any pending reads. In practice, the return value is rarely used. Note that only those fields passed as keys of the hash reference in $data will be inserted. Any other fields in the row will have their default column values.

Example

```
my %new_user = (
    -nickname  => 'perfesir',
    -fakeemail => 'perf@some.uni',
    -sig       => 'π',
);
$slashdb->sqlInsert('users', \%new_user);
```

---

sqlQuote — escapes any special database characters in a string

Synopsis

```
my $quotedval = $slashdb->sqlQuote($value);
```

sqlQuote escapes any special characters within a string so they will not break a SQL statement or otherwise interfere with database processing. This can be used safely on values that may not normally need to be quoted. However, it should not be used twice on the same value. It exists as a helper for sqlDo.

Example

```
# from sqlUpdate()
foreach (keys %$data) {
```

```
        if (s/^-//) {
        $sql .= "\n  $_ = $data->{-$_},";
        } else {
        $sql .= "\n $_ = " .
        $self->sqlQuote($data->{$_}) . ',';
        }
    }
```

sqlDo — executes an arbitrary SQL statement

Synopsis

```
    my $rows = $slashdb->sqlDo($sql);
```

sqlDo prepares and executes an arbitrary SQL statement in one fell swoop. It performs no processing or quoting, passing the contents of $sql to the database ver-
batim. When an error occurs, it logs the failed SQL statement and returns a false
value. If the statement succeeds, it returns the number of affected rows. Note that
if the statement succeeds but affected zero rows, the return value will be the special Perl value 0E0, which evaluates to "zero but true". This function can be used
destructively. Be very careful, especially if anything in $sql can come from outside
of the Slash code itself.

Example

```
    # don't do this unless you really really mean it
    my $rows = $slashdb->sqlDo("DROP DATABASE slash");
    if ($rows) {
        print "It was nice while it lasted.\n";
    } else {
        print "Dodged a bullet there!\n";
    }
```

sqlCount — returns the number of rows in a table

Synopsis

```
    my $rows = $slashdb->sqlCount($table);
    my $rows = $slashdb->sqlCount($table, $where);
```

sqlCount is a simple function that counts the number of rows in a table or tables.
The $table parameter is a string containing the name of a table or a comma-sepa-
rated list of unique table names from which to count the rows. (If multiple tables
are selected, the returned value will be the Cartesian product of the number of
rows from each table, not the sum of the number of rows.) The $where parameter
is optional. If provided, the keyword WHERE will be prepended, and the resulting
clause will be added as a WHERE clause to the SQL statement.

Example

```
my $users = $slashdb->sqlCount('users');
print "$users active users on the system.\n";
```

Display Functions

The following functions are useful for building and modifying program output. The primary method is *slashDisplay*, which will be used in nearly every program.

---

slashDisplay — processes and displays (or returns) a named template

Synopsis

```
slashDisplay($templatename, \%values);
slashDisplay($templatename, \%values, \%options);
my $page = slashDisplay($templatename, \%values, \%options);
```

This function is the heart of Slash's powerful template system. It fetches the appropriate template based on user access, preferences, and form values; processes the template based on the values; and either prints it to the user or returns it to the calling code. The first parameter is a string containing the base name of the template. The second parameter is a hash reference of variables and values to pass to the template, as described in Appendix C. The third parameter is optional. If provided, it must be a hash ref. Valid keys are:

Return

> If true, returns the processed template data instead of printing it. The default is false (print the data).

Nocomm

> If true, does not include HTML comments to identify the processed template. The default is false (print the comments).

Section

> Prefers a template from the provided Section, overriding the user's current Section. The default Sections are default and light. This unfortunately named option has very little in common with Story Sections. If an invalid Section or a Section of NONE is provided, Slash will use default instead.

Page

> Prefers a template associated with a page other than the user's current page. By default, a user accessing the *users.pl* applet is considered to be on the users page. If the selected page does not exist for the template, if this option is not provided, or if NONE is specified, misc will be used instead.

This function returns true or false depending on the success of the template processing. If the *Return* option is specified, it will instead return the processed template data. As a side effect, this causes templates to be compiled and cached.

When passed a name, the function first looks for a template with the appropriate name assigned to the current page. If none exists, it looks for a default template with the proper name. Without even this default, it must return an error. Template Sections are handled similarly.

Example

```
my $user     = getCurrentUser;
my $form     = getCurrentForm();
my $slashdb  = getCurrentDB();

my $sid      = $form->{sid};
my $story    = $slashdb->getStory($sid);
my $topic    = $slashdb->getTopic($story->{tid});
my $author   = $slashdb->getAuthor($story->{uid},

slashDisplay('dispStory', {
        user         => $user,
        story        => $story,
        topic        => $topic,
        author       => $author,
        section      => $sect->{title},
        displayLinks => $form->{nohtml},
}, {
        NoComm       => 1,
});
```

---

getDescriptions — returns a hash reference of key pairs used to build an HTML select widget

Synopsis

```
my $desc = $slashdb->getDescriptions($codetype);
my $desc = $slashdb->getDescriptions($codetype, $option);
my $desc = $slashdb->getDescriptions($codetype, $option, $cache);
my $desc = $slashdb->getDescriptions($codetype, $option, $cache, $altdescs);
```

getDescriptions builds and returns a hash reference that can be used in an HTML select statement. This provides an easy way to allow users to select from several configurable options, stored in the database. The first parameter, $codetype, is a string used as a key to a hash of common descriptions. This can be either one of the descriptions in the following list or the hash passed in as the optional $altdescs parameter. The $option parameter is used to clarify some of these descriptions further. If the $cache value is true, the function will consult the database directly, instead of consulting a cache for the descriptions.

sortcodes

> The comment sorting styles.

generic

> Any type of entry in the `code_param` table. The `$optional` parameter must be a valid type.

statuscodes

> The valid Story status codes (`archived`, `normal`, or `refreshing`).

blocktype

> The available block types (`color`, `static`, `portald`).

tzcodes

> The available time zone codes (MDT, GMT) and their offsets from GMT, in seconds.

tzdescription

> The available time zone codes and longer descriptions.

dateformats

> Examples of the available date-formatting options.

datecodes

> The `strftime()` formats for the available date-formatting options.

discussiontypes

> The available types for a discussion (`enabled`, `recycling`, `read-only`).

commentmodes

> The comment display modes (`flat`, `nested`, `thread`, `nocomment`).

threshcodes

> The comment threshhold codes and their descriptions.

threshcode_values

> Just the comment threshold codes.

postmodes

> The comment posting formatting modes.

isolatemodes

> The Section isolation modes (`part of site`, `standalone`).

issuemodes

> The Story issue mode settings (`standalone`, `neither`, `article based`, `issue based`).

vars

> The available configuration variables.

topics
> Topic IDs and their descriptive texts.

topics_all
> Topic IDs and their descriptive texts (no difference between this and *topics*).

topics_section
> Topics assigned to the particular Section, in which the Section is given as the `$option` parameter.

maillist
> The mailing list options for which users can sign up.

session_login
> The options for the length of a login session.

displaycodes
> The options for displaying a Story (`sitewide`, `within a Section`, `not displayed`).

commentcodes
> The options for allowing or disallowing comments on a Story.

sections
> The available Sections of a site and their descriptive titles.

static_block
> Available static blocks, in which the value of the `$option` parameter is greater than the block's seclev field. Pass a user's `seclev` as the value to retrieve a list of the static blocks he can edit.

portald_block
> A list of the portald blocks. This also respects the `$option` parameter.

color_block
> A list of color blocks. This uses `$option` as well.

authors
> The user IDs and nicknames of site Authors.

admins
> The user IDs and nicknames of site administrators.

users
> The user IDs and nicknames of all users.

templates
> The templates present in the database.

templatesbypage
> The templates corresponding to the page named in the $option parameter.

templatesbysection
> The templates corresponding to the Section named in the $option parameter.

keywords
> The keywords from the related_links table.

pages
> The available pages to which templates can be assigned.

templatesections
> The available Sections to which templates can be assigned.

sectionblocks
> The blocks and their titles that are currently active.

plugins
> The installed plugins and their descriptions.

site_info
> The site installation variables and their values.

topic-sections
> The available Sections that contain the Topic listed in $option.

forms
> The names of forms to which content filters can be applied.

journal_discuss
> The discussion options for a journal entry (comments enabled or disabled).

Example

```
use Slash::DB;

# from users.pl
my $session = $slashdb->getDescriptions('session_login');
my $session_select = createSelect('session_login', $session,
    $user_edit->{session_login}, 1);

slashDisplay('changePasswd', {
    useredit => $user_edit,
    title => $title,
    session => $session_select,
});
```

isAnon — tests to see if the given user ID belongs to the Anonymous User

Synopsis

```
isAnon($uid);
```

isAnon is a quick but effective way to test if a given user is registered or not. It returns true if the user is anonymous, false otherwise. This function handles non-UIDs safely, so it can be used where a user structure is not fully built. It is exported from *Slash::Utility::Environment.*

Example

```
use Slash::Utility;
return if isAnon($user->{uid});
```

---

doEmail — sends email to a user

Synopsis

```
doEmail($address, $subject, $content);
doEmail($address, $subject, $content, $code);
doEmail($address, $subject, $content, $code, $precedence);
doEmail($address, $subject, $content, undef, $precedence);
```

doEmail sends a message to a user. Normally, this is an email. The first three parameters are required and are treated as the destination address, mail subject, and content of the email message. This is exported from *Slash::Utility::System.* The optional $precedence parameter can be used to set the precedence of the message. This is a widely supported but unstandard option for mail servers. The only available option is *bulk.*

This function integrates tightly to the standard messaging plugin. If it is installed, the $code parameter can be used to distinguish between messages that should be sent as email and those that should be sent through the web interface. The available options are taken from the code_param table of the deliverymodes type. The value 0 sends an email, while 1 sends a web message. The available values may change in future versions, so it may be wiser to choose these from the database.

Example

```
use Slash::Utility;

my $mode = $slashdb->sqlSelect('code', 'code_param', 'name=E-mail');
doEmail('hemos@slashdot.org', 'finished!', <<MESSAGE, $mode);
Hi Jeff,

I've finished the book.  Tell Bella hello from Uncle chromatic!
-- c

MESSAGE
```

E

Slash Configuration Variables

The **vars** table holds all of the configuration variables for a Slash site. These can be divided into several logical groups. This appendix lists the most important variables by name and default value and offers brief descriptions. The program in Example E-1 can be used to generate a similar list for later versions and create a printable copy of current variables.

Example E-1. slashvarlist.pl

```perl
#!/usr/bin/perl -w

use strict;

use Slash;
use Slash::Utility;

my $virtual_user = shift || 'slash';
createEnvironment($virtual_user);
my $slashdb = getCurrentDB();

print <<HEADER;
Slash Configuration Variables

Name      => Value (Description)
-----------------------------
HEADER

my $sth = $slashdb->sqlSelectMany('name, value, description', 'vars');
while(my $row = $sth->fetchrow_hashref()) {
        print "$row->{name}       => $row->{value} ($row->{description})\n";
}

print "Generated at " . scalar localtime . " by $0\n";
```

Variable Tables

The variables in Table E-1 are set by *install-slashsite*, when first creating a new site. These will all differ between systems, and many will differ between sites. Modifying these variables can render site features unusable.

Table E-1. Site configuration variables

Name	Default value	Description
absolutedir	*http://firewheel*	Absolute base URL of site; used for creating links external to site that need a complete URL
adminmail	root	The destination address for administrative reports
basedir	*/usr/local/slash/site/firewheel/htdocs*	The base directory containing HTML and Perl files
basedomain	firewheel	The site domain
cookiedomain		The base domain for cookies (normally left blank)
cookiepath	/	The base path for cookies
datadir	*/usr/local/slash/site/firewheel*	The site's root directory in the system
http_proxy	*http://proxy.firewheel*	The outgoing proxy (if any) needed to retrieve content from remote sites
imagedir	*//firewheel/images*	The absolute URL of the image directory
logdir	*/usr/local/slash/site/firewheel/logs*	The directory containing site logs
mailfrom	root	The email address used when sending email to users
rootdir	*//firewheel*	The base URL of the site, used for creating on-site links that need protocol-inspecific URL (so site can be used via HTTP and HTTPS at the same time)

Table E-1. Site configuration variables (continued)

Name	Default value	Description
sbindir	*/usr/local/slash/sbin*	The location of *sbin* programs on the system
siteadmin	admin	The site administrator
siteadmin_name	Slash Admin	The pretty name for the site administrator
sitename	Slash Site	The name of the site
sitepublisher	Me	The entity that publishes the site
siteid	firewheel	The unique ID for this site
siteowner	slash	The associated system user for the site (see the section "Before You Begin" in Chapter 2)
slashdir	*/usr/local/slash*	The Slash home directory
slogan	Slash Site	The slogan of the site
smtp_server	localhost	The name of the site mailserver
stats_reports	root	The destination address for daily status reports

Some variables control the behavior of the moderation and meta-moderation systems (described in more detail in the section "Moderation Configuration Variables" in Chapter 6). Unlike some other variables, many of the following variables in Table E-2 are meant to be tweaked. Most variables starting with m1_ or m2_ are used in the moderation and meta-moderation algorithms.

Table E-2. Moderation and karma variables

Name	Default value	Description
badkarma	−10	The karma level below which users receive a −1 comment score penalty.

Table E-2. Moderation and karma variables (continued)

Name	Default value	Description
badreasons	4	The number of reasons in *reasons* that subtract a point from a comment score.
comment_maxscore	5	The maximum comment score.
comment_minscore	−1	The minimum comment score.
goodkarma	25	The value above which users receive a +1 posting bonus.
lastComments	0	The number of comments when the moderation task last ran.
m1_eligible_hitcount	3	The number of times a user must hit */comments.pl* before becoming eligible to moderate.
m1_eligible_percentage	0.8	The ratio of users eligible to moderate to the total number of users (the oldest 80% of user accounts are eligible).
m1_pointgrant_end	0.8888	Ending percentage into the pool of eligible moderators (the last 11% of eligible moderators are skipped).
m1_pointgrant_start	0.167	Starting percentage into the pool of eligible moderators (the first 16.7% of eligible moderators are skipped).
m2_batchsize	50	The maximum number of meta-moderations reconciled each time the moderator task runs.
m2_bonus	+1	The bonus for participating in meta-moderation.

Table E-2. Moderation and karma variables (continued)

Name	Default value	Description
m2_comments	10	The maximum number of comments presented to a user in meta-moderation.
m2_consensus	9	The number of times a moderation must be meta-moderated before it can be reconciled (best kept an odd number).
m2_consensus_trigger	0.75	The weighted average of consensus votes to dissenter votes which determines a "clear victory" in M2.
m2_dissension_penalty	−1	The karmic penalty assessed for a dissenting meta-moderation.
m2_maxbonus	12	The maximum bonus that can be earned by participating in meta-moderation, usually half of goodkarma.
m2_minority_trigger	0.05	The percentage of dissenting votes to consenting votes below which a meta-moderator will be assessed a meta-moderation penalty.
m2_modlog_pos	0	The last moderation ID processed by a meta-moderator, used to select the newest moderatable comments.
m2_modlog_cycles	0	The number of times meta-moderation has processed the entire moderation log.

Table E-2. Moderation and karma variables (continued)

Name	Default value	Description
m2_reward_pool	4	The number of points to split between meta-moderators per moderation. Users cannot receive more than 1 point from the point pool.
m2_userpercentage	0.9	The ratio of eligible meta-moderators to the number of total users (the newest 10% of users are ineligible).
maxkarma	50	The maximum karma a user can accumulate.
maxpoints	5	The maximum number of points any moderator can have at one time.
maxtokens	40	The number of tokens required to receive moderation points.
minkarma	−25	The minimum karma to which a user can sink.
moderatord_catchup_count	2	If a backup database is used, the number of times the moderator task will wait for replication to catch up before processing moderations.
moderatord_catchup_sleep	2	The number of seconds the moderator task will sleep if it needs to loop to wait for replication.

Table E-2. Moderation and karma variables (continued)

Name	Default value	Description
moderatord_lag_threshold	100,000	The maximum number of updates a replicated database can be behind before the moderation task must exit.
moderatord_debug_info	1	A flag to log additional moderation info into slashd.log. This is quite verbose, so use it only when necessary.
reasons	Normal | Offtopic | Flamebait | Troll | Redundant | Insightful | Interesting | Informative | Funny | Overrated | Underrated	The moderation labels to apply to comments. The first is neutral. The next badreasons reasons assess a penalty. The last two are not available for meta-moderation.
stir	3	The number of days before unused moderator points expire.
tokenspercomment	6	The number of tokens generated per each new comment.
tokensperpoint	8	The number of tokens required to "purchase" a moderation point.
token_retention	0.25	The percentage of leftover tokens a user is allowed to keep after trading them for moderation points.

Several variables control site features (see Table E-3). For the most part, these variables are set either to off (with a value of 0) or on (1).

Table E-3. Site features

Name	Default value	Description
allow_anonymous	1	Allows non–logged-in users to post.
allow_moderation	1	Allows use of the moderation system.
articles_only	0	Show only Stories in the Articles Section when listing new submissions in the Admin menu.
authors_unlimited	1	Authors have unlimited moderation points.
cache_enabled	1	Enables content caching.
comment_cache_debug	1	Debugs _comment_text cache activity to server log.
delete_old_stories	0	Deletes Stories and discussions that are older than the archive_delay.
do_expiry	1	Expires users (they must reconfirm their accounts).
mod_same_subnet_forbid	1	Forbids users from moderating any comments posted from their subnet.
newsletter_body	0	Prints the body text of Stories, not just the introductions, in the daily newsletter.
panic	0	Scales back features (such as when the site receives extra traffic). The values are 0 (normal), 1 (no frills), and 2 (essentials only).
poll_cache	0	Caches poll question and results on the homepage for users, to save database hits.
poll_discussions	1	Allows discussions on polls.
run_ads	0	Allows the site to run banner ads.
search_google	0	Disables local search, preferring Google.
send_mail	1	Allows the system to send email messages.
slashd_verbosity	2	How much information *slashd* and *runtask* should write to the log (see the section "slashd" in Chapter 11).
submiss_ts	1	Prints the timestamp of a submission in Submissions view.
submiss_view	1	Allows users to view the Submission queue.
template_post_chomp	0	Automatically chomps whitespace after directives when processing templates. The values are 0 (no), 1 (yes), and 2 (collapse whitespace).
template_pre_chomp	0	Automatically chomps whitespace before directives when processing templates. The values are the same as for template_post_chomp.
template_show_comments	1	Shows HTML comments before and after each processed template (see the *Slash::Display* documentation).
use_dept	1	Uses the Dept. field when displaying Stories.

Several variables exist to help curb abusive users (see Table E-4). As discussed in the section "Managing Users" in Chapter 8, these are technological approaches to a social problem. You may find that some of these settings annoy valued users more than they stop miscreants.

Table E-4. Abuse variables

Name	Default value	Description
approvedtags	B I P A LI OL UL EM BR TT STRONG BLOCKQUOTE DIV	The HTML tags allowed when submitting a comment or a Story.
comments_response_limit	20	The minimum number of seconds allowed between following a *Reply* and submitting a comment.
comments_speed_limit	120	The minimum number of seconds allowed between posting comments.
formkey_timeframe	14,400	The number of seconds in which a formkey can be checked.
max_comments_allowed	30	The maximum number of comments a user can post in one day.
max_discussions_allowed	3	The maximum number of discussions a user can create, per day (unused).
max_submissions_allowed	20	The maximum number of Stories a user can submit, per day.
max_users_allowed	50	The maximum number of changes a user can submit to his info, per day (unused).
max_users_unusedfk	30	The maximum number of unused formkeys a user can have active in formkey_timeframe.
max_comments_unusedfk	10	The maximum number of unused formkeys a user can have for comments.
max_submissions_unusedfk	10	The maximum number of unused formkeys a user is allowed to have active for submissions.
max_discussions_unusedfk	10	The maximum number of unused formkeys a user is allowed for new discussions.

Table E-4. Abuse variables (continued)

Name	Default value	Description
submissions_speed_limit	300	The minimum number of seconds a user must wait between separate submissions.
users_speed_limit	20	The minimum number of seconds a user must wait between changes to her preferences.
max_submission_size	32,000	The maximum allowed size of submission before a warning message is displayed.
lenient_formkeys	0	How lenient formkeys should be. If 0, the formkey is validated against the user's IP address. If 1, it is validated against either the IP address or the user's subnet. The latter is more lenient.

Several variables govern the content and frequency of the RSS feeds automatically published by Slash (see Table E-5). Unless you know what changes you need, you are safe modifying only the img, publisher, rights, and subject variables.

Table E-5. RDF publishing variables

Name	Default value	Description
rdfencoding	ISO-8859-1	The character encoding used in the site's feeds.
rdfimg	*http://firewheel/images/topics/topicslash.gif*	The URL of an icon subscriber sites can display with site headlines.
rdfitemdesc	0	How much of the introtext field to include in item descriptions. If 0, none will be included. If 1, the entire field will be included. Any other integer will be interpreted as the number of characters to include.

Table E-5. RDF publishing variables (continued)

Name	Default value	Description
rdflanguage	en-us	The language encoding of the site.
rdfpublisher	Me	The value of the publisher field in the channel description.
rdfrights	Copyright © 2000, Me	The value of the copyright field in the channel description.
rdfsubject	Technology	The value of the subject field in the channel description.
rdfupdatebase	1970-01-01T00:00+00:00	The value of the updateBase field in the channel description.
rdfupdatefrequency	1	The value of the updateFrequency field in the channel description; how often to update per rdfupdateperiod.
rdfupdateperiod	hourly	The value of the updatePeriod field in the channel description; how often to update.

The variables shown in Table E-6 govern the behavior of the comment and discussion systems.

Table E-6. Discussion configuration variables

Name	Default value	Description
breaking	100	The maximum number of comments to display on a single page before breaking them onto multiple pages.
comment_cache_max_hours	96	The age, in hours, at which comments are no longer cached.
comment_cache_max_keys	3,000	The maximum number of keys in the _comment_text cache.

Table E-6. Discussion configuration variables (continued)

Name	Default value	Description
comment_cache_purge_max_frac	0.75	The fraction of max_keys to target when purging the _comment_text cache.
comment_cache_purge_min_comm	50	The minimum number of comments allowed in a discussion before forcing a cache purge.
comment_cache_purge_min_req	5	The minimum number of times a discussion must be requested before forcing a cache purge.
defaultcommentstatus	0	The default code for article comments (no comments, normal, or read-only).
defaultdisplaystatus	0	The display status for a Story (display or do not display).
discussion_archive	15	The number of days until discussions are set to read-only.
discussion_create_seclev	1	The seclev required to create new discussions.
discussion_default_topic	1	The tid of the default Topic of user-created discussions.
discussionrecyle	0	The length of the recycle period, in days, of a discussion.
discussions_speed_limit	300	The delay, in seconds, before a user can create a new discussion.
max_depth	7	The maximum displayable depth for comment nesting.
modviewseclev	100	The minimum seclev required to see moderation statistics attached to comments.
nesting_maxdepth	4	The maximum depth to which <BLOCKQUOTE>-type tags can be nested.

Table E-6. Discussion configuration variables (continued)

Name	Default value	Description
user_comment_display_default	24	The number of comments to display on user info pages.

Slash uses some variables as convenient cubbyholes for site data (see Table E-7). Many of these keep track of the last time something happened.

Table E-7. Data storage

Name	Default value	Description
currentqid	1	The Current Question on the homepage pollbooth
daily_last	2000-01-01 01:01:01	Last time dailyStuff was run (GMT)
lastsrandsec	awards	Last block used in the semi-random block
runtask_verbosity	2	How much information runtask should write to slashd.log (0–2 or empty string to use slashd_verbosity).
totalComments	1	Total number of comments posted
totalhits	383	Total number of hits the site has had thus far
writestatus	dirty	Simple Boolean to determine if homepage needs rewriting

A few configuration variables defy easy classification. Several are important, though (see Table E-8).

Table E-8. And the rest . . .

Name	Default value	Description
admin_timeout	30	The time in minutes before an idle admin session ends and is deleted from the sessions table.
anonymous_coward_uid	1	The UID of the Anonymous User account.

Table E-8. And the rest . . . (continued)

Name	Default value	Description
apache_cache	3,600	The maximum number of seconds the cache should be active before being refreshed.
archive_delay	60	The number of days until a Story can be archived.
backup_db_user		The virtual user associated with a database that can be used for intensive database access. This is appropriate only in a carefully controlled and replicated environment. (This field is blank by default.)
block_expire	3,600	The default expiration time for the block cache.
daily_attime	00:00:00	The time of day at which to run dailyStuff (in time zone daily_tz, 00:00:00–23:59:59)
daily_tz	EST	The base time zone for running dailyStuff.
defaultsection	Articles	The name of the default Section to display.
defaulttopic	1	The tid of the default Topic to use.
fancyboxwidth	200	The pixel width of fancy boxes.
id_md5_vislength	5	The number of characters to display for ipid/subnetid.
mainfontface	verdana, helvetica, arial	The preferred font faces to use in <FONT> tags.
story_expire	600	The default expiration time, in seconds, for the Story cache.
submission_bonus	3	The number of karma points given to a user for an accepted submission.
submit_categories	Back	Extra categories for submissions.
template_cache_size	0	The number of templates to store in the cache (0 = unlimited).
titlebar_width	100%	The width of the titlebar.
updatemin	5	How often, in minutes, *slashd* should check to see if things need to be udpated.

Table E-8. And the rest ... (continued)

Name	Default value	Description
user_submitter_display_default	24	The number of submitted Stories to display on user info pages.
users_show_info_seclev	0	The minimum seclev needed to view user info pages.

Index

We'd like to hear your suggestions for improving our indexes. Send email to *index@oreilly.com.*

A

absolute URLs, changing relative URLs to, 125

absolutedir configuration variable, 49

abuse by users, protecting against (see anti-abuse features, Slash)

access_log database table, 184

accesslog table, storing user requests in, 118

accounts

  administrative, setting up, 38

  Author, creating and deleting, 17

  user, 8

    Author editing of, 44-47

    establishing for Slash installation, 24

    root, 28

    Slash, 37

administration, 44-50, 156-168

  Admin menu, 44

    blocks, creating and editing , 132

    Comment Filters link, 79

    content filters, editing, 147

    Info link to site_info table, 187

    Keywords link to related_links database, 54, 188

    menus table, entries in, 187

    n Submissions link, 63

    Sections link, 96

    suppressing for header function printing, 143

    Template Editor, 134

  administrator sessions, tracking, 188

  configuration variables, modifying, 47-50

  FAQ page for user questions, 106

  polls, 129

  programs stored in sbin/ directory, 177

  Slash utilities, using, 164-168

  tasks, 156-164

  (see also Author interface; Authors)

adminmail configuration variable, 49

admin_timeout configuration variable, 237

ads (banner), customizing, 136-138

allow_anonymous configuration variable, 61, 76

Alt Text field (ALT attribute, <IMG>), 92

alternation, regular expression matches, 80

Always Display mode, 57

and (&&) operator, 197

Andover.Net, 4

anonymous blocks, 199

anonymous posting, 48, 76, 114

anonymous users

  Anonymous User account, 8

    UID for, 237

  detecting, 224

  submitting Stories as, 61

anonymous_coward_uid configuration variable, 237

answers to poll questions, 130, 187

anti-abuse features, Slash, 116-119

  banning abusive users by IPIDs and NetIDs, 117

  configuration variables, 232

  formkeys, 117

Apache web server, 19

  ad management modules, 136

  Apache module, 22

  applets running in, 21

  banned users list, rejecting requests from users on, 118

  building with mod_perl, 32-34

  configuring, 38

    commenting global handler declaration out of httpd.conf, 39

  directives enabling installed sites (slash.conf), 175

  directives to set up virtual host for site, 176

  help, online resources for, 25

  home directory, creating, 30

  logs, location of, 177

  request cycle, 169-172

  starting, 39

  web site for Apache, 32

apache_cache configuration variable, 237

Apache::Cookie objects, 171

Apache::ModuleConfig module, 169

Apache::Registry module, 39, 171

API, Slash, 208-224

appearance, customizing for sites, 131-135

applets, 20

  admin.pl, 44, 147

  Apache request cycle, called during, 171

  htdocs/ directory, stored in, 177

  Print plugin, 141

  Slash environment, setting up for, 209

  users.pl, 206

About the Authors

chromatic lives in the Pacific Northwest and is a freelance writer and programmer. He is a frequent contributor to Slashdot and to Slash itself and wrote the Everything Bible for the Everything Development Company. Having once written Perl while riding a camel near the Pyramids of Giza, he became a Perl Guru, dispensing advice at Perlmonks, performing Perl 5 Kwalitee Assurance, and running the Jellybean project. He also plays guitar, writes non–non-fiction, crosses Extreme Programming with Free Software, attempts to raise succulents, and has two cats and a dog. chromatic is not his real name; he never filled in his email settings, but was taken seriously anyway.

Brian "Krow" Aker has spent the last decade working on projects to promote communities, information, and publishing in the digital world. He has worked on the Virtual Hospital and has built data warehouses for groups such as the Army Corps of Engineers. He currently works as the "database thug and Apache guy" for OSDN on the web site system that makes slashdot.org tick and is an instructor in the Perl Certification Course at the University of Washington. For kicks, he writes oddball Apache, MySQL, and Perl modules. Since he prefers rain and storms over most any type of weather, he lives in Seattle, Washington.

Dave Krieger is a software developer and security consultant who has been working in the Internet industry since 1992 and developing for the Web since 1995; his clients have included Apple Computer, Digital Equipment Corporation, Compaq, Palm Computing, Dow Jones, and Synopsys. He co-founded Agorics, Inc., a software development consultancy, in 1993. Dave was the scientific technical consultant to TV's *Star Trek: The Next Generation* for the 1989–91 seasons, while still a graduate student at UCLA. He lives in the San Francisco Bay Area.

Colophon

Our look is the result of reader comments, our own experimentation, and feedback from distribution channels. Distinctive covers complement our distinctive approach to technical topics, breathing personality and life into potentially dry subjects.

The animals on the cover of *Running Weblogs with Slash* are crows. Crows belong to the family *Corvidae*. The American Crow (Corvus *brachyrynchos*) is 17 to 21 inches long when fully grown and weighs approximately 1 lb. Crows in the wild can live to be approximately 10 years old (the oldest known wild American Crow lived to a whopping 29 1/2), but they are often carried off prematurely by predators and disease. Crows are omnivorous and will eat just about anything, from insects, worms, and mice, to berries and corn, to food scraps discarded by humans. An adult crow needs 11 ounces of food each day. Crows' black coloration helps to protect them from predators at night and allows them to easily identify other members of their species during the day, when they are highly visible.

Crows are believed to be the most intelligent of all birds. They exhibit many characteristics generally considered to be indications of higher intelligence, including problem solving, toolmaking, and the ability to play, as well as excellent memory, communication, and mimicry skills. Crows are also extremely social—not only will crows defend and protect their own families, but they will come to the aid of unrelated crows in need or distress. They live in large extended family groups and typically mate for life. Crows are cooperative breeders—while males do not usually incubate the eggs, they do bring food and guard the nest. Offspring remain with their parents for one to six years and help their parents raise their new broods. In the fall and winter, crows gather in roosts to sleep at night. Crow roosts can range from small scattered roosts of under 100 individuals to the spectacularly large roosts of hundreds of thousands or even more than a million crows.

Matt Hutchinson was the production editor and the copyeditor for *Running Weblogs with Slash*. Rachel Wheeler and Sheryl Avruch provided quality control. Ellen Troutman-Zaig wrote the index.

Emma Colby designed the cover of this book, based on a series design by Edie Freedman. The cover image is an original illustration created by Susan Hart. Emma Colby and Melanie Wang produced the cover layout with QuarkXPress 4.1 using Adobe's ITC Garamond font.

Melanie Wang designed the interior layout based on a series design by Nancy Priest. The print version of this book was created by translating the DocBook XML markup of its source files into a set of gtroff macros using a filter developed at O'Reilly & Associates by Norman Walsh. Steve Talbott designed and wrote the underlying macro set on the basis of the GNU *troff –gs* macros; Lenny Muellner adapted them to XML and implemented the book design. The GNU groff text formatter Version 1.11.1 was used to generate PostScript output. The text and heading fonts are ITC Garamond Light and Garamond Book; the code font is Constant Willison. The illustrations that appear in the book were produced by Robert Romano and Jessamyn Read using Macromedia FreeHand 9 and Adobe Photoshop 6. This colophon was written by Rachel Wheeler.

 # *More Titles from O'Reilly*

Web Administration

Webmaster in a Nutshell, 2nd Edition

By Stephen Spainhour & Robert Eckstein
2nd Edition June 1999
540 pages, ISBN 1-56592-325-1

This indispensable book takes all the essential reference information for the Web and pulls it together into one volume. It covers HTML 4.0, CSS, XML, CGI, SSI, JavaScript 1.2, PHP, HTTP 1.1, and administration for the Apache server.

Apache: The Definitive Guide, 2nd Edition

By Ben Laurie & Peter Laurie
2nd Edition February 1999
388 pages, Includes CD-ROM
ISBN 1-56592-528-9

Written and reviewed by key members of the Apache group, this book is the only complete guide on the market that describes how to obtain, set up, and secure the Apache software on both Unix and Windows systems. The second edition fully describes Windows support and all the other Apache 1.3 features. Includes CD-ROM with Apache sources and demo sites discussed in the book.

Web Performance Tuning

By Patrick Killelea
1st Edition October 1998
374 pages, ISBN 1-56592-379-0

Web Performance Tuning hits the ground running and gives concrete advice for improving crippled web performance right away. For anyone who has waited too long for a web page to display or watched servers slow to a crawl, this book includes tips on tuning the server software, operating system, network, and the web browser itself.

Web Security, Privacy & Commerce, 2nd Edition

By Simson Garfinkel with Gene Spafford
2nd Edition December 2001 (est.)
768 pages (est.), ISBN 0-596-00045-6

Web Security, Privacy & Commerce cuts through the front-page sensationalism and examines the major issues facing e-commerce. It reveals what the real risks are and how to minimize them. Dramatically expanded from the first edition, it includes new information about PKI, privacy, and e-commerce and examines what works or doesn't work on today's web. Destined to be the classic reference on web security risks and the techniques and technologies that protect users, organizations, systems, and networks.

Building Internet Firewalls, 2nd Edition

By Elizabeth D. Zwicky, Simon Cooper,
& D. Brent Chapman
2nd Edition June 2000
894 pages, ISBN 1-56592-871-7

Completely revised and much expanded, this second edition of the highly respected and best-selling *Building Internet Firewalls* now covers Unix, Linux, and Windows NT. It's a practical and detailed guide that provides step-by-step explanations of how to design and install firewalls, and how to configure Internet services to work with a firewall. It covers a wide range of services and protocols. It also contains a complete list of resources, including the location of many publicly available firewalls construction tools.

Apache Pocket Reference

By Andrew Ford
1st Edition June 2000
110 pages, ISBN 1-56592-706-0

The *Apache Pocket Reference*, a companion volume to *Writing Apache Modules with Perl and C* and *Apache: The Definitive Guide*, covers Apache 1.3.12. It provides a summary of command-line options, configuration directives, and modules, and covers Apache support utilities.

Linux

Using Samba

By Peter Kelly, Perry Donham
& David Collier-Brown
1st Edition November 1999
416 pages, Includes CD-ROM
ISBN 1-56592-449-5

Samba turns a Unix or Linux system into a
file and print server for Microsoft Windows
network clients. This complete guide to
Samba administration covers basic 2.0 con-
figuration, security, logging, and troubleshooting. Whether you're
playing on one note or a full three-octave range, this book will
help you maintain an efficient and secure server. Includes a
CD-ROM of sources and ready-to-install binaries.

Managing & Using MySQL, 2nd Edition

By George Reese, Randy Jay Yarger & Tim King
2nd Edition January 2002 (est.)
504 pages (est.), ISBN 0-596-00211-4

This edition retains the best features of the
first edition, while adding the latest on
MySQL and the relevant programming language interfaces, with more complete reference information. The administration section
is greatly enhanced; the programming lan-
guage chapters have been updated—especially the Perl and PHP
chapters—and new additions include chapters on security and
extending MySQL and a system tables reference.

Linux Network Administrator's Guide, 2nd Edition

By Olaf Kirch & Terry Dawson
2nd Edition June 2000
506 pages, ISBN 1-56592-400-2

Fully updated, this comprehensive, impres-
sive introduction to networking on Linux
now covers firewalls, including the use of
ipchains and iptables (netfilter), masquerad-
ing, and accounting. Other new topics
include Novell (NCP/IPX) support and INN
(news administration). Original material on serial connections,
UUCP, routing and DNS, mail and News, SLIP and PPP, NFS, and
NIS has been thoroughly updated.

Understanding the Linux Kernel

By Daniel P. Bovet & Marco Cesati
1st Edition October 2000
650 pages, ISBN 0-596-00002-2

Understanding the Linux Kernel helps readers understand how Linux performs best and
how it meets the challenge of different envi-
ronments. The authors introduce each topic
by explaining its importance, and show how
kernel operations relate to the utilities that
are familiar to Unix programmers and users.

UNIX Power Tools, 2nd Edition

By Jerry Peek, Tim O'Reilly & Mike Loukides
2nd Edition August 1997
1120 pages, Includes CD-ROM
ISBN 1-56592-260-3

Loaded with practical advice about almost
every aspect of Unix, this second edition of
UNIX Power Tools addresses the technology
that Unix users face today. You'll find thor-
ough coverage of POSIX utilities, including
GNU versions, detailed bash and tcsh shell coverage, a strong
emphasis on Perl, and a CD-ROM that contains the best freeware
available.

Linux Device Drivers, 2nd Edition

By Alessandro Rubini & Jonathan Corbet
2nd Edition June 2001
586 pages, ISBN 0-59600-008-1

This practical guide is for anyone who wants
to support computer peripherals under the
Linux operating system. It shows step-by-step
how to write a driver for character devices,
block devices, and network interfaces, illus-
trating with examples you can compile and
run. The second edition covers Kernel 2.4 and adds discussions
of symmetric multiprocessing (SMP), Universal Serial Bus (USB),
and some new platforms.

O'REILLY®

TO ORDER: **800-998-9938** • **order@oreilly.com** • **www.oreilly.com**
ONLINE EDITIONS OF MOST O'REILLY TITLES ARE AVAILABLE BY SUBSCRIPTION AT **safari.oreilly.com**
ALSO AVAILABLE AT MOST RETAIL AND ONLINE BOOKSTORES

How to stay in touch with O'Reilly

1. Visit Our Award-Winning Web Site

http://www.oreilly.com/

- ★ "Top 100 Sites on the Web" —PC Magazine
- ★ "Top 5% Web sites" —Point Communications
- ★ "3-Star site" —The McKinley Group

Our web site contains a library of comprehensive product information (including book excerpts and tables of contents), downloadable software, background articles, interviews with technology leaders, links to relevant sites, book cover art, and more. File us in your Bookmarks or Hotlist!

2. Join Our Email Mailing Lists

New Product Releases
To receive automatic email with brief descriptions of all new O'Reilly products as they are released, send email to:
ora-news-subscribe@lists.oreilly.com
Put the following information in the first line of your message (not in the Subject field):
subscribe ora-news

O'Reilly Events
If you'd also like us to send information about trade show events, special promotions, and other O'Reilly events, send email to:
ora-news-subscribe@lists.oreilly.com
Put the following information in the first line of your message (not in the Subject field):
subscribe ora-events

3. Get Examples from Our Books via FTP

There are two ways to access an archive of example files from our books:

Regular FTP
- ftp to:
  ftp.oreilly.com
  (login: anonymous
  password: your email address)
- Point your web browser to:
  ftp://ftp.oreilly.com/

FTPMAIL
- Send an email message to:
  ftpmail@online.oreilly.com
  (Write "help" in the message body)

4. Contact Us via Email

order@oreilly.com
To place a book or software order online. Good for North American and international customers.

subscriptions@oreilly.com
To place an order for any of our newsletters or periodicals.

books@oreilly.com
General questions about any of our books.

cs@oreilly.com
For answers to problems regarding your order or our products.

booktech@oreilly.com
For book content technical questions or corrections.

proposals@oreilly.com
To submit new book or software proposals to our editors and product managers.

international@oreilly.com
For information about our international distributors or translation queries. For a list of our distributors outside of North America check out:
http://www.oreilly.com/distributors.html

5. Work with Us

Check out our website for current employment opportunites:
http://jobs.oreilly.com/

O'Reilly & Associates, Inc.
1005 Gravenstein Hwy North
Sebastopol, CA 95472 USA
TEL 707-829-0515 or 800-998-9938
(6am to 5pm PST)
FAX 707-829-0104

Titles from O'Reilly

PROGRAMMING

C++: The Core Language
Practical C++ Programming
Practical C Programming, 3rd Ed.
High Performance Computing,
 2nd Ed.
Programming Embedded Systems in
 C and C++
Mastering Algorithms in C
Advanced C++ Techniques
POSIX 4: Programming for
 the Real World
POSIX Programmer's Guide
Power Programming with RPC
UNIX Systems Programming
 for SVR4
Pthreads Programming
CVS Pocket Reference
Advanced Oracle PL/SQL
Oracle PL/SQL Guide to Oracle8i
 Features
Oracle PL/SQL Programming,
 2nd Ed.
Oracle Built-in Packages
Oracle PL/SQL Developer's
 Workbook
Oracle Web Applications
Oracle PL/SQL Language
 Pocket Reference
Oracle PL/SQL Built-ins
 Pocket Reference
Oracle SQL*Plus:
 The Definitive Guide
Oracle SQL*Plus Pocket Reference
Oracle Essentials
Oracle Database Administration
Oracle Internal Services
Oracle SAP
Guide to Writing DCE Applications
Understanding DCE
Visual Basic Shell Programming
VB/VBA in a Nutshell: The Language
Access Database Design
 & Programming, 2nd Ed.
Writing Word Macros
Applying RCS and SCCS
Checking C Programs with Lint
VB Controls in a Nutshell
Developing Asp Components,
 2nd Ed.
Learning WML & WMLScript
Writing Excel Macros
Windows 32 API Programming with
 Visual Basic
ADO: The Definitive Guide

USING THE INTERNET

Internet in a Nutshell
Smileys
Managing Mailing Lists

WEB

Apache: The Definitive Guide,
 2nd Ed.
Apache Pocket Reference
ASP in a Nutshell, 2nd Ed.
Cascading Style Sheets
Designing Web Audio
Designing with JavaScript, 2nd Ed.
DocBook: The Definitive Guide
Dynamic HTML:
 The Definitive Reference
HTML Pocket Reference
Information Architecture
 for the WWW
JavaScript: The Definitive Guide,
 3rd Ed.
Java & XML, 2nd Ed.
JavaScript Application Cookbook
JavaScript Pocket Reference
Practical Internet Groupware
PHP Pocket Reference
Programming Coldfusion
Photoshop for the Web, 2nd Ed.
Web Design in a Nutshell, 2nd Ed.
Webmaster in a Nutshell, 2nd Ed.
Web Navigation: Designing the
 User Experience
Web Performance Tuning
Web Security & Commerce
Writing Apache Modules
 with Perl and C

UNIX

SCO UNIX in a Nutshell
Tcl/Tk in a Nutshell
The Unix CD Bookshelf, 2nd Ed.
UNIX in a Nutshell,
 System V Edition, 3rd Ed.
Learning the Unix Operating System,
 4th Ed.
Learning vi, 6th Ed.
Learning the Korn Shell
Learning GNU Emacs, 2nd Ed.
Using csh & tcsh
Learning the bash Shell, 2nd Ed.
GNU Emacs Pocket Reference
Exploring Expect
Tcl/Tk Tools
Tcl/Tk in a Nutshell
Python Pocket Reference

USING WINDOWS

Windows Me: The Missing Manual
PC Hardware in a Nutshell
Optimizing Windows for Games,
 Graphics, and Multimedia
Outlook 2000 in a Nutshell
Word 2000 in a Nutshell
Excel 2000 in a Nutshell
Windows 2000 Pro:
 The Missing Manual

JAVA SERIES

Developing Java Beans
Creating Effective JavaHelp
Enterprise JavaBeans, 3rd Ed.
Java Cryptography
Java Distributed Computing
Java Enterprise in a Nutshell
Java Examples in a Nutshell, 2nd Ed.
Java Foundation Classes
 in a Nutshell
Java in a Nutshell, 3rd Ed.
Java Internationalization
Java I/O
Java Native Methods
Java Network Programming, 2nd Ed.
Java Performance Tuning
Java Security
Java Servlet Programming
Java ServerPages
Java Threads, 2nd Ed.
Jini in a Nutshell
Learning Java

GRAPHICS & MULTIMEDIA

MP3: The Definitive Guide
Director in a Nutshell
Lingo in a Nutshell

X WINDOW

Vol. 1: Xlib Programming Manual
Vol. 2: Xlib Reference Manual
Vol. 4M: X Toolkit Intrinsics
 Programming Manual, Motif Ed.
Vol. 5: X Toolkit Intrinsics Reference
 Manual
Vol. 6A: Motif Programming Manual
Vol. 6B: Motif Reference Manual,
 2nd Ed.

PERL

Advanced Perl Programming
CGI Programming with Perl, 2nd Ed.
Learning Perl, 2nd Ed.
Learning Perl for Win32 Systems
Learning Perl/Tk
Mastering Algorithms with Perl
Mastering Regular Expressions
Perl Cookbook
Perl in a Nutshell
Programming Perl, 3rd Ed.
Perl CD Bookshelf
Perl Resource Kit – Win32 Ed.
Perl/Tk Pocket Reference
Perl 5 Pocket Reference, 3rd Ed.

MAC

AppleScript in a Nutshell
AppleWorks 6: The Missing Manual
Crossing Platforms
iMovie: The Missing Manual
Mac OS in a Nutshell
Mac OS 9: The Missing Manual
REALbasic: The Definitive Guide

LINUX

Learning Red Hat Linux
Linux Device Drivers, 2nd Ed.
Linux Network Administrator's
 Guide, 2nd Ed.
Running Linux, 3rd Ed.
Linux in a Nutshell, 3rd Ed.
Linux Multimedia Guide

SYSTEM ADMINISTRATION

Practical UNIX & Internet Security,
 2nd Ed.
Building Internet Firewalls, 2nd Ed.
PGP: Pretty Good Privacy
SSH, The Secure Shell:
 The Definitive Guide
DNS and BIND, 3rd Ed.
The Networking CD Bookshelf
Virtual Private Networks, 2nd Ed.
TCP/IP Network Administration,
 2nd Ed.
sendmail Desktop Reference
Managing Usenet
Using & Managing PPP
Managing IP Networks
 with Cisco Routers
Networking Personal Computers
 with TCP/IP
Unix Backup & Recovery
Essential System Administration,
 2nd Ed.
Perl for System Administration
Managing NFS and NIS
Vol. 8: X Window System
 Administrator's Guide
Using Samba
UNIX Power Tools, 2nd Ed.
DNS on Windows NT
Windows NT TCP/IP Network
 Administration
DHCP for Windows 2000
Essential Windows NT System
 Administration
Managing Windows NT Logons
Managing the Windows 2000
 Registry

OTHER TITLES

PalmPilot: The Ultimate Guide,
 2nd Ed.
Palm Programming:
 The Developer's Guide

International Distributors

http://international.oreilly.com/distributors.html • *international@oreilly.com*

UK, EUROPE, MIDDLE EAST, AND AFRICA (EXCEPT FRANCE, GERMANY, AUSTRIA, SWITZERLAND, LUXEMBOURG, AND LIECHTENSTEIN)

INQUIRIES

O'Reilly UK Limited
4 Castle Street
Farnham
Surrey, GU9 7HS
United Kingdom
Telephone: 44-1252-711776
Fax: 44-1252-734211
Email: information@oreilly.co.uk

ORDERS

Wiley Distribution Services Ltd.
1 Oldlands Way
Bognor Regis
West Sussex PO22 9SA
United Kingdom
Telephone: 44-1243-843294
UK Freephone: 0800-243207
Fax: 44-1243-843302 (Europe/EU orders)
or 44-1243-843274 (Middle East/Africa)
Email: cs-books@wiley.co.uk

FRANCE

INQUIRIES & ORDERS

Éditions O'Reilly
18 rue Séguier
75006 Paris, France
Tel: 33-1-40-51-71-89
Fax: 33-1-40-51-72-26
Email: france@oreilly.fr

GERMANY, SWITZERLAND, AUSTRIA, LUXEMBOURG, AND LIECHTENSTEIN

INQUIRIES & ORDERS

O'Reilly Verlag
Balthasarstr. 81
D-50670 Köln, Germany
Telephone: 49-221-973160-91
Fax: 49-221-973160-8
Email: anfragen@oreilly.de (inquiries)
Email: order@oreilly.de (orders)

CANADA

(FRENCH LANGUAGE BOOKS)
Les Éditions Flammarion ltée
375, Avenue Laurier Ouest
Montréal (Québec) H2V 2K3
Tel: 1-514-277-8807
Fax: 1-514-278-2085
Email: info@flammarion.qc.ca

HONG KONG

City Discount Subscription Service, Ltd.
Unit A, 6th Floor, Yan's Tower
27 Wong Chuk Hang Road
Aberdeen, Hong Kong
Tel: 852-2580-3539
Fax: 852-2580-6463
Email: citydis@ppn.com.hk

KOREA

Hanbit Media, Inc.
Chungmu Bldg. 210
Yonnam-dong 568-33
Mapo-gu
Seoul, Korea
Tel: 822-325-0397
Fax: 822-325-9697
Email: hant93@chollian.dacom.co.kr

PHILIPPINES

Global Publishing
G/F Benavides Garden
1186 Benavides Street
Manila, Philippines
Tel: 632-254-8949/632-252-2582
Fax: 632-734-5060/632-252-2733
Email: globalp@pacific.net.ph

TAIWAN

O'Reilly Taiwan
1st Floor, No. 21, Lane 295
Section 1, Fu-Shing South Road
Taipei, 106 Taiwan
Tel: 886-2-27099669
Fax: 886-2-27038802
Email: mori@oreilly.com

INDIA

Shroff Publishers & Distributors Pvt. Ltd.
12, "Roseland", 2nd Floor
180, Waterfield Road, Bandra (West)
Mumbai 400 050
Tel: 91-22-641-1800/643-9910
Fax: 91-22-643-2422
Email: spd@vsnl.com

CHINA

O'Reilly Beijing
SIGMA Building, Suite B809
No. 49 Zhichun Road
Haidian District
Beijing, China PR 100080
Tel: 86-10-8809-7475
Fax: 86-10-8809-7463
Email: beijing@oreilly.com

JAPAN

O'Reilly Japan, Inc.
Yotsuya Y's Building
7 Banch 6, Honshio-cho
Shinjuku-ku
Tokyo 160-0003 Japan
Tel: 81-3-3356-5227
Fax: 81-3-3356-5261
Email: japan@oreilly.com

SINGAPORE, INDONESIA, MALAYSIA, AND THAILAND

TransQuest Publishers Pte Ltd
30 Old Toh Tuck Road #05-02
Sembawang Kimtrans Logistics Centre
Singapore 597654
Tel: 65-4623112
Fax: 65-4625761
Email: wendiw@transquest.com.sg

AUSTRALIA

Woodslane Pty., Ltd.
7/5 Vuko Place
Warriewood NSW 2102
Australia
Tel: 61-2-9970-5111
Fax: 61-2-9970-5002
Email: info@woodslane.com.au

NEW ZEALAND

Woodslane New Zealand, Ltd.
21 Cooks Street (P.O. Box 575)
Waganui, New Zealand
Tel: 64-6-347-6543
Fax: 64-6-345-4840
Email: info@woodslane.com.au

ARGENTINA

Distribuidora Cuspide
Suipacha 764
1008 Buenos Aires
Argentina
Phone: 54-11-4322-8868
Fax: 54-11-4322-3456
Email: libros@cuspide.com

ALL OTHER COUNTRIES

O'Reilly & Associates, Inc.
1005 Gravenstein Hwy North
Sebastopol, CA 95472 USA
Tel: 707-829-0515
Fax: 707-829-0104
Email: order@oreilly.com

O'REILLY®

TO ORDER: **800-998-9938** • order@oreilly.com • www.oreilly.com
ONLINE EDITIONS OF MOST O'REILLY TITLES ARE AVAILABLE BY SUBSCRIPTION AT **safari.oreilly.com**
ALSO AVAILABLE AT MOST RETAIL AND ONLINE BOOKSTORES